APR 19 '76

# Science Policies of Industrial Nations

edited by
**T. Dixon Long
Christopher Wright**

# Science Policies of Industrial Nations
## Case Studies of the United States, Soviet Union, United Kingdom, France, Japan, and Sweden

PRAEGER SPECIAL STUDIES IN INTERNATIONAL POLITICS AND GOVERNMENT

**Praeger Publishers** New York Washington London

Library of Congress Cataloging in Publication Data
Main entry under title:

Science policies of industrial nations.

(Praeger special studies in international politics
and government)
Bibliography:  p.
Includes index.
1.  Science and state.   2.  Technology and state.
I.  Long, Theodore Dixon, 1933—      II.  Wright,
Christopher, 1926—
Q125. S183          338. 4'7'5          74-13616
ISBN 0-275-05600-7

PRAEGER PUBLISHERS
111 Fourth Avenue, New York, N.Y. 10003, U.S.A.

Published in the United States of America in 1975
by Praeger Publishers, Inc.

Printed in the United States of America

1896101

The idea for this group of country studies grew out of two study groups sponsored by the Institute for the Study of Science in Human Affairs of Columbia University, in October 1970, and April 1971. *
Following very wide-ranging discussions of the role of science and technology in history, culture, domestic politics, and international relations, the convenors determined that an effort should be made to exploit existing knowledge of the most fully documented of these issues. It was quite clear that a high level of industrialization, with consequent implications for national policy, formed a powerful common theme. The programs of the Organization for Economic Cooperation and Development's Directorate for Scientific Affairs, and of UNESCO's Science Policy Division, had established significant bodies of factual material. It seemed logical to submit these, along with a growing literature of academic policy analysis, to a comparative and critical review.

The choice of countries for study was dictated primarily by the existence of a small number of recognized specialists. The conspicuous absence of West Germany and, perhaps equally, Italy, testifies to the slow process by which this new cadre of specialists is emerging. Other omissions, such as the small western European nations, the industrialized members of the British Commonwealth, and the more industrial of the eastern European nations, are explained primarily by the paucity of information. It was the hope of the study group, however, that this initial set of case studies might lead to further efforts grouping some of the nations mentioned above. A high priority should also be assigned to comparative analysis of science policies of developing nations. But because of very great differences in the data base and in overall national strategies, quite different criteria of analysis will have to be established.

There was also a significant element of rational calculation in the selection and arrangement of these national case studies. Science policies of the "superpowers" have been of overriding interest to students of the role of modern science and technology, as well as to analysts of the content and interaction of national policies generally. Yet the published output—largely in English—has been concerned overwhelmingly with the experience of the United States. The hope

---

*Participants were: Ingemar Dorfer, Harold Fruchtbaum, Robert Gilpin, Loren Graham, Sanford Lakoff, T. Dixon Long, Harvey M. Sapolsky, Jurgen Schmandt, Eugene Uyeki, Norman Vig, and Christopher Wright.

here is to rectify that situation, without at the same time presuming to furnish an authoritative critique of the massive literature dealing with the United States. Thus one chapter treats the background and development of science policy in the Soviet Union, and another chapter offers a review of some American perspectives on science policy. These two chapters, plus a chapter on Great Britain, establish an important set of references for consideration of the three other chapters. The centralized management of science and technology in the Soviet Union, on the one hand, and the persistent conflict regarding the proper combination of freedom and control in the United States and Great Britain, locate significant cluster points on the historical and the contemporary spectrum.

Following the studies of the Soviet Union and the United Kingdom, three chapters dealing with France, Japan, and Sweden illustrate how variously the linkages among science, technology, history, and ideology have given in each case a unique style and direction. They also illustrate how each author has used somewhat differently the materials of his trade. While the editors and contributors include one historian (Graham), two philosophers (Schmandt and Wright), and four political scientists (Dorfer, Gilpin, Long, and Vig), all have tried to view contemporary science policy in a setting of historical, cultural, and geographic constraints. All the contributors emphasize the heavy imprint on postwar science policy of trends and concepts from the late nineteenth century. This seems to suggest that the condition of constant and rapid change that accompanies a high level of industrialization has still, fundamentally, a strong evolutionary dimension.

The editors have not attempted to enforce—and the contributors evidently would not have been coerced to accept—a narrow, agreed definition of "science policy." It was broadly understood that, for the mid-nineteenth century, those who practiced the scientific method expanded from a band of gentlemen amateurs to a diverse community whose activities ranged from inquiry into fundamental natural and social processes to applications for profit, welfare, and security. It was also understood that these activities, especially as a result of World War II and the global political relations that grew out of it, have come under the direct or indirect control of national government to a degree hardly anticipated either by scientists or by government officials. Finally, the contributors shared an appreciation of the extent to which the hopes and fears of the masses in industrial society are founded upon expectations about science and technology and molded by the techniques and artifacts that science-based technology makes available.

So that this volume may serve as an initial guide for teaching, research, and publication of various kinds, the editors have prepared a bibliographic appendix summarizing, for each of the national case studies, material relevant to the study of science and technology policy in that nation. These lists are not simply a compilation of footnotes, they form a selection from those and other appropriate sources.

This volume would not have been possible without the patience and cooperation of the contributors, for which the editors take this opportunity to express their thanks. Typing of various portions of the manuscript was done by Florence Maier and Margaret MacDowell of the Division of Interdisciplinary Studies in Social Science, Case Western Reserve University.

# CONTENTS

ix

## LIST OF TABLES

## LIST OF FIGURES

# LIST OF ABBREVIATIONS

| | |
|---|---|
| ACSP | Advisory Council on Scientific Policy (U. K.) |
| AEA | Atomic Energy Authority (U. K.) |
| CATS | Colleges of Advanced Technology (U. K.) |
| CCRST | Advisory Committee for Scientific and Technical Research (France) |
| CEA | Atomic Energy Commission (Fr.) |
| CERN | Centre Europeene pour la Recherche Nucleaive |
| CNRS | National Center for Scientific Research (Fr.) |
| CSP | Council for Scientific Policy (U. K.) |
| CST | Council for Science and Technology (Japan) |
| DGRST | General Delegation for Science and Technology Research (Fr.) |
| DRME | Directorate of Research and Testing (Fr.) |
| DRPC | Defence Research Policy Committee (U. K.) |
| DSIR | Department of Scientific and Industrial Research (U. K.) |
| EEC | European Economic Community |
| EPA | Economic Planning Agency (Japan) |
| JSC | Japan Science Council |
| MINTECH | Ministry of Technology (U. K.) |
| NRDC | National Research Development Corporation (U. K.) |
| OECD | Organization for Economic Cooperation and Development |
| RANN | Research Applied to National Needs (U. S.) |
| R&D | Research and Development |
| SAC | Science Advisory Council (Sweden) |
| STA | Science and Technology Agency (Japan) |
| . . | (in tables) data nonexistent or negligible |

# Science Policies of Industrial Nations

CHAPTER

# 1

## SCIENCE POLICY INSTITUTIONS IN SIX COUNTRIES

T. Dixon Long
Christopher Wright

THE HISTORICAL FRAMEWORK

Science policy—the generally accepted shorthand form for science and technology policy—is of rather recent origin. Between the late nineteenth century and World War I, the development of science and technology in Western Europe and North America became increasingly intertwined with the central policy-making role of the state. Prominent among the new relationships were the impact of science and technology on military weaponry; the professionalization of science and engineering and their incorporation into the civil services; and the emergence of national governments as the major patrons, if not principal clients, of science and technology in the fields that bear on health, welfare, and the provision of public services. The first definition of patterns and practices now known as science policies dates roughly from the Edwardian era, although precise dates differ from country to country.

The country studies in this volume show that the deepest roots of contemporary science policy started to grow much earlier in some countries than in others; France, for example, had a tradition of interaction between science and government predating the Napoleonic period. Russia, on the other hand did not truly begin to organize itself for making and carrying out science policies until a few years after the 1918 revolution, despite the founding of its Academy of Science under Peter the Great. Still different is the case of Japan, which had no tradition and little knowledge of science (in the western sense) until after the political revolution that occurred in 1868, yet through the rapid introduction of western military and industrial science and technology thereafter was able to defeat a European military power—Russia—in months.

From World War I, it is possible to identify and trace institutional developments, patterns of behavior, and relationships among actors

1

that constitute the fundamental elements of contemporary science policy in the industrial nations. In the major areas of national policy and politics since then, science and technology have been at issue. Questions of national prestige and survival, manifested in terms of military power and conflict, are the most obvious illustration. Throughout the interwar period, the currency of national competition was "bigger and better battleships." The primary requirement was increasingly sophisticated weapons. Supporting this effort were industrial production and services that could be mobilized in support of large-scale and far-flung military operations.

Economic depression and the coming of war muted the influence of science and technology on the general public welfare. But developments in the control and eradication of epidemic disease, and the national and international extension of transportation and communication systems, show that the process was continuing, even accelerating. Furthermore, the scientific and the industrial revolutions were merging, and the effects were evident in ever widening circles. Whether in the Soviet Union and Japan—where the motivation was desire to "catch up with the West"—or Great Britain and the United States—where economic crisis gave birth to the welfare state—science and technology were in analogous situations. J. D. Bernal was among the first to recognize this fact and articulate the proposition that science and technology have a "social function" that can be exploited to satisfy human needs. [1]

In this larger historical frame, the massive impact of science and technology on the conduct of World War II appears less a transition than a magnification of forces and movements already afoot. Atomic weapons, operations research, science advisors, and teamwork in research were among the technological and social inventions that marked the war and its aftermath. They represented the evolution of larger technological and social processes. Weapons of mass destruction and their associated delivery systems had become the principal elements of influence in the industrial world. They required the development and maintenance of new institutions, such as national laboratories and strategic forces, which in turn required new concepts and mechanisms of control. Constant awareness of the destructive capacity of atomic weapons, together with advanced delivery systems, permeated science policy development for a quarter of a century.

POSTWAR DEVELOPMENTS AND PROSPECTS

It is not certain even now whether the formulation of postwar national policies for the use and support of science and technology in general has become dissociated from the policies, technologies, and organizations of weapons development. Of the countries examined

2

here, four have been deeply engaged in the military nuclear field, although Great Britain from the mid-1950s ceased to be actively involved. While Japan has no nuclear arms, it is systematically reducing the lead-time that would be required to mobilize civilian capability to military purposes. Sweden also has no nuclear arms, but she does have a significant nuclear power industry and a very important military aircraft program. Weapons and weapons-oriented industries clearly remain a major ingredient in the organization and conduct of national science policy in these nations.

Higher education and the training of professionals in the industrial nations studied here have steadily shifted emphasis from general culture to technical specialization. Primary and secondary education systems have become more oriented toward preparation of the most promising students for college and specialized university training. Graduate education has become a larger-scale enterprise, less personalized in the classic master-apprentice model and better integrated into national systems of peer evaluation and accreditation.

In all the countries studied here, scientists and engineers have emerged as new elites, having particular forms of peer-group relations and making special contributions to the function of the body politic. Like lawyers, physicians, and soldiers, scientists and engineers have come to occupy the ambivalent position of the specialist who knows too much to be permitted the unregulated practice of his specialty. As the newest professional group to achieve this status, scientists still lack the range of institutional forms and behavioral patterns of their predecessors. Except in the Soviet Union, however, these attributes of elitism appear to be developing predictably, towards the establishment of professional interest groups and greater individual involvement in politics and public administration.

The most prominent manifestations of the contemporary relationship between science and national policymaking are the advisory and coordinating mechanisms which operate in all the countries studied here. That such organizations exist at all is the principal fact; that they do not adhere to a common pattern, or even perform a common set of functions, is of secondary importance, particularly in view of the widely different conditions and purposes that brought them into existence and have kept them in being.

The performance of science advisory bodies can be appraised in several different ways. Their impact on military research and development, for example, is a crucial, though somewhat shadowy, activity. While little is known about the process in the Soviet Union, it is clear that this is a distinct and dominant function there as well as in the U.S., Great Britain, and France. The coordination of military with civilian policymaking in science and technology is another significant dimension. Available information suggests that the Soviet capability is rather substantial, the British rather limited, and the U.S. somewhere between. Japan and Sweden are special cases, the first because of the absence of overt military research and development (R&D), and the second because of the very small size of the entire national R&D enterprise. National comparisons of nonmilitary sectors are not as revealing, mainly because of the dominance of military oriented research and, until very recently, the neglect of significant distinctions in the ways in which different sectors relate to science and technology.

Mechanisms for coordination are even more diverse than the activities coordinated. The Soviet system of coordination through a state committee that is effectively a subcommittee of the Council of Ministers appears to be a powerful and unique method, although it has been relatively inaccessible to analysts, as Loren Graham's chapter of this volume shows. However, some observers see advantages in the concept of central political control and administrative responsibility at the highest levels of national policymaking.

The Japanese also make use of a subcommittee of the Cabinet, but--as Long points out in his chapter--this is a nominal arrangement. The functions of the Science and Technology Council (on which the ministers sit) are actually carried out by professional appointed members of the council. Effective coordination is achieved at the budgetary level, but there it embraces less than half the national R&D budget.

Coordination in Great Britain is based on overlapping membership of sectoral advisory councils and a central advisory council, a quasirationalized example of the "old-boy network," described in detail by Norman Vig in his chapter. A somewhat superpowered version of the same approach is used in Sweden, where—Dorfer's chapter shows—it is more efficient because the society is much smaller and has a more closely integrated "establishment" group.

There is little overt central coordination in the U.S., but a complex and loose arrangement of personal contacts manages to maintain a network of communication among government agencies, private busi firms, and educational and research organizations. In France, a highly rational set of coordinative functions is supported by a large organization. As Gilpin makes clear in his chapter, however, this organization has no power against political directives that may reflect bad judgement, poor timing, ignorance, or national vanity—problems that are anything but unique to the French situation.

Although the study of science policy has focused almost entirely on the perspectives, processes, and institutions of a particular society and its government, it is revealing to consider the development of national science policies as responses to a set of needs common to advanced, industrial societies. By considering the needs of the most advanced sectors as if they were needs of entire societies, the present country studies suggest that science policies are a phenomenon not of a postindustrial society but of one that is hyperindustrial. Precisely those demands and expectations raised by advancing industrialization require wider, more rapid, and more persistent applications

4

of science and technology. If industrial societies are not to be strangled by their very affluence, it is likely that these expanding applications will be the responsibility of the public authorities, or will reflect their guidance and policy-making capabilities.

In all of the countries examined here, science policymaking has been understood as the prerogative of the national or central government. In the functional sense, of course, policymaking may be extremely pluralistic, as in the U.S., or highly centralized, as in France. But one critical difference between science policies and other kinds of policies appears to be the relative indifference, as yet, of local and other subnational levels of government to the problem-solving capabilities of modern science and technology. This is, of course, merely another illustration of the preoccupation of practitioners and students primarily with questions of national security and only secondarily with large-scale approaches to the application of science and technology in the fields of health, welfare, and public services.

Although governments below national levels are not yet seriously engaged in the development of science policies—except perhaps in the United States—the contrary is true of nongovernmental institutions. In both market and managed economies, science and technology have policy implications for large-scale business organizations, principally for manufacturing firms, but also to a considerable degree in banking, insurance, transport, and construction, as well as other parts of the service sector. For example, automobile manufacturers have mechanisms for considering and adopting self-interested positions on questions of transportation research. Banks and other financial institutions have modest means of exploring or putting forward views on the impact of investment decisions on alternative types of industrial innovation. The policy-making function is gradually being dispersed as nongovernmental actors recognize the implications of scientific advance and technological development not simply as elements of their internal policy but in terms of their impact on an entire national society.

INSTITUTIONAL ACTORS

The framework for analysis of science policy that emerges from these country studies reflects primarily an institutional approach. Because of the increased status and institutionalization of science, its essential policy elements are, in general order of importance, governmental policy-making institutions at the national level, scientific and technological organizations themselves, and institutions cutting across the fabric of both the governmental and the scientific enterprises, such as private firms and international organizations.

Government policy-making institutions have mobilized science and technology for the pursuit of national, rather than local, regional,

5

or international needs. The post-World War II development of science advisory bodies made it clear that their principal concern was with the interaction of "basic research and national goals."[2] Although the claims of minorities, municipalities, regions, and other distinctive environments were stridently voiced and effectively pursued, there seemed little temptation for science advisory bodies to address themselves to these concerns. The reports of science advisory bodies to prime ministers and presidents have consistently focused on issues that are national in scale, or of concern to the entire nation or mankind in general, such as health, population, security, education, and energy.

Below the level of policy advice, administrative agencies for carrying out large-scale technical missions have also been uniquely national in focus. In space and atomic energy, administration has been inextricably engaged with the problem of national security. It is also significant that no established department of government has been considered capable of mounting the effort required in these new areas, and newly established government departments in fields such as transportation did not seem to acquire the special status of the technical agency. In most countries, the merger of national security and economic considerations has been uniquely evident in the "big" science and technology enterprises.

The organizations charged with support of basic research, such as the research councils of the U. K. and the National Science Foundation and National Institute of Health in the U. S., are national in scope. They have, among other responsibilities, that of functioning as a "balance wheel," to ensure the nurture of fields that, in uncontrolled competition for resources, might receive less than the minimum required for survival. They have been charged with maintaining the health of science and technology on a national scale.

The coordination of research and development expenditures of the national government is an emerging institutional function of national government. As an OECD study pointed out several years ago, these are generally either an ex post or an ex ante activity.[3] In the case of the U. S., information was formerly collected through special analyses of the budget, and initiatives were taken informally but effectively by the president's science adviser in his relations with the budget bureau. In Japan and even more so in France, one agency is charged with coordinating the budget submissions of other departments and agencies. Until the postwar recognition of science as a national resource, management of research and development expenditure was never delegated to a single agency.

Controversy continues as to whether centralized or decentralized institutions for science policymaking and execution are more appropriate. The fact is that in each country studied here, some of the governmental institutions embody one perspective and some the other. Clearly, science and technology have been too pervasive to be held

6

within the programmatic or statutory limits of a single organ of government. Despite efforts to centralize a major portion of the policy-making function, this has occurred in only one of the countries represented, the Soviet Union.

Compared with the emphasis on the institutions of government, relatively less attention is given in these studies to the development of a political role either of institutions of science and engineering, or to international institutions as actors in the arena of national science policymaking. The direction of development of the scientific and engineering communities seems quite clear. Over the past century or so, the individual experimenter or man of learning—who was perhaps primarily recognized in the role of gentleman or cleric—has become a representative of a new professional class. Their modes of development have similar features that recur from country to country: a large increase in numbers, subdivision into numerous technical specialities, and relative absence, until recently, of political awareness or participation in the formulation of national policy.

One explanation for the fact that scientists and engineers do not play a more active political role through their professional organizations is the focus of these organizations exclusively on technical communication and peer evaluation. Though it is more typical of the scientific than of the engineering societies, these organizations publish journals and arrange meetings. Under intense pressure from within or outside, such an organization is sometimes able to take positions of advocacy or to provide partisan support, but its capacity to act directly is constrained by the mechanisms which control professional advancement. The effectiveness of these organizations in restricting or otherwise delimiting the range of opportunities to mobilize science for public policy purposes is substantial.

On the other hand, over the past quarter century there has been a steady evolution in the nature of vehicles of scientific communication, as they have also become vehicles of public policy information and even opinion. The professional societies of the Anglo-Saxon countries, and to a lesser extent the Continental countries, are undertaking some responsibility for studies of the impact of their professions on the general society. This trend is still too new for conclusions to be drawn about the corollary development of direct action mechanisms. One example, the involvement of scientists and engineers in public interest action groups, may even turn out to be aberrant. But the general drift is manifest in all the nations represented in this study (excepting the Soviet Union) and is illustrated internationally by movements such as the Pugwash Conferences on Science and World Affairs and the Club of Rome.

Perhaps for national security reasons, science and technology continue to be organized around national means of support, communication, and control. In some cases, such as Eastern and Western Europe, institutional developments have responded to efforts towards economic and political integration. But in general, professional organization has gone forward most intensively on a national plane, despite early associations of individual scholars and experimenters that were regional or international in scope and universalistic in the concept of the disciplines involved. Although there is nothing inevitable about the national style of development, in view of the simultaneousness of the professionalization of science and engineering and the spread of nationalist ideology and organization, it is not surprising.

As for institutions cutting across the governmental and scientific, there is a current practical interest in the large-scale internationally active corporation, and an emerging theoretical focus on transnational activities affecting science policy. These include traditional cultural and international movements related to labor, business, voluntary associations, and professional societies, as well as political and religious movements. However, international organizations concerned with science and technology are limited in the practical sense to three types: private voluntary and professional organizations, business firms, and intergovernmental organizations. For example, research-intensive firms in the natural resource and energy fields and intergovernmental organizations in the agriculture and health fields have sufficient resources to enable them to participate in national policy with global implications, as well as to take action themselves with significant large-scale effects on the natural environment, human health, and political behavior.

Nevertheless, none of the country studies gives attention specifically to the role of international institutions for the reasons that the studies were intended to address the question of internal governmental mechanisms, and only indirectly take into account the impact of foreign policy considerations, as in the study of Great Britain, or of the large corporations, as in the Swedish study.


## THE ROLE OF THE SCIENTIST


While the major focus of these studies is on institutions, some important minor themes also emerge. The most prominent of these is the status of the scientist as both expert and partisan. In the United States and Great Britain, the argument has often been summarized in the question of whether science advisors should be "on tap or on top." In the Soviet Union, the question is whether the emerging scientific elite are conscious of their power and prerogatives as professionals. The issue takes a somewhat different form in each country, but fundamentally it stems from situations in which scientists occupy extremely influential positions while explicitly or implicitly invoking the neutral, objective, truth-seeking character of science.

Two dimensions of this issue are gradually emerging as under-standing of science and public policy becomes more sophisticated and widespread in the industrial nations. The first is the lobbying activities of scientists in support of partisan political issues, even though the political role of established professional societies is nascent and, indeed, may be stillborn as a result of strong counter efforts on the part of some scientists. Scientists also hold many important adminis-trative posts in a large number of government agencies, where research and development activities supply service-to-line functions such as housing, transportation, natural resources, and communications.

## TOOLS FOR ANALYSIS

A quite different theme is the development of tools of analysis for improving the effectiveness of national science policies, especially through better understanding of the policies themselves. These tools include four kinds having different degrees of sophistication. First, budget analysis is beginning to be an important tool for science policymakers and students of science policy. The budget was selected as the point of entry into the science policy-making process by admin-istrative agencies in France and Japan. Budgetary techniques have been intermittently applied in the U.S. and Great Britain, depending to a considerable degree on changing arrangements for centralized advice and policymaking. While it is difficult to make an explicit statement about the Soviet system, the Academy of Sciences clearly has a powerful opportunity which may be expressed through influence on the budget.

Second, manpower policies and more broadly the supply of human resources and the assessment of educational needs are increasingly seen to be central to the concerns of science policymakers. Scientific and engineering manpower has been a persistent focus of innovative and reformist efforts in Great Britain and Sweden. It became a major issue in the United States following Sputnik, when it was thought that the Soviet Union was pursuing much more effective manpower policies. Upon examination, Soviet policies appeared to have severe limitations along with the advantages of a high degree of central direction. In still another manifestation of this issue, France and Japan have been plagued with continuing difficulties in attempting to increase the availability of general higher education while expanding the supply of designated technical skills and retaining the elitist character of the system.

Third, analysis of the character and productivity of individual fields of science has become increasingly important to national policymakers, who look to key fields such as physics and chemistry

9

to contribute to military preparedness and national prestige. In the Soviet Union, the academy system appears to delegate this responsibility almost entirely to the scientific community, while in Great Britain and the United States it is performed by a mixture of scientists, officials, and other public persons. Japan, France, and Sweden give a dominant role to the administrator. Yet in none of the countries studied does one method emerge as clearly superior or even satisfactory. Experimentation is still the dominant mode, accompanied by a substantial amount of confusion and disagreement regarding the object and the feasibility of such analysis.

Fourth, assessment of the impacts of technology (and to a limited extent of scientific research) on society is a widely recognized need, though not an art widely practiced by the governments of industrial nations. However, interesting combinations of scientists, legal scholars, administrators, citizens, and others are being proposed—and in some limited ways engaged in real issues—with the aim of anticipating and insofar as possible avoiding the most damaging effects of large new private and public undertakings. The provisions of the National Environmental Policy Act of 1969, and the recently established Office of Technology Assessment—both in the United States—are examples of this effort.

## CONCLUSIONS

These studies are retrospective rather than prospective, but because of the increasing importance of science and technology, policies aimed at their control and utilization should in the future be more accessible to comparison and analysis. The study of institutional structures through which societies act in the area of science policy promises to provide an important as well as interesting point of entry for future study.

The problems with which science policy must cope are increasingly global in scale, even though the major centers of decision and action remain in the governments of industrial nations. There are many means whereby some portion of a nation's resources—physical and psychological—may contribute to global objectives, yet the bulk are allocated in terms of domestic purposes only. The fundamental impetus in global activities is imbedded in the self-interest of nation-states and the competition among them for national security, national wealth, and national prestige. For this reason, this set of studies focuses on the science policies of industrial nations.

10

## NOTES

1. J. D. Bernal, The Social Function of Science (London: Routledge, 1939).
2. See NAS, Basic Research and National Goals (US, GPO, 1965).
3. OECD, Government and the Allocation of Resources to Science (Paris, 1966).

CHAPTER

# 2

## THE DEVELOPMENT
## OF SCIENCE POLICY
## IN THE SOVIET UNION
Loren R. Graham

Of the nations discussed in this volume, the Soviet Union is perhaps the most removed from general patterns. It is the only nation with an economy in which there is no private capital. It is, further, a nation in which, at least in theory, every institution has coordinated its activity with national plans since the late 1920s. In addition, it is a nation with an explicit commitment to science, including a value system and a philosophical worldview based on science, which is unmatched in intensity by any other nation in the world. Both as an independent topic and for comparative purposes, a consideration of Soviet attitudes and policies toward science seems, therefore, to be appropriate in this study of science policy in industrialized nations.

In discussing in historical terms the development of science policy and planning in different nations, it is important to distinguish between temporary or specific efforts, on the one hand, and continuing national efforts, on the other. If one is looking for moments in history when governments attempted to formulate policies toward specific problems of a scientific or technical nature (reorganization of technical education, mobilization for a war, and so forth), a multitude of examples before the present century can be identified. If, however, one is looking for the moment when a nation first attempted to formulate a

This paper contains several revised short sections from three of my earlier publications on Soviet science as well as original material. These earlier publications were: The Soviet Academy of Sciences and the Communist Party, 1927-1932 (Princeton: Princeton University Press 1967); "Science Policy and Planning in the USSR," Survey (July 1967): 61-79; and "Reorganization of the U.S.S.R. Academy of Sciences," in Peter H. Juviler and Henry W. Morton, eds., Soviet Policy-Making (New York: Praeger, 1967), pp. 133-61.

12

policy towards science and technology as a whole and to sustain and revise that policy over time, the first important instance was the Soviet Union in the 1920s. This effort was plagued with difficulties of great complexity, both political and technical, and in the final analysis must be judged as only partially successful. Furthermore, the most vital efforts to formulate science policies were curtailed early in the 1930s by the advent of Stalinism. Nevertheless, the Soviet Union was the first nation fully to recognize science as a national resource, systematically to commit large portions of its budget to the promotion of research, and to attempt to plan the progress of scientific development.

## THE PREREVOLUTIONARY HERITAGE

In order to understand the policies of the Soviet government towards science, it is necessary first to examine the characteristics of the scientific tradition which it inherited from the tsarist government. Russia, in 1917, possessed a remarkably strong foundation in the sciences. The names of Lomonosov, Lobachevsky, Butlerov, Mendeleyev, Chebyshev, Sechenov, and Pavlov are only a few of those indicating by 1917 that Russia had already produced a whole series of great scientists. Furthermore, its Academy of Sciences, founded in 1725, and its great universities, such as those of Moscow and St. Petersburg, dating to the mid-eighteenth and early nineteenth centuries, were the foci of significant scientific research long before the revolutionary overturn of 1917. As is the case with every nation, the scientific institutions in Russia bore the marks of the specific political and economic evolution of their national milieu, and Russian scientists were known for certain strengths and weaknesses.

Perhaps the first characteristic of science in imperial Russia that the observer would notice was the uncommonly large role played by the central government. In other European countries the governments nourished—in varying degrees—the scientific centers that spontaneously sprouted in the environment of increasing material and intellectual achievement, but in Russia the government was forced to import such centers complete. When Russia emerged as a state in the European system, in the early eighteenth century, it possessed no significant centers of scientific studies; the responsibility for the creation of such institutions fell, therefore, upon the imperial government. The formation of educational and scientific institutions was, for Peter the Great (1672-1725), a necessary step for the strengthening and modernization of Russia, not essentially different in his mind from the development of a navy or of industries capable of producing modern arms.

13

This pattern of central, state control of science and education was, with only a few exceptions, continued throughout the history of the empire. The important scientists of Russia received their salaries from the government, and the budgets of their institutions were similarly derived from the government. If they offended official sensibilities by their political activities, their professional careers were likely to suffer. Even their publications were subject to governmental control, although in the natural sciences censorship was only occasionally a problem.

By the end of the empire, a few important exceptions to the government's monopoly over the administration and patronage of learning had appeared. Several wealthy merchants and industrialists provided money for philanthropic funds devoted to the promotion of knowledge, and even several private educational and scientific institutions were established.[1] Nonetheless, these private efforts were much less numerous and noteworthy in Russia than in other leading European nations, such as France, Britain, and Germany. To the end of their tenure, the rulers of imperial Russia resented private initiative in any field, including science and learning. It was seen as a potential source of political power opposed to the regime. Therefore, they attempted to maintain control over the entire educational and scientific establishment. This tradition of state control passed into the hands of the new Soviet government in 1917 and has remained a characteristic of Soviet science and education to the present day.

The strongest tradition in Russian science before the revolution was probably mathematics, a tradition created and sustained by a series of brilliant scholars of whom N. I. Lobachevsky, M. V. Ostrogradsky, V. I. Buniakovsky, and P. L. Chebyshev are examples; this tradition seems to have had little connection with economic needs or applications. In St. Petersburg and Moscow there existed schools of mathematicians formed around an absorption in abstract theory which passed through several generations.

Lobachevsky's development of non-Euclidean geometry is frequently cited, even today, as a prime example of the way in which mathematicians can produce systems which, at the time of their development, have no apparent application at all. Lobachevsky himself regarded his work as an intellectually interesting but essentially useless achievement.

The strength of Russian mathematics before 1917 poses an interesting problem for historians of science who wish to explain science in terms of its socioeconomic roots. It is possible to view Russian mathematics in this light, but only by means of an unusual extension and deepening of the normal socioeconomic interpretation. Instead of seeing Russian mathematics as a result of technical demands placed upon scientists by native industries or technological needs, one may wish to see it as a curious product of the impact of theoretical science

14

from Western Europe on a country with a great lack of native industry but with an intelligentsia sufficiently large to do important scientific work. In such an environment, it may not be surprising that the initial scientific achievements have a disconnected, greenhouse character, that is, that they are not easily related to the economic needs of the country, although they probably are related to the economic state of the country.

It would be interesting to compare the initial nineteenth-century achievements of Russians in mathematics and chemical theory with the first steps of underdeveloped countries in science today. In this highly speculative area one thing is clear, however: the Bolshevik modern-izers of the post-1917 period believed, apparently correctly, that Russia's scientific tradition was abnormally skewed to the side of pure science, and they made enormous efforts, described below, to redress this balance.

Another great tradition in prerevolutionary Russian science, that of chemistry, can be compared to mathematics in its theoretical emphasis. To be sure, the greatest figure here—Mendeleyev—is less simple to categorize than the lonely genius Lobachevsky, since Mendeleyev had very strong interests in industrial chemistry. He toured the centers of the petroleum industry in the United States, wrote extensively on chemical industry, and served as an ideological spokesman for builders of Russian capitalism such as Count S. Witte and the Association of Industry and Trade.[2] Nonetheless, Mendeleyev's principal achievement—the formulation of the periodic table of the elements—was a momentous feat in conceptualization rather than application. Mendeleyev was unsuccessful in his efforts to establish large industrial research institutions.

To the end of its reign, the tsarist government was ambiguous in its attitudes toward the development of industry and industrial research. While it saw the advantages of industrial power, it feared the political consequences of industrial pressure groups and the rise of the middle class, which was intrinsic to modernization. The government would have preferred to combine, somehow, political autocracy with economic modernization, but it never found a successful plan for reaching this goal. Consequently, scientists such as Mendeleyev, who saw the great technological possibilities for Russia in chemical research and industry, met with a series of insuperable obstacles in the policies of the tsarist government. Mendeleyev objected strenuously, for example, to the governmental regulations on the petroleum industry around Baku, which hobbled the development of research and industry.

Mendeleyev's plight points toward the most important reason for the relative lack of applied research in prerevolutionary Russia: the underdevelopment of Russian industry. Industry was the logical focus of applied research, as was illustrated in the industrial chemical laboratories of Germany in the last half of the nineteenth century. In Russia, however, large-scale industry started considerably later

15

than in Germany. Furthermore, when industrial expansion did develop toward the end of the century, it was to an unusual degree a result of foreign investment and under foreign control. French, German, and Swedish industrialists depended on research bases in their own countries and were little interested in establishing or assisting industrial laboratories in Russia, where they sought instead raw materials and inexpensive labor.

Another area in which Russians were leaders before the revolution was the earth and life sciences, particularly those aspects of these sciences for which expeditionary research was particularly appropriate. Here the geography of the Russian empire left a considerable imprint on Russian research. The vast expanse of the Russian lands—from the Arctic to Central Asia, from seashores to great deserts, from the steppes of Europe to the volcanoes of Kamchatka—became an object of expeditionary research in the same way that the American West was studied in the United States. The specimen collections stemming from this work—particularly the mastodon remains and the ethnographic data on Siberian tribes—had a great impact on European science; these specimens form the core of the existing great collections in Leningrad. The Russians also produced outstanding works long before the revolution in such areas as geological and topographical surveys and in soil science, subjects with quite obvious practical implications, but surprisingly little effort was made before the twentieth century to integrate and apply this information for the purposes of economic exploitation. Instead, the Russians developed ever further their penchant for compiling enormous specimen collections and writing lengthy descriptive works.

The prerevolutionary emphasis on pure science and spectacular descriptions of the earth sciences was in part a result of the desire of Russian scientists to prove the worth of science in Russia. They were often not content with restricted topics of investigation; they desired topics either of grander scale than elsewhere or deeper in theory. This desire to pursue research which would gain prestige for Russia, easily identifiable in the writings of such men as Lomonosov and Mendeleyev, prompted Russian scientists to stay abreast of the latest developments in western Europe, even though on the level of applied science Russia was much further behind. Thus Russia tried to compete in the area of science which, at her stage of development, benefited her least: advanced theoretical research.

By the beginning of the twentieth century, a discernible turn away from the traditional Russian absorption in pure and descriptive science was underway; this change would surely have intensified even if the revolution had not taken place. The number of Russian engineering schools and technical institutes steadily increased. Russian capitalism grew impressively, and with it the demand for technical knowledge. With the advent of World War I, the Academy of Sciences turned a small part of its attention to applied science for the first time in decades. In 1915, it created the Commission for the Study of Natural Resources, an organization which, in modified form, would have a long history in the Soviet period. The primary duty of the new body was to serve as a technological advisory committee for war needs, but its activities in the area of industrial research and minerals exploration were important to the economy as a whole. The Commission for the Study of Natural Resources should be recognized as a significant prerevolutionary predecessor of the new forms of research bodies in the applied sciences which the Soviet government urged in the late 1920s. Indeed, the commission served as an organizational model during the later attempts to give science a more planned and applied direction. Since the commission was founded by geologists, and since expeditionary work is particularly amenable to planning, it is not surprising that among the early leaders of planned science in Soviet Russia were geologists who had established their reputations before the revolution, such as A. P. Karpinskii, V. I. Vernadskii, and A. E. Fersman.[3]

Another characteristic of Russian science before the revolution, which would continue to have influence after that political event, was the importance of the Imperial Academy of Sciences compared to other scientific institutions. In western Europe, the first learned societies had been established in the seventeenth or early eighteenth centuries, long after the first universities but before the industrial revolution; their later evolution was affected both by the subsequent changes in the older universities and the advent of industrialization. When these societies first appeared, they represented the "new science" of the seventeenth century and were opposed to the system of thought in the universities, which the new scientists considered to be an arid scholasticism. The early publications of these societies reveal what a mixture of interests they served and what diverse writers contributed to them—some articles were written by aristocratic dilettantes in science, others by great theoreticians such as Descartes and Newton, still others were directed toward such goals as shipbuilding and agriculture. As learning grew in western Europe and society there became more complex and specialized, many of these interests became the special concerns of other groups and institutions. With the growth of industry in the nineteenth century, the application of knowledge to commercial interests became more and more the concern of leading industrialists and financiers, people with sufficient capital to assume the risks involved in the development of new goods. As these other institutions assumed important functions earlier performed by learned societies, the latter became largely honorific or social in character. Industrial laboratories, particularly in Germany, were becoming the centers of research for commercial purposes; governmental institutions were beginning to assume responsibility for the development of knowledge to be used for general or humanitarian purposes, such as health and communication; and the universities were becoming the seats of

17

theoretical research. The development, in the universities, of graduate education in the sciences transformed these institutions to a degree almost unrecognizable to a person accustomed to the form of universities which existed in the seventeenth and early eighteenth centuries, when the learned societies first developed. In sum, the early functions of the learned societies—both in the practical arts and in the generation of new knowledge—were being assumed in western Europe and America in the late nineteenth century by other institutions. As a result, the old learned societies had largely lost instrumental importance and become instead prestigious organizations meeting rarely and doing little actual work on their own.

These same trends were discernible in late nineteenth-century Russia, but the situation was nonetheless considerably different. In contrast to western Europe, the Academy of Sciences in Russia preceded the universities in date of foundation and won an important governmental position before their advent. To be sure, after reforms in 1863, the universities in Russia developed very impressively; more and more significant scientific research was being performed in university settings. It was clear that within a few decades, if trends continued uninterrupted (they did not), the universities would thoroughly displace the old Academy of Sciences as a center of research, just as the universities in western Europe had done. By the end of the century, the universities, taken as a whole, were already considerably more important than the academy in the Russian scientific establishment. Yet it was also true that the academy was stronger than its west European counterparts and, indeed, was probably more important in Russian science than any one of the universities. It was particularly significant in its sponsorship of learned publications. Furthermore, the hand of political oppression fell more heavily upon the universities than upon the academy, particularly in the period leading up to and immediately after the 1905 revolution, when hundreds of university scholars were dismissed from their posts. The tsarist government distrusted the politicized university professors more than it did the members of the academy, and the latter institution probably inadvertently benefited from this distrust. The permanent secretary of the academy in the years after 1904, S. F. Ol'denburg, dreamed of a renaissance of Russia, a blooming of its scientific and cultural potential, with the Academy of Sciences playing the role of a scientific and cultural directorate of the nation. It seems clear that before 1917, Ol'denburg and several other intellectual leaders in Russia already hoped to avoid the pattern of education and research which they saw developing in western Europe and instead to create new institutional forms. At any rate, until the end of the old regime the Imperial Academy of Sciences managed to cling—despite increasing competition—to its claim to be "the highest scientific institution" in Russia. When the Communist leaders inherited this extraordinary institution, they had to decide what to do with it—abolish it, as the Academie des

18

Sciences in France had been abolished in the wake of the French revolution; support it at approximately the existing level; or build a structure of scientific research in which it would be the central and critical element. The decision which was finally reached was related— although not, of course, determined—by the relative strength of the Academy in 1917.

## EARLY SOVIET ATTITUDES TOWARDS SCIENCE

No previous government in history was as committed to the idea of science as that of the Bolsheviks in 1917. Those who see a neces- sary contradiction between ideology and science may object to this observation, since the Communist commitment to science was without question ideological. The Bolsheviks, however, saw their ideology as being synonymous with science, and they promised from the start the patronage of science on an unprecedented scale. Science was to them particularly appropriate as a remedy for the ills of Russia. It would conquer Russia both as a state of mind and as a state of nature. It would overcome the medieval mysticism of the church, while pro- viding the key to the country's natural riches.

Science would thus be one of the most influential allies of the Soviet state, and one of the major goals of the early Soviet leaders was to provide the best conditions for its development. They believed that within every society there existed an "environment for science" which helped or hindered the development of science and technology. A number of variables could theoretically be adjusted in the hope of creating the optimum environment: the form of the educational system, the system of rewards, the provision of material support (laboratories, equipment, operating funds), the economic environment, and even the value system. The Communist rulers of Soviet Russia stated repeatedly that they intended to construct the ideal society for science.

Among the early Soviet leaders, the belief was strong that they, the revolutionary Russian Marxists, were themselves symbols of the values of rationality and science. They had executed a revolution on the basis of what they considered to be a scientific analysis of social history. Several of the leaders, including Lenin, wrote highly theoret- ical works, not only on economics and politics but also on scientific and philosophic topics. Lenin had written before the revolution on philosophic aspects of modern physics, Trotsky had once been a star mathematics student who caused his teacher grief by deserting the subject for politics, and Bukharin was deeply interested in scientific topics. All of them believed that the old regime had repressed the development of science and education in Russia; they all foresaw that the revolution would lead to the flourishing of a new culture in which science would play a prominent role. In short, in the view of its leaders, the revolution was synonymous with science in the affairs of men.

Favorable towards science as the predominant attitude among early Soviet Communists was, there were a few tensions and contradictory elements as well. Russian factory workers, who had been by far the most important source of strength to the Bolshviks in 1917, were ambiguous in their attitude toward scientists and technical specialists. The scientists and engineers were frequently seen by the workers as members of the despised bourgeoisie, and, indeed, the great majority of Russian scientists and technicians in the immediate postrevolutionary period were of middle-class background. One colorful leader of the left segment of the Russian proletariat spoke in the early 1920s of the technical specialists as "remnants of the past, by all their nature closely, unalterably bound to the bourgeois system that we aim to destroy."[4] However, the potentiality for conflict was only in part a result of class and cultural differences; it was also a product of the classic dispute between the principles of political democracy and specialized knowledge. Just who would run the new Soviet state, the Russian proletariat or white-collar specialists? Who would administer the Soviet factories, the workers employed there, or directors with training in engineering and industrial economics? Who would decide which expensive scientific research projects would be financed by the new government, the workers in their assemblies (the soviets), or the scientists themselves?

The contradictory views of the left Communists and the workers' groups toward science and technology came out most clearly in the 1920-21 debates of a much larger and politically more important issue: the trade union controversy. The details of this debate have been discussed elsewhere;[5] the final result of the discussion was to deprive the trade unions in the Soviet Union of any real political power of their own and to place factory management on the basis of the principle of one-man leadership instead of the earlier principle of collective workers' control. A similar development occurred in the workers' and peasants' legislative councils, which became of much less importance than the organs of the Communist party. In the course of the debates, several of the partisans of workers' control spoke out not only against the political apparatus of control in the Soviet economy and government but against the concept of privilege associated with specialized knowledge as well. The workers saw that the equation of socialism with science could take on a tendency opposed to their interests, if the logical deduction were drawn that the socialist state should therefore be run by scientists and technicians rather than by workers.

This dispute over whether technical decisions with social implications should be made by specialists or nonspecialists is common to all modern societies, although it appears in very different forms. It surfaced in the United States during the 1960s in the discussions of

20

large appropriations for research projects such as elementary particle
accelerators and space exploration. Citizens without technical
educations were not willing to leave such decisions in the hands of
specialists. In the Soviet Union, the tension has been expressed in
different ways. Stalin manipulated some of these feelings quite
brutally in the 1930s, when he staged political trials of technical
specialists at which they were charged with economic sabotage. The
accusations were usually false, but the popular animosity toward
technical specialists and their middle-class aspirations was in part
genuine. With the education of Soviet engineers and scientists who
have spent their entire lives in Soviet society and who cannot therefore
be accused of having prerevolutionary, bourgeois backgrounds, the
potency of this issue has greatly declined. The tension in the Soviet
Union between workers and scientists has been largely replaced today
by a tension between political bureaucrats and scientists. The old
issue still lingers on, however, in a different and much milder form
in the occasional complaints in the newspapers from Soviet factory
workers who observe that white-collar workers usually enjoy greater
privileges and prestige than blue-collar workers, despite the ceremon-
ial praise by government officials of the proletariat.

## EARLY SOVIET ACHIEVEMENTS

In the 1920s, when the idea of formulating science policies was
much more novel than today, a great discussion of the topic occurred
in the Soviet Union. It was in this period that Soviet scholars and
leaders first asked such questions as: "Can science be planned?"
"What aspects of science are most amenable to planning?" "What
are the first steps a nation should take toward formulating a science
policy?" "What organizational forms are best suited for planning
research and what forms are best suited for actually carrying out
research?" Although these questions were never fully answered, the
suggestions given in the Soviet Union in the 1920s are intellectually
interesting and continue to influence Soviet science today. This is
particularly true on the topic of organizational forms.

Planning was, and is, the preferred method of socialist and
Communist theorists in all human activities, and particularly economics.
Science, however, presents unique problems as an object of planning.
Among the Soviet advocates of a planned economic system in the
1920s, one could find many who would insist that theoretical research
in the natural sciences cannot be planned in any genuine sense.
They argue that there is an essential difference between science,
where progress depends on the discovery of unknown facts and the
construction of new hypotheses at indefinite times in the future, and
industrial production, which requires the converging of at least

21

theoretically ascertainable quantities of materials, properly trained personnel, and equipment. These Soviet authors emphasized that the path of scientific research is frequently determined by what was most recently learned. The most ardent opponents of the planning of science in the 1920s—frequently older scientists with considerable hostility toward the regime itself—maintained that there is something essentially creative and mystical about advanced theoretical research which totally defies rational investigation. Even among the Marxists who wrote on the planning of science there was a great spectrum of opinions, ranging from the denial of any significant difference between physical and mental labor, and therefore a firm belief in the planning of science as of industry, to an affirmation of the inherently intuitiveness of the process of discovery.

Despite the great differences of opinion, the idea of the planning of science was rather widely accepted by the late 1920s; different people merely defined this idea in quite different ways. To some, planning of science meant making science responsive to the needs of Soviet industry; to people holding this opinion, the real planning would occur among the economic planners, the scientists and engineers would merely serve the economic plan which the economists formulated and the government approved. To others, the planning of science meant providing for the supply of materiel and personnel to research institutes in a rational fashion, avoiding the bottlenecks so common in the early Soviet economy. To still others, the planning of science was essentially the planning of higher education. But to a fourth group—the one most interesting in retrospect—the planning of science meant the meshing together of judgements about the future of two relatively independent elements: on the one hand, the future needs of Soviet society; on the other, new developments which one could reasonably expect to occur in science and technology. These writers emphasized that what the Soviet Union needed first was more thorough knowledge of the existing scientific establishment. How many scientists of every category did the Soviet Union possess? What were their strengths and weaknesses?

The first step, then, in planning science was the gathering of empirical information. In the years between 1921 and 1934, workers at the Academy of Sciences made statistical and organizational surveys of the scientific personnel and institutions of the USSR which were remarkable in their detail and in their awareness of the potential of science and scientific institutions as natural resources. Anticipating similar work in other countries by more than a decade, the multivolume surveys, not to mention less ambitious handbooks and outlines, provided an enormous amount of data for the study of the growth of scientific disciplines and institutions in Russia. [6] The organizational surveys were conducted by a commission of the Academy of Sciences called "Science and Scientific Workers of the USSR," under the principal direction of S. F. Ol'denburg, permanent secretary of the

Academy of Sciences. One volume, published in 1930, covered the activities of 1,227 scientific research establishments and 151 higher educational institutions with 411 different departments. It included not only academies, universities, and research institutes, but also scientific societies, associations of doctors and other professions, and local organizations. The emphasis was on the gathering of new data which could be used according to the new techniques of the social sciences for the exploration of the sociology and political administration of science—and even for investigations of the social and genetic sources of creativity. [7]

One of the most important tasks of Soviet administrators in fostering science and technology was the development of rational, efficient work habits. Any traditional state embarking upon a modernization drive will attempt to eliminate peasant attitudes and work habits. The scientific management of labor was a major concern of Soviet planners in the 1920s. The effort to increase efficiency included time-and-motion studies for Russian factory workers, inspired in large part by the work of the American expert on labor efficiency, Frederick Winslow Taylor, but went far beyond to actual attempts to use the same approach on scientific research.

Soviet authors attempted to modernize scientific research by improving research techniques and the use of laboratory equipment; by proposing reforms in publication and indexing operations; by calling for information-retrieval systems, including primitive computers; and by developing quantitative criteria for evaluating the effectiveness of scientific research. A few even launched psychological and sociological studies of the nature of scientific creativity. [8] The assumption underlying all this activity was that scientific research could be submitted to analysis, its principles could be ascertained, and its conduct improved. Unfortunately, most of this research was abandoned in the early 1930s as the social sciences withered under Stalin's authoritarian policies. A rebirth would come in the 1950s.

Even before Stalin's ascendancy, the scientific management of research movement ran into opposition. Just as factory workers usually resented time-and-motion study engineers whose ultimate goal was to obtain more effective labor at less cost, so also many scientific researchers resented efforts to make research more productive. Among the scientists with prerevolutionary educations, the idea of "planning science" often continued to be held in suspicion. It was also obvious that frequently the controls designed to facilitate science planning were used for political purposes—to ensure loyalty to the regime. Even among some of the enthusiastic supporters of the goals of the new state, the management specialists continued to be distrusted. A. A. Bogdanov, one of the spokesmen for the proletarian culture movement but also a person who respected science, felt that the leaders of the science planning effort placed too much emphasis

23

on technical specialists and management engineers, who he feared might emerge as an elite replacing both the workers and the Communist Party.

The scientific management of the research movement revolved essentially around the problem of increasing individual creativity rather than thematic planning or the establishment of national priorities in science. Despite all the writing about the planning of science which one can find in the Soviet journals of the 1920s, the only moment when these major problems received full attention was at the First All-Union Conference on the Planning of Scientific-Research Work in Moscow from April 6-11, 1931. [9] Almost a thousand delegates, including over six hundred scientific workers and twenty full members of the Academy of Sciences, attended the conference. Nikolai Bukharin's keynote speech on the methodology of planning science marked a high degree of sophistication in the approach of Communist planners to the problems of charting the development of scientific research. Representatives of scientific researchers in agriculture, health, transport, and industry spoke on the problems of the planning of science in their particular areas.

Bukharin, who took an active role in administering scientific research as a member of several governmental committees, was a strong advocate of the planning of science. His major contribution to the debate was the definition of the phases of science which, in his view, were amenable to planning:

1. The determination of the share of the country's labor and budgetary resources which would be devoted to science. Bukharin gave scientific research the highest of all priorities, higher even than that of heavy industry.

2. The logistic support of scientific-research institutions. Again Bukharin assigned the highest priority to science, recognizing that fitful logistic support of a laboratory is more damaging than the same kind of support to an industry.

3. Geographical placement of scientific-research institutions. Bukharin called for the elimination of the old St. Petersburg center, and sketched the model for such provincial centers of science that Novosibirsk later became.

4. The supply of scientific researchers. Bukharin asked for the planned training of scientists, according to need.

5. The subjects of research. Bukharin recognized serious difficulties in actually planning the topics of research, but called for emphasis on those themes of research which would be of the most service to socialist construction. He granted allotments of free, unprogrammed time to all researchers.

24

# THE SOVIET BASE

## The Idea of the Scientific-Research Institute

Perhaps the most innovative and permanent reform which the Soviet Union enacted in the 1920s was the establishment of the idea of the research institute. There are, of course, research institutes in all scientific nations today, and there were quite a few even in the 1920s; one might doubt, therefore, that the Soviet idea of a research institute is in any way extraordinary. To a western scientist who has spent considerable time in the Soviet Union, however, it will be obvious that the term "scientific-research institute" (<u>nauchno-issledovatel'skii institut</u>) has a stature and a meaning in the Soviet Union that it does not have in any western country. Almost all outstanding scientists in the Soviet Union are members of an institute or have connections with one. (The main exception is university scientists, but faculty members without institute connections play a remarkably small role in Soviet research.) Institutes are the basic research units in the various academies of sciences and in the industrial ministries. The archetypical institute is in the USSR Academy of Sciences. In the entire academy system (including the republic academies) there are about six hundred institutes today; many more fall under the industrial ministries. Certain streets in Moscow, Leningrad, Novosibirsk, and Kiev are lined on both sides with institutes. These organizations form the determining milieus of their members; they often allot housing to their researchers, they largely determine their status, their international contacts, including the opportunity to travel abroad, and, of course, their pay. The institutes contain scholars in all fields—history and philosophy, for example, as well as physics and chemistry. In each field there are two or three institutes recognized as the best; once a person has reached that level there appears to be less transfer of members among institutes than there is among American universities (at least until positions became scarce in the U. S.). New institutes have occasionally been created on the demand of star scientists; Novosibirsk is well known for its institutes of this type, more often headed by younger scholars than in Moscow or Leningrad.

The idea of the institute was a result of conscious deliberation in the 1920s. At that time, the concept of research in specialized institutes—as distinguished from research in universities or conventional academies—was relatively new in all countries. The Soviet leaders looked over their shoulders at the new types of research organizations developing in the West and attempted not only to catch

25

up but actually to anticipate western trends. In the process, they promoted the idea of the specialized research institute to an unheralded prominence.

All over western Europe and America, in the first decades of the twentieth century, scientists frequently spoke of the need to find new forms of organization for scientific research. Germany, which led the way in the cultivation of pure research at university centers, also led in the first efforts to form integrated research institutes. These efforts sprang from the groups of industrial chemists in Germany in the 1860s and 1870s who established new norms in the direction of scientific and technological research. Later developments, especially in physics and chemistry, determined the prosperous future of the research institute. Developments in electronics opened possibilities for diverse applications which could be exploited only through the cooperative labor of many highly trained engineers and technicians. These institutes were sponsored by both private industry and governments; the Kaiser Wilhelm Institutes were, as the Russians noted, quite significant as prototypes of research institutes depending, at least partially, upon governmental funds. Other governmental institutions which were observed by the Soviet planners were the British National Physical Laboratory and Department of Scientific and Industrial Research, and the French National Center of Scientific Research. In the United States, the most prominent early institutes were in private industries, such as the General Electric Company and the Bell Telephone Company.

With their strong sense of historical evolution, the Soviet planners of the 1920s believed that they saw a clear trend in these new institutions. The west European and American developments indicated to them that the important research of this century would not be done in the old academies or the universities but in these institutes. After returning in 1926 from an inspection tour of scientific institutions in Germany, France, and England, the permanent secretary of the Russian Academy of Sciences, S. F. Ol'denburg, wrote, "If the eighteenth century was the century of academies, while the nineteenth was the century of universities, then the twentieth century is becoming the century of research institutes."[10] The Communist party leader Bukharin agreed on the importance of new organizational forms, noting in 1931 that history was moving into a new era in which future progress depended much less on the individual inventor or scholar and much more on the large, organized research laboratory.[11] Academician N. I. Vavilov, a geneticist, agreed that they were witnessing a revolution in world science which demanded new methods: "From the work of solitary scientists, we are shifting to collectivism. Modern institutes and laboratories are, so to speak, 'factories of scientific thought.'"[12]

The particular form which the new Soviet research institutes took was a result of a combination of factors: the above analysis of trends in the West; the strong tradition of the Academy system in Russia;

the need to make a closer link between practical and theoretical science; and the principles of a socialist economy. The fact that consolidation of research units was a trend in the West confirmed the opinion of the Soviet analysts of science that they were on the right track. The unique strength of the Academy of Sciences, compared to other scientific institutions in Russia, led them to believe that the academy was the logical framework to contain the leading institutes. The fact that the Soviet Union was building a socialist economy meant that the institutes deeply involved in industrial technology would not be attached to a single company—as was usually the case in the United States—but instead would serve industry as a whole. Soviet planners frequently commented that only a socialist economy could avoid the wasteful duplication in research which they saw between competing firms in capitalist countries. In sum, the idea of the new Soviet research institute was a hybrid of western and native Soviet elements.

The institutes have now developed over forty years in the Soviet Union with rather small changes. The new form was unquestionably a successful one. In all the recent debates over reform of scientific research in the Soviet Union, no one proposed radically altering the institute system. Indeed, that system is now one of the most prominent features of Soviet academic life. At the same time, one can now see that the Soviet reformers of science of the 1920s and 1930s may have carried their extrapolation of historical trends too far, particularly in their de-emphasis of university research and in their wish for the organizational separation of industrial research from individual plants. Universities in the West have not lost their positions as centers of theoretical research and, in at least some cases, provide important centers for the fruitful combination of teaching and research. Further-more, industrial research which is located close to factory production is more likely to be utilized quickly than when it is far away in a centralized institute under different administration. A number of Soviet scientists have indicated in recent years that a mixed pattern, including research in academic institutes, university departments, and plant laboratories, possesses genuine virtues. One of the products of the exchange of scientists in recent years between the Soviet Union and other nations has been a greater appreciation, on both hands, of the respective strengths of different research patterns.


The Planning System for Science


In the years immediately after the revolution, the government was not successful in establishing central control over the scientific establishment. Furthermore, since the Soviet Union was not formed legally until 1922, and did not possess a constitution until 1924, it was logical for the first committees concerned with science to be

27

subordinate to the republic governments (component states of the USSR) rather than to central authorities in Moscow. In the first years of Soviet power, the old centers of science, such as the Academy of Sciences, continued their research as before the revolution. The result of this lack of coordination in science was a proliferation of local planning bodies for science under the republics. Soviet authorities always assumed that some day there would be one central planning organ for science working with the existing central economic and political organs, but that goal receded deeper into the future. When the Soviet Union finally, in the late 1920s, made serious attempts to establish centralized planning, the field was cluttered with various other governmental and semigovernmental committees with ambiguous powers.[13]

In the early 1920s each republic possessed, under its Commissariat of Education, a Chief Administration of Scientific Institutions responsible for the formulation of policy for science on the level of the republics. By far the most important of these scientific administrations was that of the Russian republic, which supervised the Academy of Sciences, the research laboratories belonging to the universities, and also many of the independent research institutes. The closest approach to the nationwide coordination of science which occurred in the 1920s was the effort the several scientific administrations made at their infrequent conferences. These meetings were the scenes of many jurisdictional disputes between the scientific administrations, the universities, the Academy of Sciences, and the central governmental organs. The Academy of Sciences repeatedly accused the Russian Scientific Administration of bureaucratic interference in scientific affairs.[14]

The first technological task which the Soviet government approached on a planned basis was the electrification of the country; the famous Governmental Commission for the Electrification of Russia (GOELRO) was established February 21, 1920. The plan was not viewed simply as a schedule for electrification but as a method for transforming the entire country on the basis of heavy industrialization. Lenin's well-known slogan, "Communism is Soviet power plus electrification of the whole country," conveys the fervor of the times.

Many competing planning organs for science evolved in the early 1920s. Despite the fragmentation of authority, the grand dream of the rational, centralized state, not only planning scientifically but planning science, was not forgotten. After the adoption of the 1924 constitution, and the formation of all-union (central, or federal) governing organs, the debate over a supreme planning organ broke out afresh, with greater intensity than ever before. Now it seemed natural that a permanent central science committee, directly under the USSR Council of Commissars, should take over the functions previously performed on the republic level. Some persons said that since the committee would be in charge of science throughout the country, it should have full rank as the Commissariat of Science. Even the idea that the Academy of Sciences itself might be transformed into such a body was considered. Another possible contender was the Communist Academy (called the Socialist Academy from 1918 to 1923) which had from its first days been considered a counterbalance to the bourgeois influence of the old intelligentsia.

The period immediately after 1924 was, along with the period after 1956, the moment when a central coordinating body was most expected to appear. The severe economic crisis had by this time passed, and the discussion of the methodology of long-range industrial planning in these years inevitably involved science and technology. Yet, strangely enough, the much talked about national coordinating center for science was not created. The opposition of the republic authorities, particularly those of the Ukraine, was one reason for not centralizing science policy. So also was the lack of enthusiasm for the planning of science among several of the leading natural scientists of the USSR Academy of Sciences. The most important reason, however, for the absence of a central science policy committee was the loss of the innovative character of Soviet government as a result of the deadening effect of Stalinism. [15] The idea of a rational state which would create new models in developing science policies faded into the background. It was revived partially after Stalin's death.

Soviet Science During Stalin's Tenure

By the mid-1930s, Soviet science had taken on the basic organizational features which have remained constant to the present day, despite numerous small reforms in the last fifteen years. Research was concentrated in three distinct pyramids: (1) the academy system, headed by the USSR Academy of Sciences, but including academies for each of the republics as well; (2) the institutions of higher education, such as the universities and technical institutes; (3) the ministerial research establishments, usually industrial research institutes.

Although the USSR Academy of Sciences enjoyed more prestige than any other single organization in Soviet science and also exercized the greatest influence, it contained only a small portion of all the active scientific workers. Its status was based on the universally acknowledged fact that it contained the most talented scientific thinkers in the country.

Theoretically, the work of all three of these pyramids was coordinated by the State Planning Commission of the Council of Ministers, which was responsible for the five-year economic plans. This coordination succeeded in a gross fashion—for example, the development

29

and production of metal alloys, electronic equipment, aviation technology, and synthetic fibers involved contact among all three branches of research. On most topics, however, the individual pyramid controlled its own work. Indeed, each institute usually based its future research plan on past work and on the opinions of its leading scientists. Even the industrial ministries, directly involved with national economic planning, were given appreciable leeway in looking after their own research needs.

Informal and unofficial arrangements gradually became much more important than legal definitions of authority. A multiplicity of different committees and governmental organs with clashing jurisdictions gradually assumed responsibility for the formulation of science policy. In moments of important disputes over science, resolution usually occurred on the all-union level, or in the highest organs of the Communist party, or even by Stalin's personal intervention. At other moments, decisions were made in a rather haphazard fashion on local levels.

During the period from the mid-1930s to the mid 1950s, Soviet science planning was characterized by emphasis on an ultimate product: an increase in production of heavy industry. This emphasis was frequently antithetical to broad social planning. In addition, Stalin's purges took a heavy toll of the intellectuals and economic planners who had given an enthusiastic and innovative tone to the debates of the 1920s.

In several areas of science, such as genetics, political controls extended to the substance of science itself. Attracted by Lysenko's promises of quick practical gains from the use of his agricultural techniques, Stalin supported a series of resolutions governing the administration of research which placed Lysenko and his followers in control of important sections of the educational, agricultural, and scientific establishments. Paradoxically, Lysenko's inability to understand modern molecular biology was combined with an extraordinary talent for currying political favor; he managed to maintain himself, with many ups and downs, long after Stalin's death, until finally discredited in 1965. [16]

During World War II, the Soviet planning system performed rather well, sided by the intense unity evoked by the war effort. Soviet planners successfully mobilized industries, transferred wholesale many plants to areas outside the German line of advance (an accomplishment little appreciated in the West), developed tanks and planes which performed well under extreme trials, and handled the logistic complexities of warfare, including the reception and distribution of immense quantities of lend-lease material.

The wartime mobilization of science and technology was, of course, common to all the nations involved in the struggle. The evidence indicates, however, that the longterm impact of the war on the organization of science and technology was actually less in the Soviet Union than in the other allied nations. The reason for the difference was simply that Soviet science and technology were already under the control of the Communist party and, consequently, relatively few new principles needed to be established in order for political directives to flow throughout the scientific and technological establishment. The basic system of controls, which had been created before the war, continued during the conflict and persisted into the peacetime period.

Unattractive to most intellectuals as this Stalinist system of controls was, it should also be recognized that during its existence the Soviet state fulfilled certain impressive humanitarian goals, as well as industrial and military ones. Illiteracy in the Soviet Union was drastically reduced by means of campaigns embracing both children and adults, and the educational system expanded strikingly at all levels. Perhaps most impressive, from a social welfare point of view, was the expansion of medicine and, even more important, the creation of a system for the distribution of medical services. This system, despite certain qualitative faults, was a tremendous improvement for the Soviet population and continues to be a model for many nations today. At the time of Stalin's death in 1953, there were more physicians in the Soviet Union on a per capita basis than in any other nation in the world with the possible exception of Israel, where most of the physicians were immigrants. 17 During the quarter of century of Stalin's rule, the number of medical doctors in the Soviet Union quadrupled, the construction of dispensaries and hospitals kept pace, and infant mortality precipitously declined. Historians of the Soviet Union will have to consider this impressive social product of Stalin's reign along with the frightful violence of collectivization and the purges. The complexity of historical judgements is once again revealed. Medicine is probably the area of science which has most unambiguously benefited man during the last half-century; the relative improvement of the health of the citizens of the Soviet Union during this period has been dramatic. This improvement was more a result of social organization than of independent developments in medical research.

## CHALLENGES TO SOVIET SCIENCE POLICY

### The New Needs of Soviet Society after World War II

In the early phase of industrial expansion before the war, immediate practical needs were the most significant determinants of research. Marxist theory had been developed to justify this emphasis by stressing the need to tie theory to practice in science as well as philosophy. As Marx commented, the need was not only to interpret

31

the world but to change it. Technology is man's most obvious means of changing the world. Soviet planners of the 1930s believed it was actually immoral for geologists to study rock strata simply to determine the age of the earth, because oil deposits were desperately needed and geologists were scarce. Even the social sciences had to adhere to pragmatic standards; anthropologists studied "Soviet man as a productive force" in the quest for ways to improve the efficiency of the worker or peasant. Men who had been educated as theoretical physicists were occasionally allocated to projects that called for mechanical engineers. Members of the academies of sciences were required to make trips to lecture workers on the close connections between science and production and to observe at first hand the engineering problems confronting factory directors. The assignment of theoreticians to engineering tasks was inherently wasteful on a longterm time scale, but this system of allocation was rationalized with the argument that so long as the Soviet Union remained a backward nation in both industry and science, it could obtain from western nations the basic knowledge needed for the improvement of its technology.

After World War II, the national goal of Soviet science and technology slowly shifted. The steady rise in the nation's industrial strength contributed to its self-confidence and permitted a longer view at priorities. The growing number of engineering graduates enabled planners to make a more appropriate allocation of scientists and engineers; no longer did theoreticians need to enter directly into the processes of factory production. The industrial plants began to create their own research and development laboratories and were thus freed of complete dependence on central institutes. Furthermore, as the general level of research in the USSR approached that in the other advanced countries, the Soviets had to provide more and more of their own basic scientific knowledge. As V. Glushkov, vice-president of the Ukrainian Academy of Sciences remarked

> In the future the role of pure science will be constantly growing. As long as we had the task of catching up with the technological development of the capitalist West, we could afford to devote less attention to long-range research, making wide use of the scientific and technological experience accumulated abroad. But those who are marching ahead have no one to learn from. [18]

One of the obstacles to a reform of Soviet science was ideological in nature. The Marxist concept most closely connected to the reform of research concerned the position of science relative to the productive forces of society. Is scientific research a derivative function of social organization, or is it an independent activity that may, at least on occasion, itself determine the direction of social activity?

The emphasis of the Soviet writers of the 1930s was on the impact of society on science. Soviet scientists after the war, however, began to speak more and more frequently of the "inner logic" or "self-flow" of science, and of the impact this relatively autonomous science had upon society, instead of society upon science.

It took time for the new thinking of the scientists to be reflected in the writings of the government's ideologists after the war. According to textbooks of Marxism-Leninism of the late Stalinist period, the fundamental elements of social life were: (1) the productive forces of society (manpower, machinery, technology, natural resources), (2) the corresponding productive relations (socialist, capitalist, feudal) which together with the productive forces, form the economic base of society, and (3) the ideological superstructure of society (law, morality, religion, art, and so forth) which develop not independently but in response to changes in the economic base. The theoreticians of the 1930s and 1940s usually assigned science to the superstructure, believing in the creation not only of a new, class-oriented literature and art but also of a new science. It was believed that "science is one of the highest, if not the highest of the layers of the superstructure."[19] The linguist N. Ia. Marr regarded as a part of the superstructure not only language but also the "highest ideologies," including art, philosophy, and science. If this view had prevailed, a reform of scientific research in the Soviet Union that had as its goal the granting of more independence to theoretical research would have been difficult to reconcile with Marxist theory.

The belief that science was a part of the superstructure and therefore a derivative function of society became increasingly awkward, even in the Stalinist period. Marxist theory postulated, for example, that each epoch (feudalism, capitalism, socialism) had its own superstructure, and emphasized the discontinuities separating the stages. When a new economic base was formed, the old superstructure must fall. While a Marxist might accept the theory that the Soviet Union needed a complete break with the capitalist superstructure in such fields as philosophy and art, he could hardly hold the same view with regard to science. The development of science was obviously additive, and Soviet scientists had begun where their tsarist predecessors left off.

Scientific theory was becoming too independent and potent a force in society to be regarded as a mere reflection of economic relations. Of course, there remained a certain persuasiveness to Engels' remark that "If a technical demand appears in a society, then it will move science ahead more than ten universities,"[20] but by World War II this statement was obviously only a partial description at best of the complex relationship of science and society. Science no longer served merely as the minion of industry, answering the demands placed on it. It also, by giving birth to discoveries that shaped technology, was creating industries that were not anticipated by economic planners or obviously caused by industrial demand; and it was modifying social relations in ways not predicted by social theorists. Far from being merely a part of the derivative superstructure, science seemed, in addition, to be related in some important fashion with the formative economic base.

Late in his life, Stalin initiated an important reevaluation of the role of science. In his Letters on Linguistics, he advanced several new theories, the effects of which in the areas of language and politics (but not in the field of science) are well known abroad. [21] Stalin introduced the concept of social activities that are a part of neither the base nor the superstructure, and stated that science is one of these activities. Discussion of these theories has continued to the present. They were an issue in the debate over the reform of Soviet science, since they affected the autonomy of the theoretical sciences.

The growing prestige of the fundamental sciences was reflected after Stalin's death in the 1961 Party Program which stated that "science will become, in the full sense of the word, a direct productive force." This statement left no doubt that science would soon be considered a major independent element of the economic base, a motive force which did not depend primarily on social organization or industrial production for its advancement. [22]

The Great Debate of Science Policy
in the Late 1950s

In the late 1950s, a few years after Stalin's death, a spirited debate over the administration of science broke out in the Soviet Union. The changing needs of Soviet society discussed above were important causes of the debate, as was the belief by scientists that the political thaw occurring throughout Soviet society should be extended to science. In addition, the achievements of Soviet space scientists had dramatically elevated their prestige. Soviet science and technology were now highly appreciated internationally; it seemed to Soviet scientists that it was an appropriate moment to raise the independence of science domestically.

The major complaint of the scientists in the academy was that they were forced to spend too much of their time worrying about practical applications and thus did not have enough time and funds for theoretical research. The president of the academy, A. N. Nesmeianov, wrote in 1955 that there were too many engineers in the academy; he also observed that government and party officials continually interrupted the research of the members of the Academy with requests for solutions to narrow production problems. [23]

To the scientists' surprise, Nesmeianov's plea was picked up by Nikita Khrushchev himself, who commented in February 1956, that a

34

thorough reform of scientific research was needed. [24] He returned to the theme three years later; it was clear that the poorly educated and unsophisticated Khrushchev had somehow grasped the essence of the problem, that it was time to shift the priorities of the academy from industrialization to the further expansion of knowledge: "The time has come . . . to reorganize the work in the Academy of Sciences. . . . I think that a difficult situation has arisen in some scientific institutions in the Academy. Some scientists may disagree with me, but I consider it unwise for the Academy of Sciences to take on questions of metallurgy and coal mining. After all, these areas were not within the Academy's domain earlier. . . . Think over this problem, comrades, and make suggestions on it."[25]

Khrushchev's invitation for a full debate was immediately accepted. The ensuing discussion soon revealed much disagreement among the scientists and engineers about the correct organization for Soviet science. In earlier years, when Stalin emphasized unity, they usually kept their disagreements to themselves; now divisions and quarrels that had simmered for decades boiled over into public view. During the peak of the polemics in 1959, four general positions could be discerned: that of the theoreticians of the natural sciences, that of the engineers, that of the representatives of the local research institutions, such as the republic academies of science, and that of the university professors.

The most aggressive proponent of the natural scientists' position was Nikolai Semenov, a chemist who won the Nobel Prize in 1956 for his research on the theory of chemical reactions. In an article in August 1959, in the leading government newspaper, Semenov advanced an outspoken defense of theoretical scientific research together with a sharp criticism of the past interpretation of the Marxist principle concerning the unity of theory and practice, to the advantage of the applied sciences. [26] He maintained that there was no necessity for engineers in the academy. Science is not an appendage of industry, he argued, but has its own independent assignment, which is the "thorough study of nature and the internal mechanism of phenomena and the mastery on man's behalf of hitherto concealed natural forces." He considered it a gross oversimplification to maintain that science receives all of its stimulation from production. Did industry ever hint at the possibility of unleashing atomic energy, he asked? On the contrary, atomic energy was the fruit of pure science. (Semenov dodged here the question of how much influence military requirements had on the time and place in which atomic energy appeared.) To Semenov, a sophisticated understanding of science would reveal that there are two rather independent sources of scientific advance: the demands of production, which he thought Soviet planners steadfastly emphasized, and the internal logic of science itself, which he thought Soviet planners ignored.

Semenov believed that responsibility for research in the two different areas of pure and applied science should be assigned to separate research organizations. In his view, the Academy of Sciences should be primarily responsible for theoretical research, and the engineering institutes should be removed from the academy and placed under the control of the industrial ministries. Whenever a theoretical problem was solved by the academy's theoreticians, the results could then be turned over to the appropriate industrial authorities.

Semenov also called for a recognition of the fact that the planning of theoretical research had never worked well. "The output of the Academy's scientific endeavors," he wrote, "is not material processed by machine but scientific truth, which can never be planned in detail." Therefore, he recommended that the authority of the central administration in the academy be diminished, and that leading researchers be granted greater authority to investigate those topics which seemed most important to them.

The leading spokesman for the engineers —and the chief opponent of the point of view expressed by Semenov--was Ivan Bardin, the head of the department of the academy which contained most of the engineering institutes. Bardin had been one of the first engineers ever elected to the academy, and he flatly accused Semenov of trying to erase the past thirty years by advocating a return to the academy of prerevolutionary times, which had been an ivory tower of theoretical research. Bardin pointedly asked, "Just why must the USSR Academy of Sciences, which was awakened to the need for contact with life by V.I. Lenin, constrict the range of its work and retreat to the position of the ill-remembered Imperial Academy of Sciences?"[27]

The most important reason for the emotional content of Bardin's reply was Semenov's proposal to oust the engineers from the academy, thereby depriving them of the title of "academician," which carries greater prestige than any other professional title in the Soviet Union. Underlying the whole debate, of course, was the tension between theorists and practical men which has appeared in scientific organizations all over the world. Engineers have often suspected that theorists have considered them intellectually and socially inferior. In the Soviet Union this same tension existed, despite the fact that in the first decades of that nation's existence the practical life of the engineer was constantly praised in official writings, novels, and films. It is interesting that the ethos of the pure scientist was not destroyed by this social emphasis but, on the contrary, retained extraordinary strength.

The contest between the engineers and the fundamental scientists was now fully joined. However, the organizational issue involved was not a simple, two-sided question. Other factions of the scientific and technical intelligentsia submitted their opinions on the organization of Soviet science. V. Kirillin, who later emerged as a leading administrator of Soviet research, emphasized the need for decentraliza-

36

tion, a point which was echoed by many local scientists from provincial areas who feared central controls. Kirillin wrote, "We must reject the idea that a central organ can plan and coordinate all the scientific work being conducted in the various institutes, laboratories, and higher educational institutions in the Soviet Union. As a matter of fact, the number of scientific research institutes and higher educational establishments in our country is around 3,000. . . . It is difficult to imagine any sort of single, central institution."[28]

Another difference of opinion frequently expressed in the debates was that between researchers in the academy system and those in the universities. The criticism of the Soviet academy by the professors harked back to a rivalry that had existed during much of the nineteenth century, when the faculty members of the universities reprimanded the academicians for their political conservatism and their disregard of pedagogical and industrial concerns. Despite the underdevelopment of research in Soviet universities, a few fields, such as mathematics — had prospered there. Several university mathematicians reproached the chemists and physicists of the Academy of Sciences for their assumption that only in the academy could truly advanced research be performed. They pointed out that the average age of researchers was lower in the universities than in the institutes of the academy, and that in fields such as theoretical mathematics youth was an intellectual advantage.[29]

The debates of the 1950s involved dozens of articles and many more viewpoints than can be described here.[30] Out of this period of discussion stemmed a series of changes in the administration of Soviet science.

### The Reforms

In the period 1961-65, the system of science administration in the Soviet Union was reformed three times. In these changes, the opinions of Semenov and his colleagues seemed to be the most influential, although a variety of conflicting interests has been represented. The first reform was announced on April 12, 1961, the day Yuri Gagarin made the first circumnavigation of the globe by artificial satellite.[31] This 1961 decree, issued jointly by the Central Committee of the Communist Party and the Council of Ministers of the USSR, stipulated that narrow engineering institutes would be removed from the academy and placed under the jurisdiction of the industrial ministries. That this change was designed to permit the academy to concentrate upon fundamental research was clearly indicated in the decree: "The work of the Academy should be focused primarily on the most important long-run problems of science that are undergoing rapid development."

The decree also established a new organization, superior to the academy and in charge of all Soviet science. This organization has

37

continued to the present day, although its name and its function have been altered in the interim. Originally named the State Committee for the Coordination of Scientific Research, this body was given power to allocate research projects and recommend budgetary support (for approval by the Council of Ministers) for research projects in all three research pyramids: The academies, the universities, and the industrial ministries. As will become clear, the system never performed in quite this fashion.

The Committee for the Coordination of Scientific Research found that the direction of engineering research in industry was considerably easier than the control of theoretical research in the republic and all-union academies. As a governmental committee, its interests were primarily in technology rather than in pure science, and even though it had legal power to coordinate the work of the Academy of Sciences, it only rarely used that authority. Instead, the leading members of the academy maintained most of the controlling influence in their institutions simply by demonstrating their superior knowledge of their subjects and by pointing to their past records as successful researchers. This situation was partially recognized in the second reform, in April 1963, which strengthened the position of the Academy of Sciences of the USSR as the coordinator of theoretical research throughout the Soviet Union.[32] The academy was even given authority to direct research in the universities as well, an authority which led to many conflicts and was only partially successful. (Today the university in Novosibirsk is under the control of the Siberian branch of the Academy, but the older universities have maintained their autonomy.)

In 1965, the top committee coordinating science was renamed the State Committee for Science and Technology. It is today, in principle, the supreme coordinator of science and technology in the Soviet Union. However, several of its administrators have admitted in articles and in interviews with foreigners that its responsibilities are primarily in technology and not in theoretical science. In the latter area, the Academy of Sciences continues its rather independent role.

In order to coordinate research cutting across institutions and disciplines the State Committee on Science and Technology has relied increasingly on a form of organization known as "scientific councils." These councils are appointed on an ad hoc basis to discuss research policies toward particular problems or subjects and bring together leading scientists, engineers, government administrators, and economic planners from many different institutions. Although their function is purely advisory, they often make suggestions which are then implemented by the appropriate ministry or research institution. The scientific councils are the most successful foci for the mixing of advice from all three research pyramids and from the government and party.

RECENT FEATURES OF SOVIET SCIENCE POLICY

Factors Working Against the Reforms

In retrospect, it can be seen that despite their apparent success the reforms of the early 1960s faced formidable obstacles. The leading theoretical physicists and chemists who provided the most important impetus for the reform movement had goals which were not identical with those of government and party leaders who gave them important temporary support. The theoreticians were aiming for a new era of free research in which all questions about matter were equally justified and in which they would no longer have to defend their research in terms of its practical consequences. They were weary of having to pretend that even the most abstract mathematical formulation of elementary particle theory, or the development of alternative algebras, or investigations of theories of chemical bonds would have inevitable practical effects which would justify the expense of the research to government bureaucrats.

The government and party leaders, on the other hand, were willing to support some of the reform requests because they correctly saw that the Soviet Union had moved into a new era in which it would have to shift, at least relatively, from the gross indexes of industrial production to a broad support of the whole scientific-technological enterprise of an advanced nation, including endorsement of theoretical research with no apparent application. The political leaders had noticed that the value of theoretical research did not consist entirely in its practical utility; for a nation to be a leader in high-energy physics or space exploration brought international prestige similar to showing the flag in foreign ports. It appeared that a happy alliance of bureaucrat and pure scientist might be possible.

Soon that alliance broke down as it became clear just how far the bureaucrats had been all along from accepting the ethos of "science for science's sake." They still made demands on the scientists, although frequently different ones than they had expressed in earlier decades. One demand which continued from the 1950s and, indeed, intensified, was that the Soviet Union compete successfully with other nations in certain areas of science, particularly with the United States.

The effects of competition distorted the profile of research in both the United States and the Soviet Union, causing incredible wastes of money, and frustrating many scientists. The effects in military technology, resulting in the rapid obsolescence of weapons of staggering cost, are obvious. Norman Vig has written in this volume that the rate of advancement of military technology in the 1960s in the U. S.

39

and the USSR was so rapid that Great Britain had to scrap its own missiles and supersonic aircraft and abandon the competition. The price of success paid in the United States and the Soviet Union included the neglect of social needs and the restriction of research in certain areas. The similar effects of competition in space exploration are so evident that they do not require repetition. Somewhat less obvious were the effects of rivalry in even theoretical areas of physics, chemistry, biology, and mathematics.

The 1960s were the years in which the phenomenon which I have called the "Blueberry Effect" was most pronounced in affecting the science policies of the United States and the USSR. The term comes from observing my six-year-old daughter and her friend picking wild blueberries while on vacation. I suggested that they compete to see who could pick the most blueberries in ten minutes. Contrary to my expectation that they would strike out in different directions in the woods in the hope of coming upon a lush bush that the other would not find, the two girls literally stuck elbow-to-elbow during the entire time, secure in the knowledge that each would get approximately half of whatever was discovered. The desire for security overwhelmed the willingness to take risks.

In the 1960s, administrators in the Soviet Union and the United States preferred being at each other's elbows in research and development to the chance of being lost alone in the woods. Even mathematicians lobbying for money from Congress spoke of Soviet progress in their field, and Soviet scientists revealed to their American colleagues that the best way to obtain money was to speak of what the Americans were doing on the same topic. Although these effects are impossible to measure, such competitive considerations undoubtedly influenced the profile of scientific research and restricted the freedom of researchers. Money was plentiful for performing the research which administrators thought crucial, and scarce for other purposes. The harm in this approach was not so much in the idea of setting priorities in research as it was in the particular priorities which were established. One of the most interesting breaks in this postwar pattern of the interrelationship of Soviet and American policies toward technology came later, in the 1970s, when the United States began to break out of the framework of the Blueberry Effect by refusing to build the supersonic transport (despite impressive Soviet achievements), by cutting down on space research, and by considering reduction of military research and development. It is still too early to tell whether these developments are permanent or temporary, and it is also not clear that they have yet had appreciable effects on Soviet science policies.

The ultimate obstacle to the reforms of the early 1960s in the Soviet Union was that the leaders of the Communist party desired not a relaxation of controls over scientists but a redefinition of the goals of such controls in accord with the new perception of national interest and prestige. The political leaders agreed that no longer should the primary concern of scientists be basic industrialization, as it had been under Stalin. They insisted that the scientists continue to accept as social responsibilities the needs of a new, more sophisticated industry, and the requirements of a Soviet Government with global interests. Information theory, automated industry, new military technology, synthetic fibers, space exploration, plastics, lasers, microminiaturization, solid-state physics, data-processing—these were the fields presenting new demands upon scientists. In the social sciences, a new breed was also desired—mathematical economists, political scientists, specialists in arms control and game theory, foreign area experts, sociologists, computer programmers, business management experts. The worldview of these technocrats was considerably different from the pure scientists who had labored for reform, and as time went on the differences increased.

Post Reform Period

Since 1965, the Soviet system for the organization of science has undergone no major reforms, although there have been a number of minor policy shifts and much discussion of the need for additional improvements in the administration of research. The multitude of articles on science policy which have appeared in the Soviet Union in the last six or seven years seems to reflect several concerns of the governmental leadership: (1) An increasing concern about the high cost of modern scientific research and a consequent desire to economize. (2) A continuing realization that despite the growing strength of Soviet science the United States has been progressing even more rapidly in certain critical areas, such as computer technology and chemical research. (3) A continuing desire to increase industrial growth more rapidly by the use of scientific and technological innovations.

While the above concerns are those voiced most frequently by party and government leaders, the working scientists have often expressed their own worries, which frequently differ from those of the leadership, at least in emphasis. The scientists continue to call for greater autonomy in research, freer communication with foreign scientists (including travel abroad), better equipment in laboratories and institutes, better pay and privileges for scientists, and reforms in pedagogy and preparation of scientists.

Even a cursory glance at the recent speeches and articles of Soviet administrators of science will reveal their growing anxiety over the financial costs of modern science. The Soviet Union maintains a scientific establishment of approximately the same size as that of the United States, while it has a national income of less than half that of

41

the United States. The economic pressures involved are intense. In 1967, M. Millionshchikov, one of the vice-presidents of the Academy of Sciences of the USSR, asked in the leading government newspaper: "Is it really worth it to expend so much money and effort on topics so far from our vital needs as elementary particles, the explosions of supernovas, and so forth? Is there any guarantee that this expenditure of resources will not be in vain?"[33] Millionshchikov answered that the history of science illustrated that such expenditures were indeed justified, but he was clearly worried. M. V. Keldysh, the president of the academy, devoted a considerable portion of his recent speeches to the need for increasing the efficiency of scientific research.[34]

The pressing issue of expenses has been the major reason for the great attention given in recent years to cost-effectiveness studies in the Soviet Union. Soviet scholars, like their colleagues in other countries, have attempted to calculate the return on investment that has accrued from various lines of research and have then attempted to allocate priorities in research on this basis. Some progress has been made in this area, and certain institutes finance themselves through their own innovations, receiving return payments from industry. The more theoretical the research, however, the less realistic cost-effectiveness studies have been. The thought of forcing a mathematics institute or an astronomical observatory to pay its own way is recognized as absurd.

The effort to make science more efficient is also the major reason for the recent large-scale development in the USSR of the "science of science," the effort to use the methods of science on itself in order to understand and control its development. This interest represented a return to the concerns of science planners in the 1920s. The western pioneers in this field, J. D. Bernal and Derek Price, are well-known figures in the Soviet Union. Gennadi Dobrov has established a center for the science of science (naukovedenie, nauka o nauke) in Kiev.

The effort to improve the efficiency of scientific research has included a few recent investigations of the sociology of science. These studies represent a departure from past policies, since for many years sociology was almost totally undeveloped in the USSR. The collection of data on personal opinions was impossible during Stalin's rule, and not until the 1960s did social science data begin to appear in Soviet journals. In 1969, however, V. Poshataev reported that he had collected data on scientists in research institutes by asking them questions such as "What is your chief motivation for scientific work?" and "Are you satisfied with your work in the collective?"[35] The answer of the majority to the first question was "creative interest," although a few replied that their creative interest was stifled by the tight bureaucratic control in their institute. In answer to the second question, 25 respondents out of 137 in one institute replied that it was really impossible to speak of a "collective" in their institute because most of the researchers were doing individual dissertation research and never had serious general discussions with the other members of the institute. Of course, one can not draw conclusions about the motivation of Soviet researchers from such fragmentary evidence, but it is clear that Poshataev and other Soviet sociologists believe that such studies can lead to recommendations which will improve research. Poshataev, for example, recommended that group defenses of dissertations be permitted in order to improve cooperation in the institutes, and he also called for more work on the "typology of researchers" in order to learn more about why some groups of researchers work together well while others do not.

One of the main obstacles preventing the improvement of the effectiveness of scientific research in the Soviet Union has been difficulties in the supply of laboratory equipment. Both the government and individual researchers have agreed in numerous articles that institutes and laboratories often cannot obtain needed equipment, cannot get it repaired when it breaks down, and do not utilize it efficiently when they have it.

It is difficult for Americans to realize that this problem of the supply of laboratory equipment and materials is considered by Soviet scientists to be a major problem and not just a trivial difficulty. The dimensions of the difficulty of laboratory supplies are simply of a different order in the Soviet Union than in western countries. Perhaps no other topic has been the source of more complaints in recent articles by working scientists in the Soviet Union.

The Soviet system has difficulty accomplishing those functions which are best performed by local initiative and private capital, such as the supply of small quantities of sophisticated equipment and supplies. On the other hand, it performs very well those functions most appropriate for the public sector, such as the distribution of medical services to all levels of the population and the provision of public transportation (which, in turn, not surprisingly, are inadequately performed in the United States).

The problem of laboratory supplies has been attacked by Soviet scientists from several different directions. One author, writing in Pravda, called for the establishment of special supply outfits for institutes, laboratories, and construction bureaus that could provide supplies on a flexible basis and without delays.[36] Another scientist wrote in the same newspaper that a solution of this type was desperately needed. Under the present system, he reported, his institute was required to make its supply orders in May or June for the following year—everything from nails to complex apparatus—but the thematic plan of the laboratory was not approved until October, so the task of ordering supplies was literally impossible.[37] Some directors of institutes found an exit from such paradoxes by ordering equipment to cover all contingencies. Not surprisingly, much of this equipment was never taken off the shelf, a fact often cited by the government's cost-effectiveness experts.

43

In 1970, the Committee of Weights, Measures, and Instruments of the Council of Ministers of the USSR assumed a greater role in supplying research units. It was given a new and modern building on Lenin Prospect in Moscow, near the presidium of the Academy of Sciences and many of the leading research institutes. Several innovative proposals, including the establishment of "equipment pools" from which institutes could rent items, were being tested.[38] The president of the Academy, Keldysh, reported in February 1970, that the problem of supplying equipment to research institutes was gradually being alleviated.[39]

In his speeches in recent years, Keldysh has also emphasized the need for the Soviet Union to match the United States in certain critical areas of research. The success of the United States in sending manned expeditions to the moon was one sign of this competition, although perhaps a temporary one in the light of the subsequent diminishing of interest in space exploration in the United States. Most important, thought Keldysh, was the rapid progress of American scientists and engineers in areas such as computer development, chemical research, and microminiaturization.

In the United States, mutual stimulation between research and industry was particularly successful in these areas. Soviet administrators recognized that one of their biggest problems was to achieve such stimulation and a resulting introduction of innovations into production. They frequently complained that even theoretical discoveries first made by Soviet scientists often were applied to industry in the United States earlier than in the Soviet Union.[40]

One of the reasons for the greater success of the United States in applying research in industry was the differences in the organization of research in the two countries. S. Lisichkin, writing in the well-known liberal journal Novyi Mir, noted that in the United States 70 percent of scientific workers were employed in industry compared to only 2 percent in the USSR. While Lisichkin's statistics are dubious, the general point was valid: in the USSR, research laboratories in industry continue to be strikingly underdeveloped. The difference is not quite so great if one realizes that Lisichkin was not including the workers in the institutes under the control of the industrial ministries in the 2 percent, since these workers served a whole branch of industry (for example, ferrous metallurgy) rather than a particular plant. But Lisichkin recognized that the institutes under the industrial ministries were subject to different chains of command than the individual plants and, hence, were not closely connected with the actual problems of industrial production. Lisichkin also lamented the fact that researchers in industrial institutes were paid lower salaries than those in the theoretical institutes of the Academy of Sciences. He queried, "If we so constantly proclaim the need for a close tie between science and industry why is it that we do everything to make a scientist be uninterested in factory laboratories?"[41] Here Lisichkin was touching on one of the main weaknesses of research in the Soviet Union: the division between academic science and industrial application. Paradoxically, after decades of striving to bring science closer to industry, the gap remained serious. This division was a part of both the organizational apparatus of Soviet science and the Russian social ethos. The Academy of Sciences network was the locus of highly theoretical work, while the industrial ministries promoted applied research; communication between the two hierarchies, despite every effort, continued to be poor. Furthermore, the prestige of academic, theoretical science has always been high in the Soviet Union. Physicists, chemists, astronomers, and mathematicians enjoy much higher social stature than engineers and applied scientists (as is usually true in the West also), and this stature is also reflected in higher salaries and social perquisites (not so often true in the West, or, at least, not to the same degree).

The old method for the introduction of scientific innovations into production had consisted of a movement of projects along a chain of institutions in the following order: theoretical institute, construction bureau, pilot plant, industrial plant. Only the first link in this chain was usually under the administration of the Academy of Sciences; the rest fell under the industrial ministries (and sometimes the theoretical discovery was made in one of its institutes as well). Thus, a discovery made in a theoretical institute which had industrial potentialities was supposed to follow a natural evolutionary chain and eventually, if successful economically, would end up as a part of the processes of an operating plant. The weak spot in the scheme was the motivation in the final link; that is, a lack of interest on the part of most factory directors in technical innovation. They knew that the primary criterion by which they were judged was quantitative production, and they were hesitant about disrupting existing production lines in order to experiment with new methods. This lack of interest communicated up the chain of institutions with the result that many theoretical discoveries never left the institute where they were originally made.

In the late 1960s, Soviet administrators introduced a series of reforms in an effort to change this situation.[42] Laboratories and institutes were established on industrial sites and, at least in a few cases, industrial researchers were paid at rates comparable to academic researchers. Furthermore, industrial scientists were given bonuses on the basis of their success in getting process and product innovations introduced into production. In addition, factory directors were given more economic autonomy and hence greater incentive for introducing profitable innovations. It is still impossible to determine the degree of success which Soviet science administrators had in drawing research and industry more closely together. Part of the difficulty is no doubt economic; without a relatively free market and considerable leeway to alter production, factory managers do not seem to be adventurous about introducing innovations.

45

Another change in the administration of scientific research in recent years has been a much greater emphasis on contracts and subcontracts. Soviet research managers were obviously impressed by the way in which research is frequently done on contract in western countries, and in the last decade they have developed quite similar procedures. The institutes of the Academy of Sciences, the university research laboratories, and the technical institutes all now frequently accept contracts from individual plants for the execution of specific research projects. Quite a few institutes receive more than half of their income from such contracts. The contract system is thus an important feature of current Soviet research and has unquestionably helped to close the gap between industry and research.[43] It continues to be a popular and expanding method of conducting research, although administrators frequently comment that the overall research plan approved by the government is still the most important determinant of research in the institutes. In recent years a few complaints have been voiced about the contract system, many of which will sound familiar to administrators of research in other countries. Writing in 1969, A. Plonskii noted that the "one-time contract" was particularly harmful because it resulted in the expansion of a research institute which is then left in the lurch when the contract ends. The critic also believed that subcontracts adversely affected the morale of scientific workers, since the workers often never really found out what the ultimate use of their research would be and hence did not feel that they were serving social needs. Plonskii observed, in conclusion, that the contract system leads to fits and jumps in the development of research institutions rather than to the regular, long-term development of science.[44]

In 1970, an interesting debate on the organization of science broke out in the Ukrainian republic, initiated by V. P. Shelest, a talented atomic physicist who is the son of the head of the Ukrainian Communist Party.[45] Young Shelest voiced the old complaint of the theoreticians that not enough attention was being given in the Soviet Union to the fundamental sciences. He felt that the Soviet government should create new institutions on the model of the Institute for Advanced Study in Princeton, New Jersey, which he had visited and had found very impressive. Shelest's call for new emphasis on basic science was supported by a number of other Ukrainian scientists who contributed to the newspaper debate. Several of them wrote that the Soviet system for education and research was too rigid and left little room for independent creativity.

Another characteristic of Soviet science in recent years has been a wave of dissent among certain groups of Soviet scientists, paralleled by continuing and evidently increasing measures by the government to assert tighter controls. Editorials and articles in leading party publications have called for greater vigilance against bourgeois influences and for stricter discipline over scientists.[46] It is very difficult to tell to what degree these authoritarian moves by the party and government represent shifts in science policy per se (for example, further attempts to erase the reforms of the 1960s by bringing the academy under closer supervision and to force it to pay closer attention to industrial or security problems), and to what degree they are just one more attempt by the government to suppress political dissent, as it constantly endeavors to do throughout Soviet society. The positions certain prominent dissident scientists have taken, such as the physicist A. Sakharov and the geneticist Zh. Medvedev, go rather far beyond science policy questions to calls for actual political reforms. [47] Sakharov, Medvedev, and their colleagues have been careful, however, to attempt to stay within legal bounds. They have called for greater civil rights in the Soviet Union, international cooperation among all nations, the application of science to the world's problems, greater freedom of travel, and the widening of political democracy. Their most insistent demand has been that the government live up to the principles of its own constitution concerning freedom of the press and judicial guarantees.

A Slowing of Science Growth in the USSR?

In the United States there was much talk in the mid-1970s of a "turn away from science." Quite naturally, observers of the Soviet Union are curious to know if a similar phenomenon can be seen there. A moment when this issue was raised in a very pointed fashion was the Thirteenth International Congress for the History of Science, held in Moscow and Leningrad in August 1971. The two main participants in the debate which arose there were Derek Price of Yale University and S. R. Mikulinsky of the Institute for the History of Science and Technology in Moscow. Their discussions were held in one of the main auditoriums of Moscow University and attracted the attention of hundreds of scholars.

Price based his analysis on his well-known descriptions of the "exponential growth" of science in the western world since the time of the industrial revolution. According to Price, the recent expressions of dissatisfaction with science in the United States—whether by legislators who balked more and more in appropriating research funds or by undergraduates who found astrology and alchemy more interesting than astronomy and chemistry—were different manifestations of the same underlying phenomenon: the approaching of the saturation point in the growth curve of science in the United States. What lay ahead was a shift from growth described by an exponential function to that described by a standard symmetric logistic curve. In other words, Price believed that science would continue to grow in the United States in the future but at a much slower rate than previously. As he

47

commented, "It is my estimate that in the region of 1965 the U.S.A. went through the middle of the logistic, the point of inflexion, and that now it is less than half of the scientific 'size' and growth rate that would have been expected if the exponential phase had been maintainable."[48] He predicted that the long linear phase would probably last "at least until the end of the century." Price disagreed pointedly with those critics who saw the present U.S. slowdown in science as a temporary crisis, calling it instead "ultimate," in the sense that continued exponential growth of science simply could not continue to occur in the United States because only approximately "two possible orders of magnitude" were left, a reservoir of manpower and resources which would have been rapidly exhausted at the old exponential growth growth rate.

Turning to his Soviet colleagues in attendance at the congress, Price maintained that the Soviet Union, as the second most developed scientific nation in the world, "must necessarily be the next" to experience such a deceleration in scientific growth. As Price observed:

I must suppose that increasingly during the next several years the Soviet Union must experience a political and intellectual reaction against science and technology in some form or other: a curtailing of funding for research, the abandonment of 'unproductive' lines of development, a questioning of such big programs as those of space and high-energy physics, and a general retrenchment in tertiary education.[49]

In his reply to Price, which was widely distributed to foreign scientists at the congress, Mikulinsky recognized that on an abstract level Price was perfectly correct in noticing that the existing growth rates of science in developed countries could not be indefinitely maintained. As he observed, "In the USSR, throughout the period of 1961-1966, that is, in six years, the number of research workers increased by over twice. Naturally, such growth rate cannot maintain its level for a long time."[50] But Mikulinsky believed that Price had "absolutized" the exponential growth model, using it in a schematic way that failed to take into account the actual state of affairs. Mikulinsky disputed the view that the United States and the Soviet Union were approaching states of saturation in scientific growth, and he further maintained that a slowdown in the growth rates of certain quantitative indices related to science could be accompanied by a continued very rapid, or even accelerated, growth of scientific knowledge itself.

Mikulinsky believed that Price failed to put enough emphasis on the impact of society upon science, stressing instead the reverse influence, even to the extent of treating the "growth curves" as factors independent of social influence. While Price saw the flattening of the exponential curve of growth of science as one of the contributing causes for economic depression and ideological confusion, Mikulinsky saw the causal arrows as pointing in the reverse direction: the economic depression, the social problems, and the military enterprises of the United States were the root causes of the present relative decline in science there. Mikulinsky noted that although there had been a slight decline in the growth rate of scientific manpower in the USSR in recent years, the state budget of the USSR continued to grow, providing 13 billion rubles in 1971, compared to 11.9 billion in 1970.

Lastly, Mikulinsky denied the emergence of an antiscience movement in the USSR. "In our country, " he maintained, "there is no ground for political and intellectual reaction directed against science and technology. Our activities are based on the thesis that communism is inseparable from science and that an all-sided development of science and technology is a prerequisite for building a communist society. "[51]

Only the future will determine whether Price or Mikulinsky came closest to describing accurately the prospects for science in the United States and the Soviet Union. Certainly there is irony in a Soviet scholar calling an American's interpretation of history "too deterministic, " although it should be noted that the better Soviet scholars shifted long ago from simple determinism to a more sophisticated "soft determinism" in which history follows trends possessing multiple potential outcomes of varying probabilities. Participants at the congress were also struck with Mikulinsky's comment to Price that his description of "a decline of science" in the U.S. was "untimely and premature, " just as it also was for the USSR. Indeed, Mikulinsky was more optimistic about the future of science in the United States than most of the American participants at the congress.

Whether there are signs of a growing reaction against science on the part of Soviet intellectuals and youth is a very difficult question to answer. The press in the Soviet Union usually reflects a very positive tone about the relations of science and society. Signs of intellectual turmoil of any kind are much more difficult to detect there than in a western society with its rash of publications following every shift in intellectual fashion. As a person who has lived intermittently in the Soviet Union for rather long periods of time, my subjective opinion is that so far there has been no movement in the Soviet Union approaching the intensity of current criticism of science in the United States. Soviet citizens, by and large, remain convinced of the value of science. And yet, if one knows where to look, a few signs of criticism can be found. In his novel of the 1950s, Doctor Zhivago, the noted Soviet author Boris Pasternak wrote passages containing outspoken criticism of the attempt of modern geneticists to reshape life. The underlying tone was deeply religious, and Pasternak seemed to see a deep conflict between the religious approach to the world and the scientific one. Another Soviet citizen chosen for the Nobel prize in literature, Aleksandr Solzhenitsyn, wrote a play in 1960 which contained a frontal attack on science; his main protagonist at one point explodes:

'O great science!' To express such an attitude is the same as saying 'O what great intellects we are,' or, even more precisely 'O, how great I am.' People have worshipped fire and the moon and even a wooden idol, but I fear that even to worship an idol is not as base as to worship oneself. [52]

And yet, in my opinion, it would be a mistake to see the Soviet Union as inevitably passing through the same stages of intellectual fashion as the United States or other industrialized countries. The Soviet Union has a unique history; it is, furthermore, significant that the Soviet Union had neither the experience with nuclear weapons in World War II that the United States did, nor a recent bruising, divisive foreign war such as Vietnam. Both of these events have been used by critics in the United States as examples of modern horrors based on science and technology. Such criticisms, valid or not, unquestionably affected the degree of optimism and commitment to science prevalent in the United States. At the moment, the relative experience of the United States and the Soviet Union on such topics has been rather different.

CONCLUSIONS

No one would doubt that the Soviet effort to build an outstanding scientific research establishment has been successful. Soviet researchers are full members of the international scientific community and are leaders in a number of important fields. The rise of the Soviet scientific establishment in the twentieth century is one of the most rapid and spectacular developments in the history of recent science. Soviet science is certain to play an ever increasing role in international science. The Russian language is more important today than French or German in many areas of research.

However, many observers of Soviet science, including quite a few Soviet scientists themselves, have noted that in view of all of the emphasis placed upon science in the USSR and the great expenditure of resources, the totality of creative achievements—impressive as they are—is somewhat short of what one might expect. No trustworthy criteria of creative achievement exist, but whatever criteria one uses—Nobel prizes awarded, frequency of citation of scientific papers, creation of internationally influential schools of research, universally acknowledged theoretical breakthroughs—the Soviet Union

50

does not seem to rate as high as its almost unmatched quantitative effort would seem to warrant. In part this can be explained, no doubt, by the rapidity of the development of science in the Soviet Union and the consequent immaturity of many fields of work. Here, the near future will undoubtedly bring genuine changes. The isolation of the Soviet scientific community and the difficulty of the Russian language are other factors. Russian scientists who have done important work often have considerable difficulty in gaining the attention of the international community. The continuing political controls are also obstacles to creativity, as the recent wave of dissent among Soviet scientists has illustrated.

The historical evolution of Soviet science policies in the last fifty years reveals a particularly interesting interaction of two important factors in scientific development: the social and political demands of the environment and the internal development of scientific knowledge. During the first thirty-five or forty years of Soviet history, the most important determinant of Soviet science policy was the social and political environment. The overriding concern of the Soviet government during most of this period was industrialization. The period of the late 1920s to the mid-1950s was one of intense effort to modernize on the basis of heavy industry, an effort interrupted only by the even greater strain of an incredibly costly war, with its similar command tempo.

Soviet scientists in this period served the industrialization and military efforts in many important ways, but most of them looked forward to the day when they could devote themselves to the study of nature without having to worry at every turn about national needs. This characteristic of Soviet natural scientists in no way implies a disloyalty to the government or a peculiar social irresponsibility; it merely means that like scientists everywhere, they were excited by the possibility of discovering something new about the structure of matter or the nature of life, and they needed a bit more luxury of time and money and a bit more protection from ideological pressures than they were able to obtain during the modernization drive. Many of them agreed that the industrialization effort was the most important consideration of the moment. They were observing the Protestant ethic of deferring pleasure for the future while laboring in the present. Or, if one prefers a different terminology, they were following Marx's principle that a new realm of freedom can be gained only on the basis of a genuine material achievement.

From the standpoint of this analysis, the great debate over science policy of the late 1950s was a unique moment in Soviet history, a moment when briefly the desires of working Soviet scientists and the Soviet government were in agreement.

The scientists in the period after Stalin's death saw a simultaneous growth in the prestige of science —symbolized by the successful space effort —and a relaxation of political controls. Even more important, it was obvious to them that the most strained period of Soviet industrialization had been completed. The USSR by the late 1950s was a great industrial power capable of raising its citizens' living standards to general European levels, if the necessary policy decisions were made. No longer did it seem necessary to defer material and intellectual pleasures to the future.

The theoretical scientists felt that the time had come for a readjustment of science policies. The long years of emphasis of the link between science and industry had not destroyed the traditional Russian esteem of pure science. The theoreticians called for removal of the engineering interests from the Academy of Sciences, the granting of much greater autonomy to the institutes and individual scientists, and the relaxation of ideological pressures upon scientists.

The most important factor aiding the reformers was the realization by the government leaders that the Soviet Union could no longer depend on the fundamental research performed by other nations. Industrially and scientifically, the Soviet Union was now close enough to equity with other nations that it must provide its own fund of knowledge for further development. Nikita Khrushchev, the leader of the party, was an ebullient reformer who did not shrink from radically altering administrative structures. Furthermore, he favored de-Stalinization, which in science meant less ideological pressure. To be sure, Khrushchev (of peasant background) had no genuine understanding of science and out of mistaken practical considerations favored the worst charlatan in science, Lysenko, but he nonetheless was an important ally to the theoretical scientists in winning several important reforms.

Over a decade has now passed since the great policy debate of the late 1950s, and several further developments have become clear. First of all, although the theoretical scientists improved their position, it is now evident that they failed to gain that new era for fundamental research which was their goal in the 1950s. Indeed, there is considerable irony in the position of theoretical scientists in the USSR today: having freed themselves from the demands of the steel age of Soviet industrial expansion, the basic development of national power, the theoretical scientists have found themselves caught in the pressures of new national needs, in some cases dictated by military requirements, in others by the problems inherent in industrial power. These new needs have included military requirements in electronics and missiles, space exploration urged by considerations of national prestige, and new concerns for the quality of the environment. Throughout all of the recent period, the pressure for economy in research has seemingly increased, despite the growing overall budget for research.

When Soviet scientists have turned to western scientists, they have found that they, too, feel all of these pressures. The western scientists also think that military pressures and considerations of national security have distorted the profile of scientific research. They agree that governments are increasingly unwilling to finance all of the research projects and expensive equipment which scientists want. For quite a few Soviet researchers in the fundamental sciences, however, this new development has a particular irony. Some of them believe that somehow the Soviet Union missed the days of luxury which American scientists enjoyed after the war, when it was maintained that "all knowledge is equally valuable." In a certain sense, the USSR went directly from the problems of an underdeveloped nation to the problems of an overdeveloped one with no interim such as many western nations enjoyed. The Soviet scientists of the 1930s who felt they were saving for the future are still waiting.

Within the space of only one or two decades, Soviet administrators have had to turn their concerns from the fact that the Soviet Union was a backward nation to the new facts that its very success in becoming an advanced nation was, along with similar efforts in other parts of the world, rapidly destroying the environment. The problems inherent in industrial development—deterioration of the environment, congestion in transportation and communication—are very practical ones, involving engineering much more than conceptual schemes for the understanding of nature, and have tended to counter shifts toward fundamental research of the late 1950s (as has continuing military emphasis).

It has been very difficult for a Soviet factory director, who has always been promoted for his ability to increase production, to become truly concerned about the pollution caused by his factory, just as it has been difficult for the western capitalist, who has always placed his premium on the profit which he has earned, to be similarly troubled. The Soviet Union, like all other modern industrial nations, imbibed deeply of the Baconian principle that knowledge is power, and has had difficulties in adjusting to the view that true knowledge will, at least in some cases, include the desire to limit and modulate the use of power.

The one area in environmental protection where the soviet Union has demonstrated a consistent advantage over capitalist nations, however, is in the absence, as a result of systemic economic differences, of unsightly commercial districts around its major cities. The spread of commercial strips, with their garish restaurants, stores, rotating and lighted signs, and parking lots, has long been a major phenomenon of the American visual environment and has now been reproduced in parts of western Europe. The majority of Americans live near such areas, and their impact on the quality of life should not be underestimated. So far, Soviet citizens have been spared this particular form of environmental deterioration, not because of con- scious policies to preserve the countryside but simply because of the absence of private businesses. (In conversation, Soviet citizens often respond that they would not mind benefiting from the services available in such strips.)

On a much broader scale, it becomes clear that despite the unique character of the Soviet economy and the unusual organization of Soviet science and technology, the current emphases of research in the USSR is not very different from the emphases of research elsewhere. Furthermore, many of the same tensions exist there as do in other countries, such as those between political administrator and researcher, between central direction and autonomy, between pure science and engineering, between research and teaching, between industrial advancement and conservation, between expansion of knowledge and satisfaction of immediate social needs, and between research for military or strategic purposes and research for the improvement of human life. Yet, the different responses to these tensions stemming from the historically conditioned institutions and attitudes of the Soviet Union are valuable and interesting to non-Soviet observers.

## NOTES

1. See Alexander Vucinich, Science in Russian Culture, 1861-1917 (Stanford: Stanford University Press, 1970), esp. pp. 209-213.

2. Ruth Roosa, "The Association of Industry and Trade, 1906-1914: an examination of the economic views of organized industrialists in prerevolutionary Russia," unpublished Ph.D. dissertation, Columbia University, 1967.

3. See Loren R. Graham, The Soviet Academy of Sciences and the Communist Party, 1927-1932 (Princeton: Princeton University Press, 1967).

4. Alexandra Kollontai, "The Roots of the Workers' Opposition," Solidarity Pamphlet, London, 1968, p. 6.

5. Isaac Deutscher, Soviet Trade Unions: their Place in Soviet Labor Policy (New York: Royal Institute of International Affairs, 1950); Solomon M. Schwartz, Labor in the Soviet Union (New York: Praeger, 1952).

6. S.F. Ol'denburg, ed., Nauka i nauchnye rabotniki SSSR, [Science and Scientific Workers of the USSR] 4 vols. (Leningrad: 1926-1934); O. Iu. Shmidt and B. Ia. Smushkevich, Nauchnye kadry i nauchnoissledovatel'skie uchrezhdeniia SSSR [Scientific Personnel and Scientific-Research Institutions of the USSR] (Moscow: 1930); see also L. V. Sergeevich, "Zadacha sobiraniia nauki," Nauchnyi Rabotnik [The Task of Gathering Information on Science, The Scientific Worker] (September 1926): 31-34.

7. Several Soviet authors were active in the eugenics movement and believed that science would help couples choose sperm donors of great intellectual ability and thereby produce creative scientists. The most serious and talented of the Soviet eugenicists was Iu. A. Filipchenko, who carried out a detailed survey of the genealogical

backgrounds and social and ethnic origins of all the members of the Academy of Sciences from 1846 to 1924. The eugenics movement in the Soviet Union disappeared in the 1930s. See T. K. Lepin, Ia. Ia. Lus, and Iu. A. Filipchenko, "Deisvitel'nye chleny akademii nauk za poslednie 80 let (1846-1924), " Izvestiia biuro po evgenike [Full Members of the Academy of Sciences during the Last 80 years (1846-1924), Transactions of the Bureau of Eugenics] (No. 3, 1925): 7-49; also, "Spornye voprosy evgeniki, " Vestnik Kommunisticheskoi Akademii [Controversial Questions in Eugenics, Herald of the Communist Academy. ] (No. 20, 1927): 212-54.

8. See, for example, M. Dynnik, "Problema nauchnoi organizatsii nauchnogo truda, " Nauchnyi Rabotnik [The Problem of the Scientific Organization of Scientific Labor, The Scientific Worker] (January 1925): 180-92; N. P. Suvorov, "O metodakh izucheniia effektivnosti nauchnykh rabot, " Nauchnyi Rabotnik[On Methods of Studying the Effectiveness of Scientific Works, The Scientific Worker] (December 1928): 23-33; and V. V. Dobrynin, "Problema organizatsii tvorcheskogo truda, " Nauchnyi Rabotnik [The Problem of the Organization of Creative Labor, The Scientific Worker] (May-June, 1928): 54-64.

9. Vsesoiuznaia konferentsiia po planirovaniiu nauchno-issledovatel'skoi raboty, 1-ia [The First All-Union Conference on Planning Scientific-Research Work] (Moscow-Leningrad: 1931).

10. S. F. Ol'denburg, "Vpechatleniia o nauchnoi zhizni v Germanii, Frantsii i Anglii, " Nauchnyi Rabotnik [Impressions of Scientific Life in Germany, France, and England, The Scientific Worker] (February 1927): 89.

11. Vsesoiuznaia knoferentsiia po planirovaniiu nauchno-issledovatel'skoi raboty, 1-ia, op. cit., p. 20

12. "Khronika, " Nauchnyi Rabotnik [News Items, The Scientific Worker] (March 1929): 86.

13. Sources for the organization of Soviet science in the early years are: Organizatsiia nauki v pervye gody Sovetskoi vlasti [Organization of Science in the First Years of Soviet Power] (1917-1925), (Leningrad: 1968); Akademiia nauk SSSR—shtab sovetskoi nauki, [The Academy of Sciences of the USSR—Headquarters of Soviet Science] (Moscow: 1968); A. V. Kol'tsov, Lenin i stanovlenie akademii nauk kak tsentra sovetskoi nauki [Lenin and the Establishing of the Academy of Sciences as the Center of Soviet Science] Leningrad, 1969; P. N. Pospelov, ed., Lenin i akademiia nauk [Lenin and the Academy of Sciences] (Moscow: 1969).

14. G. I. Fedkin, Pravovye voprosy organizatsii nauchnoi raboty v SSSR [Legal Questions Concerning the Organization of Scientific Work in the USSR] (Moscow: 1958), p. 292.

15. The Soviet authority Fedkin acknowledged that the Communist party lost interest in science policy bodies. Ibid., p. 298.

16. See David Joravsky, The Lysenko Affair (Cambridge: Harvard University Press, 1970); Zhores Medvedev, The Rise and Fall of T. D.

55

Lysenko (New York: Columbia University Press, 1969); and Loren R. Graham, Science and Philosophy in the Soviet Union (New York: Knopf, 1972).

17. Mark Field, Soviet Socialized Medicine (New York: Macmillan, 1967), pp. 2-3, 5, and 110-11.

18. V. Glushkov, "Prokladyvat' tropy v neznaemoe, " [Blaze trails into the Unknown, ] Izvestiia (October 19, 1963).

19. S. Volfson, "Nauka i bor'ba klassov, " [Science and the Class Struggle, ] VARNITSO (February 1930): 23.

20. K. Marx and F. Engels, Izbrannye pis'ma [Collected Letters] (Moscow: 1947), p. 469.

21. J. Stalin, Marksizm i voprosy iazykoznaniia [Marxism and Problems of Linguistics] (Moscow: 1950)

22. "Programme Kommunisticheskoi Partii Sovetskogo Soiuza, " [The Program of the Communist Party of the Soviet Union, ] Pravda (July 30, 1961).

23. A. N. Newmeianov, "Zagliadyvaia v budushchee nauki, " [Looking at the Future of Science, ] Pravda (December 31, 1955): 2.

24. Pravda (February 14, 1956).

25. Ibid., (July 2, 1959).

26. N. N. Semenov, "Nauka segodnya i zavtra, " [Science Today and Tomorrow, ] Izvestiia (August 9, 1959). Semenov's article initiated a long series of articles on the same subject (see the following issues of Izvestiia: August 18, 21, 28; September 2, 6, 27; October 14, 21; November 11; December 16).

27. I. P. Bardin, "Most mezhdu teoriei i praktikoi, " [The Bridge Between Theory and Practice, ] Izvestiia (August 28, 1959).

28. V. Kirillin, "Nauka i zhizn', " [Science and Life, ] Pravda (March 13, 1959).

29. A. Kurosh, "Dorogu smelym ideiam, " [The Path to Bold Ideas, ] Izvestiia (August 18, 1959).

30. See Loren R. Graham, "Reorganization of the Academy of Sciences, " in Peter Juviler and Henry Morton, eds., Soviet Policy-Making (New York: Praeger, 1967), pp. 133-61.

31. "O merakh po uluchsheniiu koordinatsii nauchno-issledovatel' skikh rabot v strane i deiatel' nosti Akademii Nauk SSSR, " [On Measures for the Improvement of the Coordination of Scientific-Research Works and on the Activity of the Academy of Sciences of the USSR] Pravda (April 12, 1961).

32. V. M. Keldysh, "O merakh po uluchsheniiu deiatel'nosti Akademii Nauk SSSR i akademii nauk soiuznykh respublik, " [On Measures for the Improvement of the Activity of the Academy of Sciences of the USSR and the academy of sciences of the union republics] Vestnik Akademii Nauk SSSR (June 1963): 4-22.

33. M. Millionshchikov, "Dorogi poznaniia, " [Paths to Knowledge] Izvestiia (May 2, 1967): 3.

34. M. V. Keldysh, "Nauka i tekhnicheskii progress," [Science and Technological Progress] Pravda (February 4, 1970): 1-2

35. V. Poshataev, "Uchenyi v kollektive," [Scholars in the Collective] Pravda (June 7, 1969): 3.

36. V. Semenov, "Fond nauki," [The Resources of Science] Pravda (December 27, 1968): 2.

37. V. Rymalis, "Eshche raz o fondakh dlia nauki," [Another Consideration of Resources for Science] Pravda (May 31, 1969): 2.

38. See V. Arutiunov, "Kollektivnoe khoziaistvo institutov," [The Collective Economy of Institutes] Pravda (April 28, 1970): 3.

39. M. V. Keldysh, "Nauka i tekhnicheskii progress," [Science and Technological Progress] Pravda (February 4, 1970).

40. See, for example, M. D. Millionshchikov, "Partiia i nauka," [The Party and Science] Pravda (March 29, 1966): 4.

41. S. Lisichkin, "Nauchnym issledovaniiam—razumnaia organizatsiia," Novyi Mir [A Judicious Organization for Scientific Researches, New World] (August, 1967): 271.

42. "O meropriiatiiakh po povysheniiu effektivnosti raboty nauchnykh organizatsii i uskoreniiu ispol'zovaniia v narodnom khoziaistve dostizhenii nauki i tekhniki," [On Measures for the Raising of the Effectiveness of the Work of Scientific Organizations and the Acceleration of the Use of the Achievements of Science and Technology in the National Economy] Pravda (October 23, 1968): 1-2.

43. See, for example, G. Popov, "Reforma u dverei instituta," [Reform of the Doors of the Institute] Pravda (August 15, 1968): 2.

44. A. Plonskii, "Vuz i 'bol' shaia nauka,'" [The University and 'Big Science'] Pravda (April 26, 1969).

45. See Digest of the Soviet Ukrainian Press, New York, vol. XIV, no. 7 (July, 1970): 1; also, "Soviet Scientists in Ferment," in Guardian Weekly (November 7, 1970): 6.

46. N. Sviridov, "Partiinaia zabota o vospitanii nauchno-tekhnicheskoi intelligentsii," Kommunist, [Party Concern about the Education of the Scientific-Technological Intelligentsia, Communist] no. 18 (December, 1968): 36-45.

47. A. D. Sakharov, Progress, Coexistence and Intellectual Freedom, (New York: Norton, 1970); Z. A. Medvedev, The Medvedev Papers: The Plight of Soviet Science, (New York: St. Martin's Press, 1971).

48. Derek J. de Solla Price, "Is There a Decline in Big Science Countries and in Big Science Subjects?" paper read at the XIIIth International Congress for the History of Science, Moscow, August, 1971.

49. Ibid.

50. S. R. Mikulinsky, "Is a Decline in Science an Inherent Law of its Development: a-propos the paper of Prof. Derek Price," paper read at the XIIIth International Congress for the History of Science, Moscow, August, 1971.

51. Ibid.

52. Aleksandr Solzhenitsyn, "Svecha na vetru," [Candle in the Wind] Student, no. 11-12, (London, 1968): 23.

CHAPTER

# 3

## POLICIES FOR SCIENCE AND TECHNOLOGY IN GREAT BRITAIN: POSTWAR DEVELOPMENT AND REASSESSMENT
Norman J. Vig

It is the argument of this chapter that intrinsic barriers to control of scientific activities have combined with accumulated structural constraints and overriding political goals to undermine the potential for any coherent or consistent scientific and technological "strategy" after World War I. While the same is true, to a varying extent, in all advanced industrial nations, a number of specific factors in the historical development of the British economy and its social and political institutions appear to account for especially confining conditions following World War II.

I shall emphasize the institutional legacies of prewar Britain, and their consolidation in the postwar years despite rapidly rising expenditures and developmental commitments generated by the wartime experience. The result was an aborted and delayed response in establishing new governmental mechanisms for handling questions of scientific and technological priorities, as programs multiplied and expanded on a lagging resource base. This led to an institutional crisis in the early to mid-1960s. It also raises questions of public and private responsibilities which have become well-nigh insoluble.

Britain inherited greater barriers to scientific and technological modernization than did most industrial nations. Though colonial expansion and technological modernization are by no means incompatible (witness Germany and Japan), in late Victorian England they appear to have been alternative routes to economic growth. Britain has been widely criticized for failing to recognize the importance of science and education to industry before other countries (especially Germany and the United States) had established a commanding lead in developing scientific technology. Sociological and cultural explanations have been given for the resistance of industry to new techniques in general, and for its lag of science-based technology in particular. Secondary and higher education were left to the private sector and local authorities much longer than in other industrial

59

nations. Technical education, in particular, was seen as an inferior and probably futile enterprise that merited little public support.

Despite numerous warnings from individual scientists and the scientific associations, as well as calls by a royal commission for increased scientific support, little aid was given in the nineteenth century. The place of science was only gradually established among the prestigious classical disciplines in the universities. The values and attitudes of the educational elites were in turn incorporated in the civil service, with the result that entry to government administration was largely closed to those who did attain scientific and technical qualifications. Over time, the mystique of the cultured amateur, the "all-rounder" capable of serving any minister with equal impartiality and wisdom, came to pervade the higher reaches of the public service.

The Board of Education was established in 1900. It, together with the Treasury Grants Committee (later renamed the University Grants Committee), assumed general responsibility for financial grants to the universities and university colleges. In the same year, the National Physical Laboratory was founded to promote research and industrial standards testing, and in 1909 a Development Fund was added for support of agricultural and fisheries research. By this time, the Board of Education was considering a number of plans for broadening public involvement in university and industrial research.

The need for action was catalyzed by World War I. In July 1915, a White Paper proposed the creation of the Department of Scientific and Industrial Research (DSIR), which was established the following year. DSIR came to provide the bulk of funds for university and industrial research but did nothing to link education and industry closer together. It was placed under supervision of a privy council committee chaired by the lord president. This failed to engender confidence among industrialists, or give DSIR political stature among the old-line departments. Nevertheless, DSIR became the chief sponsoring agency for civil research and development over the next half century.

DSIR set the pattern for the British system of channeling research funds through semiautonomous research councils which awarded grants to universities and also maintained their own specialized laboratories. The Medical Research Council (MRC) was created in 1920 and the Agricultural Research Council (ARC) in 1931 to support basic and applied research in their fields. However, there was little overall coordination of scientific activities during the interwar period, despite attempts to strengthen administrative supervision. The position of scientists and engineers in the civil service was not significantly improved in this period. Despite immense political and economic difficulties following the governmental collapse of 1931, intellectual opinion remained divided over the issue of greater expertise in government.

I cannot do more than indicate some of the main departures during the World War II mobilization. There is no doubt that scientists came to play an unprecedented role in strategic decision-making. In the most crucial area of all—development of the atomic bomb—British scientists did much to confirm the feasibility of what became the Manhattan Project. They became an integral part of the American and Canadian teams which carried out the project, with the result that Britain was in a position to build her own reactors and atomic weapons at the end of the war.

The wartime mobilization had profound implications for future policies. The huge expansion of atomic, aviation, and electronics research was to launch Britain into the postwar arms race in advanced weaponry, despite her strained financial position. Military R&D was carried out largely in government arsenals and laboratories rather than in private industry and the universities. And notwithstanding the enhanced role of scientists in decision-making, bitter disputes emerged over the nature of scientific advice and coordination at the highest levels of government.

Among political leaders, the role of scientists in wartime fostered a mystique of the potential benefits of science in peacetime. The need for rapid expansion of research and training in the universities was recognized, and a ten-year expansion plan was designed to double the output of qualified scientists and engineers. More generally, the election campaign of 1945 gave vent to feelings that the "benefits of peace" should not be "frittered away" again as after World War I. The breakup of the wartime coalition government and rejection of Churchill's party at the polls reflected "a tremendous presumption in favor of change."[1] The Labour government which took office was committed to amelioration of longstanding social inequities and enactment of health, welfare, and employment programs in a new framework of social and economic planning. But it also felt that Britain would soon fall behind again unless industry was modernized and social problems attacked with the aid of scientific and technical knowledge.

It became increasingly apparent, however, that Britain's economic and political status had been badly undermined by the war, and that international trade and finance had to be considered in all domestic policymaking. Accumulated wartime debts and losses of markets, shipping, and capital abroad now threatened the country's survival in peace. By 1947-48, international considerations of this kind came to overshadow Labour's internal reform efforts.

Two other sets of constraints were also operative: Britain's colonial and commonwealth connections, and her commitment to the western military alliance. The colonial legacy affected British defense policies into the 1960s and hindered economic cooperation with Europe As the cold war developed, and Britain's "special relationship" with the United States deepened, the outgoing Labour government was

61

persuaded to undertake a massive rearmament program. Together with nuclear weapons development, Britain's commitments to NATO and defense of interests throughout the Near and Far East entailed enormous diversion of resources and technological capabilities from civilian industrial production.

Other major political choices affected British development and set the limits for science policies. Conservative fiscal and monetary policies contributed to the familiar "stop-go" economic pattern which retarded investment and slowed industrial growth through the 1950s. During the early 1960s, the major issues of economic stagnation, entry to Europe, and defense spending came to a head. Disillusionment reached a peak in 1963, following DeGaulle's veto of Britain's application to the European Economic Community (EEC). It was at this juncture that a "second reconstruction" was demanded, and that Harold Wilson and the Labour party jumped on science and technology as the key to Britain's economic future. But before examining the critical issues which have emerged over the past decade, it is necessary to review post-World War II science policies in some detail.

POLICIES SINCE 1945: AN OVERVIEW

The "Lessons of War" and the
Reconstruction Effort: 1945-51

At the end of the war, Britain—and other industrial nations—had come to recognize the importance of scientific research for the future security and prosperity of the world. The British were especially eager to perpetuate the brilliant successes of scientists and engineers who had been rushed into government service to aid in the Battle of Britain, in the development of new weapons systems and, ultimately, in the construction of the first atomic bomb in America. But there was also a widespread feeling in governmental and political circles (particularly the Labour party) that the discoveries of British scientists must in future be applied to a broad range of industrial and social purposes. Morrison, the deputy prime minister, stated boldly in the House of Commons that

the Government attach the very greatest importance to science. We recognize the contribution which science has made to the prosecution of the war and the achievement of victory, and we are no less desirous that science shall play its part in the constructive tasks of peace and of economic development. [2]

62

There was no disagreement on this basic proposition. Indeed, the policies which developed were given relatively little attention in Parliament and in public generally—a marked contrast to the rancorous battles fought over such issues as control of atomic energy and sponsorship of research in the United States in the same period. [3]

The lessons of the wartime mobilization were reflected in the postwar consensus. Firstly, scientific activities undertaken or supported by government should be given a permanent peacetime basis and a greater degree of coordination than in prewar days. This meant that R&D programs whould be expanded considerably under the direction of responsible officials advised by eminent representatives of the scientific and engineering communities. Secondly, the supply of qualified scientists and technologists produced by British universities and colleges was dangerously inadequate, and the educational establishment must be rapidly enlarged to increase the supply of manpower. Thirdly, British industry was conducting far too little research, and special emphasis was needed to encourage technological application to improve productivity and efficiency. However, this should be done largely through expansion of the Department of Scientific and Industrial Research, and the research associations it supported, rather than through some wholly new machinery. Fourthly, academic research generally should continue to be supported through a decentralized set of grant-awarding bodies such as DSIR and the University Grants Committee. Finally—and of greatest significance—the vast new field of defense R&D opened up by the atomic bomb and high performance aircraft should be kept primarily within government laboratories rather than contracted out to private industry, as in the U.S.

The latter decision was most crucial in the long run, since defense R&D quickly came to dominate the British postwar research effort, much as in America. In part, the decision to expand the nuclear and aviation laboratories rather than placing responsibility for development in industry indicated a belief among Labour leaders that private enterprise could not be trusted with military development. But it also reflected a general feeling that British industrial research was inadequate to handle the job; it was already years behind American firms, which had been brought into the nuclear weapons program at an early stage of World War II. A heavy burden of administrative inertia also existed, due to the prior existence of the civilian research councils which maintained government R&D establishments. Most telling, however, was the urgency felt in developing nuclear weapons and the secrecy with which the program was undertaken. Parliament was not informed about it by the prime minister for some three years, in 1948. In any event, the concentration of work on the key military field of nuclear technology, aviation, and electronics in the Ministry of Supply meant that much of the work was to remain secret for years, and that industry generally was not seen as the beneficiary of military technology, as in the U.S. [4]

The traditional separation of government, industrial, and academic research was encouraged by this system. University scientists were not generally brought into government research and development, though there was some university contract work from the beginning. And, while relationships between DSIR and other government research units and private industrial firms varied considerably, close collaboration between government and private industry remained the exception to the rule. Most importantly, civil service regulations continued to allow little flexibility in movement of personnel between government, industry, and the universities.

In some respects, however, the Attlee government sought to orient research towards the problems of reconstruction. DSIR laboratories were instructed to concentrate on projects of short-term economic and social importance, and numerous productivity studies were conducted. In 1948, the National Research Development Corporation (NRDC) was created to support inventions by private individuals, the universities, and government research teams. Operating as an independent body under the Board of Trade, NRDC has financed and patented a number of important innovations over the years (including one of the first large digital computers, the Hovercraft boat, hydrogen/oxygen fuel cells, and carbon fibers). A new research council, the Nature Conservancy, was added in 1949 to assist oceanographic, meteorological, geological, and other ecological research. The government also rapidly expanded university enrollments to increase the supply of scientific manpower. In 1945, a Cabinet committee had recommended doubling the output of scientists and engineers within a decade, and the universities were opened to returning veterans with this in mind. 5

An attempt was made to improve the machinery for scientific advice and coordination as well. Sir Henry Tizard became the government's chief scientific adviser. Tizard, who had gained enormous respect as leader of the team which developed radar in time for the German blitz of London and other British cities, had been shunted aside during the war by Lord Cherwell. However, in 1945 he was invited to head two new science policy committees, the Advisory Council on Scientific Policy (ACSP) for civil research and the Defence Research Policy Committee (DRPC) for military R&D. Although this recognized the bifurcation of civil and military research, it also sought to overcome that division by placing Tizard at the pinnacle of each and providing a common secretariat. This advisory apparatus appeared on paper to be an excellent vehicle for developing a balanced research effort. In fact, its powers were limited to general advice without executive responsibility. Sir Solly Zuckerman, more recently the government's chief scientific adviser, has pointed out the real lack of authority in this structure:

While the Council [ACSP] was not inhibited when debating a variety of problems in which no other body had a particular vested interest—for example, questions such as the growth and deployment of scientific manpower, the scale of financial support for basic research, and matters concerning certain aspects of our overseas scientific relations— throughout its existence it not surprisingly found itself impotent when it came to advising either about the use of scientific and technological resources in executive Departments of State, for example, the Defence Departments, or about the programs of the Research Councils. [6]

The ACSP was thus largely confined to informal stimulation of other agencies. It had no power to allocate funds (R&D budgets were negotiated directly with the treasury, which had no scientific staff), and no power to initiate research or determine priorities in any way. After Tizard's resignation in 1951, when ACSP and the Defence Research Committee and their staffs were separated entirely, there was even less coordination of civil and military science policies.

For the most part, therefore, the Labour government's aspirations to redeploy science and technology for social and economic purposes came to naught. Civil research expenditure was increased significantly, [7] but prewar institutional arrangements were largely consolidated in the postwar years. Science policy coordination was improved temporarily, but "mission-oriented" programs in military and other departments soon overwhelmed general policy considerations. These were all expanded in the years thereafter.

The "Defense Science" Era: 1951-57

Rearmament and weapons development reflected the major new priorities in the early 1950s, as Britain sought to establish an independent nuclear deterrent and general military capability. In this crucial period, government support for civil R&D increased slowly (even declining in some sectors in the early years), and efforts were made to halt university expansion while capital investment in facilities caught up with the postwar enrollment boom. While the output of scientists and technologists was doubled before 1956, it was not until that year that the full measure of American and Soviet manpower superiority was recognized.

The most important educational reform was consequently enacted: the Technical Education Act, which provided for the creation of ten Colleges of Advanced Technology (CATs) to award a new "university level" degree, the Diploma in Technology (Dip. Tech.). This was

65

a manifest compromise between those who wanted to raise the technical colleges to full university status and those unwilling to grant a university degree for applied technological work. Nevertheless, it began to remedy the traditional weakness in British technical education.

A significant institutional reform in 1954 was separation of nuclear research from the Ministry of Supply. Both civil and military nuclear R&D were now vested in an independent statutory corporation, the U. K. Atomic Energy Authority (AEA). [8] Completion of the hydrogen bomb and launching of a massive nuclear power program led to this change, modeled in part after the American Atomic Energy Commission (AEC) — though far less R&D was contracted out to private firms. The AEA's nuclear power program soon made Britain the international pacesetter in this field—by the 1960s, the U. K. had more installed nuclear generating capacity than the rest of the world combined and was proceeding rapidly with the design of advanced reactor prototypes — but the economics of nuclear generation remained hazardous and anticipated markets for export of commercial generating equipment largely failed to materialize. [9]

The magnitude of early investments in this program made it increasingly doubtful that Britain could maintain its leading position for long, since this required disproportionate allocation of scientific resources to one R&D sector. Civil and military nuclear development heavily influenced university research priorities as well as governmental scientific activity, with capital and project grant assistance flowing into high energy physics and related disciplines in the 1950s. By the end of the decade, as least half of all government support for civil science and technology was concentrated in this field.

The Ministry of Supply (later renamed Ministry of Aviation) continued to support civil and military aeronautical and electronics R&D. While figures on the ministry's internal funding are not available for this period, it is clear that the vast majority of supply-aviation funds were for defense aircraft projects. [10] Meanwhile, as government sponsor for the aerospace industry generally, the ministry encouraged an expansion of production capacity which later exceeded demands and saddled the public with government subsidies to the aircraft companies in the following decade.

In contrast to the general separation of civil and military research, then, the most costly fields of civilian R&D—nuclear energy and aviation—were placed in mission-oriented agencies, together with related defense work. These two fields absorbed at least half of civil research funds through the 1950s, in addition to most military R&D expenditures; and their productive marriage not only blew spending out of all proportion to reality in these sectors, but made priority planning an impossibility for ACSP or any other subcabinet body. The peak of the imbalance was probably reached in 1955-56 when over 90 percent of total government R&D support appears to have gone into defense, aviation, and atomic energy projects.

The Rise of "Civil Science"—Basic Research and Education: 1957-64

After 1956 defense research began to level off, and as the nuclear power program became operational, investments in UKAEA also grew at a more stable rate. Under the Macmillan government (1957-63) it was recognized that Britain's long-term scientific and technological status depended on a wider range of basic knowledge and skilled manpower. This was in part a response to the Russian and American breakthroughs in space technology, and in part to a more general awareness of international competition in other fields of development. A growing realization existed that British R&D expenditure was not contributing sufficiently to national economic growth, and that various fields of research had been neglected in the previous phase. This led to increasing political controversy over government R&D priorities and, by the end of the period, to far-reaching demands for reorganiza-tion of science policy machinery. However, the most striking feature of this transitional period was the greatly increased support given to basic university research and, ultimately, to higher education gener-ally.

The Conservative administration invested particularly heavily in university research facilities in these years. Lord Hailsham, the lord president and (from 1959) Minister for Science, was a firm believer in the primacy of educational development and unfettered basic re-search. [11] Under his tutelage, expenditures by the research councils were greatly increased. DSIR grants to universities and CATs expanded especially rapidly (six-fold), and overall research council funds nearly quadrupled. This rate of increase (about 25 percent a year) was probably as great as the universities could readily absorb, despite the relatively small amounts involved. [12]

Allocating funds between different fields of basic research was of growing concern to the Advisory Council on Scientific Policy, though it had no direct control over the research council budgets. From about 1960 it devoted increasing attention to "fallow fields" and "gaps" in academic research—that is, the value of more research in the biological sciences as opposed to physics—as well as to broader matters such as the balance between domestic and international programs.

There was also rising concern in the ACSP and DSIR over the economic implications of R&D. The large British R&D effort did not appear to be paying off in the industrial-economic sphere. [13] DSIR thus began a series of confidential industrial studies to assess the potential benefits of research support and, in 1959, began awarding "civil development contracts" for promising research in private indus-try. Other types of selective support and advisory services were also initiated, but DSIR had no authority to force innovation in the private sector. Meanwhile the department's growing support of university re-search raised fundamental questions about its role and functions.

67

FIGURE 3.1

Organization of British Government for Science and Technology, 1959

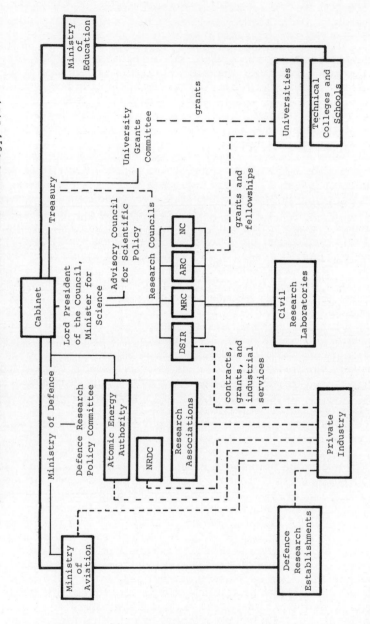

68

By 1962-63, a serious institutional crisis had developed over government aid to science and technology. Public R&D expenditure had been rising exponentially for some years, averaging 12-13 percent a year in the civil realm alone, but there was as yet no means for coordinating this expenditure or for establishing budgetary priorities (other than general treasury control). The ACSP and DSIR recognized in their annual reports that priorities must be set but declared themselves incapable of doing so. Lord Hailsham, as Minister for (rather than ''of'') Science maintained that the government's role must be limited insofar as any attempt to "control" science would destroy free inquiry and private initiative. He argued bluntly that

> the duty of organizing science in a free society, like all other important duties, begins with the individual. . . . Government is a financing, coordinating, participating, training, function. Over a large field it is not, and cannot be, directory and executive. These are functions in which the main role ought to be played by industrialists, educationalists, teachers, and scientists themselves. [14]

He went on to state that "The clue to the correct organization of science is an adequate pattern of education. I would almost go so far as to say that if we could get this right, we should, in the long run, get everything right." [15] Thus the government's chief scientific spokesman resisted all pressures to create an executive department for science and technology, holding that the traditional British system of semiautonomous research councils and university block grants provided greater assurance that worthwhile scientific projects would receive support while maintaining safeguards against political interference in free research and discovery.

Hailsham's rather dogmatic adherence to these principles in the realm of industrial and applied research, as well as basic research and education, brought growing criticism from the Labour party and others concerned with the economic and social implications of science. From 1959 onward, Labour had been seeking new issues and programs to counter their traditional working-class image. [16] The party's new program in 1961 had introduced the theme that "we live in a scientific revolution" and that it was necessary "to harness the forces released by science in the service of the community. "[17] Although there was some hesitation under Hugh Gaitskell in developing this theme, which implied a rather radical departure from the usual concerns of the party, Harold Wilson quickly elevated science and technology to a central issue after succeeding Gaitskell in early 1963. Throughout 1963 and early 1964, Wilson's campaign revolved around the theme of modernizing Britain through massive increases in government aid to civilian industrial technology and to economically and socially productive fields of research generally. Wasteful military and other "prestige" projects would be cut, and new priorities determined by a centralized Ministry of Science or Ministry of Technology. At the 1963 Scarborough Conference, Wilson promised to "harness Socialism to science, and science to Socialism" and to remake Britain "in the white heat of scientific revolution."[18]

As the Labour party developed a radical critique of the entire spectrum of R&D policies, the Conservative government moved decisively in one area—expansion of higher education—and carried out its own reorganization of scientific and educational administration. The Robbins Committee on Higher Education, appointed by the prime minister in 1961, issued its report in October 1963.[19] This report, one of the most important in postwar Britain, called for a drastic increase in university and other higher education to meet the demands of the student population.[20] At virtually the same time, another government committee—chaired by Sir Burke Trend of the Cabinet Secretariat—reported on the organization of government for civil science and technology.[21] Trend called for strengthening of the Office of the Minister for Science and reorganization of the research councils along more functional lines. It was decided by the Douglas-Home government (Macmillan had retired) in early 1964 to establish a new "federal" ministry, the Department of Education and Science, to be responsible on the one hand for general education and on the other for university education, civil science, and technology.

The Conservatives also announced plans to restructure the research councils as recommended by Trend—which entailed abolishing DSIR and replacing it with two new research councils: one for basic science and university research, and the other to handle DSIR's industrial functions. The net effect of these changes was to concentrate a broader range of responsibilities in the hands of the Secretary of State for Education and Science and his subordinate ministers without adding appreciably to the coordinating authority previously exercised by the Minister for Science.[22]

Beyond these organizational changes, there is little indication that a fundamental restructuring of science policy was contemplated by the Conservative administration prior to its electoral defeat in October 1964. In the crucial field of industrial research and development, the government was obviously divided. Although Trend's proposal for a new research council in this area (to be called the Industrial Research Development Authority) was approved by the outgoing administration, others would have preferred a separate Ministry of Technology or transfer of these functions to another established department such as the Board of Trade. The Labour party had by this time arrived at the conclusion that a stronger Technology Ministry was indeed required, incorporating the defense research functions of the Ministry of Aviation as well as the industrial programs of DSIR and other agencies such as the Atomic Energy Authority. This ministry was "to guide and stimulate a major national effort to bring advanced technology and new processes into industry," while the party would also "go beyond research and development and establish new industries, either by public enterprise or in partnership with private industry."[23]

Science policy had in fact become embroiled in partisan and ideological politics. Hailsham's conservative (or classical liberal) views on the freedom of science, when projected to applied research and industrial development, took on the appearance of traditional Tory philosophy on private enterprise. The Labour party, in attempting to revive socialist principles in the context of advanced industrial society, projected a radical counterimage of humane technological planning. In practice, neither set of doctrines was as extreme as it sounded during 1963-64, but the postwar consensus on science policy had clearly been shattered.

Global Industrial and Technological Competition: 1964-74

The new Labour government generally accepted the reforms already made by the Conservatives in the realm of basic science and education. The authority of the Department of Education and Science was, however, strengthened in allocating resources to the universities and research councils. Two "new" research councils were established as planned by the outgoing administration: the Science Research Council (SRC) to take responsibility for grants in the physical sciences and other fields previously supported by DSIR; and the Natural Environment Research Council (NERC), an expanded version of the former Nature Conservancy.[24] A Council for Scientific Policy, composed entirely of independent scientists, replaced ACSP and was given powers to advise the Secretary of State for Education and Science on the distribution of funds among the research councils. Thus there was formal authority for the first time to determine relative priorities in the research council sector.

But the most important decision of the Labour government was to abandon plans for the Industrial Research Development Authority and to create, instead, a powerful executive department for technology. The Ministry of Technology established in 1965 now replaced DSIR as the central agency for promoting industrial research. Initially, the ministry was given supervision of the major independent agencies, the Atomic Energy Authority and National Research Development Corporation, together with most of the industrial services and laboratories of DSIR. More broadly, it became the chief governmental agency concerned with advanced technological industries and ultimately with the manufacturing and power industries generally. In 1966-67, it absorbed the Ministry of Aviation and became the military R&D and procurement department, as well as sponsor for most civil research (see Figure 3. 2).

The thrust of the Labour government's "scientific revolution" was thus towards industrial innovation and reform. While provision for university research and education continued to advance rapidly (the Robbins targets were exceeded despite severe financial constraints), the Ministry of Technology emerged as the chief economic development agency. Efforts to reduce expenditure on defense, aerospace, and nuclear R&D met with some success, though on the whole these programs were run down gradually. The outstanding lesson of this experience is that (in Britain, at least, ) economic and commercial motives have come to predominate in national support of science and technology.

In part, this reflected changing attitudes toward science policy in Europe generally. Whereas in the early 1960s attention was focused on the scale of national R&D budgets and manpower, new issues came to the fore in the latter half of the decade. If there was no direct correlation between research expenditures and national economic growth rates, it became evident that western Europe might increasingly be dominated by U.S. industry and technology. This produced widespread concern over the "technology gap" dramatized by J.-J. Servan-Schreiber and others. [25] Prime Minister Wilson joined French and Italian leaders in attacking foreign technological hegemony and proposing greater European collaboration, at the same time making Britain's second effort to gain entry to the European Common Market in 1966-67.

But it was also clear that American penetration of world markets in advanced processes and goods was due as much to organizational and managerial superiority as to basic scientific and technological resources. The Labour government thus attempted to reorganize certain export industries to enable them to compete on the scale of large U.S. and multinational corporations. To a considerable extent, this implied that Britain's industrial position could be improved only if corporate management was remodeled along American lines. [26] In any event, the Ministry of Technology moved increasingly towards becoming a service department for progressive private companies seeking to compete more effectively abroad. Its official slogan became "technology for profit" rather than "harnessing science to socialism. "

Wilson's electoral victory in 1964 posed the question of what a government can do, having publicly committed itself to some kind of scientific and technological revolution. Few administrations have received—or wanted—a popular mandate of this kind; and experience in other countries does not suggest that rational science policies are easy to come by, let alone popularize. In the event, the financial ceiling caved in on Wilson, plans for R&D suffered along with others, and to most critics the promised revolution never got off the ground. [27]

72

FIGURE 3.2

Organization of British Government for Science and Technology, 1967

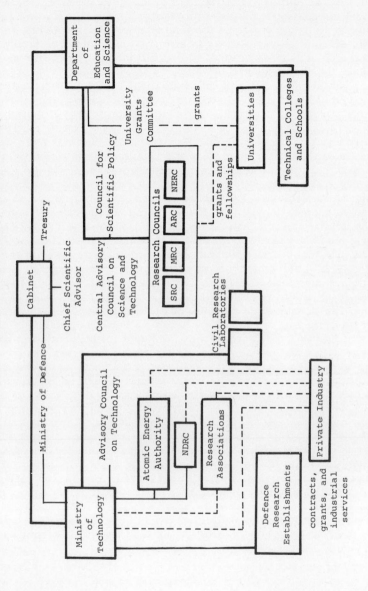

73

To be sure, behind the scenes new lines of thought, new priorities, and new problems began to emerge from Labour's experiment with planned scientific and technological modernization. But what is most significant is the extent to which the government was forced to modify its basic tenets on the role of the state in scientific matters. The difficulties encountered in attempting to "plan" or "guide" research and development in the public interest proved far more difficult than contemplated by the party intellectuals. 28

On the other hand, coordination was certainly improved in the more traditional areas of science policy. Research council budgets were considered together by the Council for Scientific Policy, which began the difficult task of assigning relative priorities to different fields of basic science. The Department of Education and Science asserted tighter administrative and financial supervision in the academic realm as the Robbins expansion progressed. On the manpower front, a strengthened Committee on Manpower Resources for Science and Technology was established under DES and Mintech. At a higher level, cooperation between these and other ministries was sought through the office of the Chief Scientific Adviser (Sir Solly Zuckerman), who also chaired a Central Advisory Council on Science and Technology. While little is known about scientific advising at the cabinet level, it would appear that this apparatus, together with a stronger cabinet secretariat, did contribute to an overall shift in national R&D priorities and to new managerial practices at the center.

The Conservative government of Edward Heath, elected in 1970, carried the drift of Labour's policies further. Responsibility for technical innovation and growth was, at least initially, shifted back towards private industry. One of the first acts of the new administration was to dismantle the Ministry of Technology and several other agencies set up by Labour to assist industrial development. Although the successor Department of Trade and Industry gradually resumed various forms of assistance, its focus was less overtly technological. Moreover, as explained below, other types of applied R&D supported by government have come to require justification in terms of "customer"(that is, private industry) needs. An increasing share of public R&D is now done under contract with potential users (both government departments and private firms). At the same time, government support has been reduced in "nonmission" areas such as research council grants for basic science. This general retrenchment reflects growing skepticism over the public benefits of much of the R&D previously supported, as well as Britain's continuing financial difficulties in the 1970s.

ISSUES IN BRITISH SCIENCE POLICY

Despite policy shifts and confining conditions, Britain has built up a large scientific and technological establishment since World

74

War II. The government has played a decisive role in this development, financing some three-quarters of all national R&D in the mid-
1950s and about half of it by the 1970s. But despite heavy R&D
investment, the British economy has continued to lag behind those
of its competitors, and research support is being scaled down to
meet more pressing financial needs. In order to understand the
reasons for this disappointing performance, it is necessary to look
more closely at the pattern of British R&D expenditure.

The British R&D Effort

Table 3.1 gives an overall picture of R&D expenditures in the
U.K. during 1961-71. It will be noted that total (public and private)
expenditure increased from £658 million in 1961-62 to £962 million
in 1967-68 (an average annual growth rate of about 7.5 percent).
The aggregate increase was somewhat greater in the latter three
years (25 percent) than in the first three (17 percent). Although the
figures for 1970-71 are not complete or entirely comparable, [29] gross
expenditure by then was well over £1billion. Of this total expenditure, government provided slightly over one-half of the funds as of
1967-68, but this proportion was declining. Private industry's share,
on the other hand, had remained fairly constant at just over 40 percent
of the total (rising to 42 percent in 1967-68).

The most striking change over the years was in the relative
proportion of government funds spent for military and civil purposes.
As late as 1964-65, defense consumed 60 percent of public R&D
funds, but by 1970-71 the 60:40 ratio had been reversed. Government
research classified as civil more than doubled over the 1965-71
period, with the research council component rising even more rapidly.
There can be little doubt, then, that the advent of the Labour government in 1964 had a significant impact on R&D priorities; civilian
projects, as well as economic projects, received greater attention
than previously.

Nevertheless, taking the decade as a whole, military, space,
and nuclear research continued to absorb the bulk of the R&D budget
(taken together, these sectors accounted for 80 percent of public
R&D spending in 1960-61 and over 56 percent in 1969-70). [30] Of
the smaller countries, only France was devoting a similar proportion
of funds to this sector at the end of the decade, largely as a result
of its belated attempt to develop nuclear weapons. Other figures
suggest that by 1970 Britain had fallen considerably behind both
France and West Germany in public expenditure for civil research
and was fast being challenged by Japan in this regard as well. [31]
Thus, while military and other "prestige" spending has declined, and
civil expenditure has greatly increased, it can be argued that Britain

75

TABLE 3.1

Research and Development in the U.K.
1961-71

| A. Government Funds | 1961-62 | | 1964-65 | | 1967-68 | | 1970-71a | |
|---|---|---|---|---|---|---|---|---|
| | millions of £ | percent | millions of £ | percent | millions of £ | percent | millions of £ | percent |
| Civil Research | 139.3 | 36.2 | 171.9 | 40.3 | 259.4 | 53.5 | 350.0 | 60.3 |
| Research Councils only[b] | (24.0) | (6.2) | (38.0) | (8.9) | (57.1) | (11.8) | (93.8) | (16.2) |
| Defense Research | 245.7 | 63.8 | 255.1 | 59.7 | 225.9 | 46.5 | 230.0 | 39.7 |
| Total | 385.0 | 100.0 | 427.0 | 100.0 | 485.3 | 100.0 | 580.0 | 100.0 |
| B. Expenditure by Source of Funds[c] | | | | | | | | |
| Government | 378.2 | 57.5 | 421.2 | 54.6 | 493.1 | 51.3 | n.a. | — |
| Universities (own funds) | 1.3 | 0.2 | 1.8 | 0.2 | 5.7 | 0.6 | n.a. | — |
| Private Industry[d] | 266.2 | 40.5 | 311.6 | 40.4 | 405.2 | 42.1 | n.a. | — |
| Other[e] | 12.0 | 1.8 | 36.8 | 4.8 | 58.1 | 6.0 | n.a. | — |
| Total | 657.7 | 100.0 | 771.4 | 100.0 | 962.1 | 100.0 | n.a. | — |

[a]Figures in this column are estimates.
[b]The Research Council funds in this line are included in the "Civil Research" total given on the
line above, and exclude some industrial and applied research funded by DSIR prior to 1965.
[c]Figures under B are actual expenditure returns for the given year; the government totals thus differ
slightly from those under A, which represent appropriations.
[d]Includes public corporations and research associations financed by private industry.
[e]Includes funds from overseas which account for slightly over half the totals in this line.

Source: Adapted from A Framework for Government Research and Development, Cmd. 4814, Dainton
Report, p. 42.

76

has nonetheless been left with a sizable deficit in publicly supported civilian R&D.[32]

Comparative statistics on the supply and employment of qualified scientific and technical personnel are exceedingly difficult to interpret, due to national differences in defining professional qualifications. But the available data suggest that the U. K. compared very favorably with her principal competitors in terms of scientific and technical manpower in the mid-1960s. Indeed, the ratio of scientists and engineers to total population and to the economically active population appeared considerably above that in Sweden, France, and Japan.[33] Other figures indicate that British national expenditure on education grew more rapidly in relation to GNP than in most nations during 1955-65, and that this expenditure was exceptionally heavily concentrated on higher education.[34] And, although degrees are not highly comparable, it appears that the U.K. had enrolled a higher percentage of the relevant age group in university and higher education courses leading to science and technology degrees than virtually any other western country.[35]

Finally, it seems evident that by the 1960s Britain's export performance was greatly dependent on "research intensive" industries such as pharmaceuticals and chemicals, electrical and nonelectrical machinery, precision instruments, and aircraft. Table 3.2 indicates that Britain, along with the United States and West Germany, was particularly dependent on such exports, though Britain's share of the world market in these exports was only slightly higher than her overall share of manufacturing trade.

Education and Manpower

Governments in Britain as elsewhere have taken it upon themselves to increase the supply of scientists and engineers as they have not done in any other category of manpower training.[36] Since the end of World War II, all administrations have singled out science and technology as the most crucial field of educational expansion. The most fruitful work of the Advisory Council on Scientific Policy was done in this area, through its Manpower Committee. This committee, chaired for the most part by Sir Solly Zuckerman in this period, was a consistent and persuasive advocate of increased output in science and (especially) technology into the 1960s. It undertook increasingly sophisticated surveys of likely supply and demand, documenting a continuing shortage of scientific and technical personnel. Even then, in its triennial surveys of 1962 and 1965, the committee indicated that it had underestimated needs for engineers in previous forecasts and that serious manpower vacancies remained

77

TABLE 3.2

Export Performance of Ten OECD Countries in Research-Intensive Industries, 1963-65
In percentage

| | Country's Share of Total Manufacturing Reports | Each Country's Share of Total World Trade in Research Intensive Industries | | Share of Research Intensive Industries in Each Country's Manufacturing Exports | |
|---|---|---|---|---|---|
| | | Excluding Air-craft and N.E. Machinery$^a$ | Including Air-craft and N.E. Machinery$^b$ | Excluding Air-craft and N.E. Machinery$^a$ | Including Air-craft and N.E. Machinery$^b$ |
| U.S.A. | 22.6 | 26.6 | 30.1 | 22.9 | 51.5 |
| Germany | 18.1 | 21.8 | 22.1 | 23.6 | 47.2 |
| U.K. | 13.2 | 12.9 | 14.2 | 19.1 | 41.9 |
| France | 9.8 | 8.9 | 7.7 | 17.7 | 30.3 |
| Japan | 8.1 | 7.5 | 5.3 | 18.0 | 25.1 |
| Italy | 7.5 | 5.7 | 5.9 | 14.7 | 30.0 |
| Netherlands | 5.9 | 7.6 | 5.3 | 25.0 | 34.6 |
| Belgium | 5.8 | 3.5 | 3.2 | 11.7 | 20.8 |
| Canada | 5.5 | 3.3 | 3.4 | 11.6 | 23.9 |
| Sweden | 3.5 | 2.2 | 2.8 | 12.1 | 31.4 |
| Total | 100.0 | 100.0 | 100.0 | 19.5 | 39.0 |

a. The sectors included are drugs, chemicals, electrical machinery, instruments.
b. Same sectors as in (a) but including aircraft and non-electrical machinery. Data compiled by the Science Policy Studies Unit, University of Sussex, England.

Source: OECD, Gaps in Technology: Analytical Report, Table 13, p. 207.

78

in industry. As a result of these and other findings, the adequacy of Britain's manpower supply remained an issue.

Currently available statistics show continuing expansion in annual output of newly trained scientists and engineers, the total increasing by about 50 percent between 1960 and 1967 (Table 3.3). The increase was substantially greater for scientists than in engineering and advanced technology, with output of the former out-distancing the latter by 1967, despite repeated government warnings on the shortage of engineers. In fact, unfilled student places existed in engineering faculties and technical colleges during this period.

The problems of manpower planning were compounded by the rapid expansion of university facilities following the Robbins Report of October 1963. As noted earlier, a university expansion program was begun in 1958-59, but in the next three or four years the percentage of applicants gaining admission declined significantly as the demand for places outran facilities.[37] At the same time, lack of research and teaching opportunities in the universities appeared to be contributing to an increasing "brain drain" to other countries. For these reasons, Robbins was instructed to examine the entire higher educational system (including the nonuniversity "further" education sector of technical colleges and teacher training institutes) with a view towards long-term development.

TABLE 3.3

New Supply of Qualified Scientists and Engineers, Great Britain (all forms of qualification)

|  | 1960 | 1962 | 1964 | 1966 | 1967 |
|---|---|---|---|---|---|
| Engineering & Technology | 8,910 | 8,819 | 10,412 | 11,696 | 12,051 |
| Science | 7,479 | 8,215 | 9,909 | 11,607 | 12,499 |
| Total | 16,389 | 17,034 | 20,321 | 23,303 | 24,550 |

Source: Table 23, Department of Education and Science and Ministry of Technology, Statistics of Science and Technology, 1970, pp. 50-51.

The Robbins Report led to a massive expansion of British higher education—from about 200,000 full-time students in 1962, to almost 500,000 a decade later. But from the perspective of manpower planning, Robbins contributed relatively little. His guiding principle was that "courses of higher education should be available for all those who are qualified by ability and attainment to pursue them and who wish to do so. "[38] Both considerations of social justice and economic growth compelled the Conservative government in this direction, and Robbins performed a notable service in attacking the traditional idea that a limited "pool of ability" inherently restricted higher educational expansion. But this focused attention on aggregate demand for places rather than on occupational or other demands for skills, on quantity rather than quality or substance, on numerical expansion rather than reform.[39] Although Robbins indicated that educational expansion was justified on economic and manpower grounds, he denied that techniques of manpower planning (that is, attempting to match educational output with occupational needs, as had been done in science and technology) or of human investment planning (attempting to measure the costs and benefits to society of different types of education) were sufficiently developed to provide a basis for educational policies.[40] He did, however, recommend a further increase in the percentage of students taking science and, especially, technology in the coming decades.[41]

Following the Robbins recommendations, the University Grants Committee and the individual university authorities incorporated special requirements for scientific and engineering facilities into their general expansion plans, the net result being highly preferential treatment for students entering the natural sciences. While university places were provided for some 60 percent of school-leavers with minimum entrance qualifications, four out of five students in the natural sciences found places. In fact, the greatest increase in student demand was not in the natural sciences but in the social sciences, where fewer than half the applicants gained university admission by the late 1960s.[42]

Meanwhile, there was no basis for estimating manpower needs for social science graduates or general assessment of the "rate of return" for different types of educational investment. This problem was further accentuated by a disturbing number of unfilled places in engineering faculties, as well as by a disproportionate increase in postgraduate students in science and technology. One university vice-chancellor stated that, "The building work of the 1960s . . . over-provided science and technology capacity to such an extent that, until the mid-1970s at least, practically all new university buildings (other than in medical schools) will be for non-laboratory subjects."[43] Many students who became politically active in the later 1960s attacked the growing emphasis on science and technology, and by the end of the decade, the specter of overproduction of graduates in some fields of science began to appear.

Nevertheless, the Council for Scientific Policy continued to express concern over the long-term supply of scientists and engineers. One of its study groups investigated the subject preferences of secondary students and was disturbed to find a general trend away from specialization in science and mathematics in sixth form.[44] Of more immediate concern than this alleged "swing from science" was the pattern of employment discovered among recent scientific and engineering graduates. A study commissioned by the Manpower Resources Committee found that a growing proportion of the most able graduates were entering academic careers or continuing postgraduate research in the basic sciences. [45] The demands for personnel generated by the university expansion program, together with the traditional prestige of academic research appeared to negate efforts to recruit graduates into the fields of greatest manpower deficiency, namely industry and school teaching. In addition to excessive concentration of scientific talent in the basic research sector, a frightening number of research-minded graduates sought employment or fellowships abroad. The dangers of the "brain drain" had been recognized for more than a decade, and it had generated considerable public controversy during Labour's run for office in 1963-64, but new evidence suggested that it grew steadily worse up to 1967, particularly among young engineers and technologists. [46] Though emigration slowed significantly thereafter, due to the new American immigration laws and declining market opportunities, it appeared that fundamental differences in the employment conditions of specialized personnel continued to put British industries at a disadvantage vis-a-vis foreign firms. [47]

By 1970, educational authorities were warning against overproduction of scientists who could not find employment in teaching and research and were ill-prepared for nonacademic occupations. Indeed, unemployment among new science graduates was already a serious problem of the 1970s. [48] Another rapid expansion of university facilities could make this oversupply of specialists even worse. Consequently, various efforts are underway to broaden the university science curriculum to produce more "generalists" suited to nonacademic (especially industrial) jobs and to direct graduate scientists into technological and secondary teaching careers.

However, the reward structure in British science continues to inhibit such changes in career preferences. Social and academic traditions still limit the prestige of many industrial and engineering professions, while the social sciences have attracted a growing share of the student population. Thus, while British manpower planning has largely succeeded in meeting aggregate demands for scientists and engineers, it has become increasingly evident that factors beyond the control of the planners persist in shaping career choices and determining the allocation of critical skills in the economy. For this reason, the Committee on Manpower Resources for Science and Technology was disbanded in 1970, and scientific manpower is now considered—along with other categories of highly qualified personnel—by the Department of Employment.

81

Priorities in Research Support

The question of priorities for research support in the universities and in the government's own research laboratories came to a head in the early 1960s. The then Advisory Council on Scientific Policy and Department of Scientific and Industrial Research came to the conclusion that new criteria for determining choices in R&D investment were urgently needed. [49] There was increasing concern over both neglected fields of basic science and allocation of funds for applied research which might contribute more directly to economic and industrial growth. The research councils financed basic and applied research in the universities, industry, and their own research stations; but, as noted earlier, there was no means for coordinating the various projects supported or for allocating funds, according to overall assessments of national deficiencies and needs.

The reorganization of 1964-65 was in part designed to remedy this weakness by restructuring the research councils and making them responsible to the Secretary of State for Education and Science, who was in turn advised by the new Council for Scientific Policy (CSP) on budgetary and other matters. Thus, for the first time formal apparatus was created for distribution of funds in the university and research council sector.

In its first report, the CSP made it clear that exponential growth in research expenditure could not continue, and that research support must be expected to level off in the years ahead. More careful forward planning and discrimination among research projects would thus be required in future. The research councils were notified that they must hereafter justify their support programs on a broader range of criteria, including social, economic, educational, and political objectives, as well as intrinsic scientific merit. The council announced that its first task was to demonstrate "how criteria for the development of science can be formulated and applied in practice."[50]

The council's report was met with protests from scientists and researchers, who questioned what appeared to be an excessively pessimistic outlook on the part of CSP. However, the financial crisis of July 1966 and its aftermath quickly sobered the scientific community as prospects of greater budgetary cutbacks appeared imminent. The council itself devoted a large portion of its second report in the following year to a defensive rationale for basic research expenditure in conditions of growing financial stringency. [51] In effect, the council was forced to shift its attention from new allocational criteria to short-term budgetary planning, in an effort to ensure adequate financing as the economic situation deteriorated. [52]

The CSP, composed of fifteen eminent scientists and backed by staff from the Department of Education and Science, sought to negotiate interim budgetary commitments in 1966-67 which would have maintained an annual increase in the science vote (appropriation) of about 10 percent over the following three years. Although this growth rate was not achieved in real terms, current spending in the research council sector continued to increase rapidly through 1970-71, and the proportion of research funds in this sector grew appreciably.[53] It thus appears that British scientific administrators were more successful in maintaining the flow of basic research funds in the late sixties than were their counterparts in the United States and some other countries.[54] However, the rate was clearly downward and was expected to be negative by 1974-75.[55]

It is difficult to say precisely how the CSP determined priorities for different fields of science, but it undoubtedly influenced the allocation of funds among the various research councils and prompted the councils to reconsider their own grant-awarding policies.[56] Since 1966-67, the Agricultural Research Council's budget has declined slightly in relation to the others, while the Medical Research Council's has increased. The Natural Environment Research Council's share grew sharply in its first years, in an effort to establish it on a par with the older councils. The Science Research Council's reduction from 53 percent in 1966-67, to about 48 percent in 1971-72, was especially noteworthy and indicated a desire to reduce support in some areas of physical science (especially basic physics research) in favor of applied research of greater social impact. However, this also reflected the lower priority given to aerospace, nuclear energy, and related defense work generally.

Evidence of changing priorities within the research councils themselves is considerable. The Science Research Council, faced with especially tight resources, undertook a thorough review of its grant policies during 1965-70.[57] In general, it sought to direct its grants and fellowships towards research of greater socioeconomic potential. Student grant applications in applied science and engineering were given preference over those in pure science, although in 1969 two-thirds of the fellowships granted to Ph.D. candidates were still in engineering. New awards were designed to attract students into industrial and secondary teaching careers, while program support was greatly increased in several interdisciplinary fields of potential industrial application or social benefit (such as automatic control engineering, polymer science, enzyme chemistry and technology, transportation, and environmental pollution control). In each case, the SRC is establishing multidisciplinary research centers at selected universities and institutes; this equipment and facilities will be shared by other scientists. In official terms, this reflects a general policy of increasing "selectivity" and "concentration" in the support of research, with "more favorable than average" treatment being given to fields and institutions of greatest potential contribution.[58]

Recent SRC policies do represent something of a departure from past operating principles. Though the research councils have always tended to support "the man" (that is, outstanding individual scientists) rather than distributing funds on the basis of institutional need, the new policies will have the effect of concentrating support in a smaller number of university research centers. This is justified in terms of maintaining a "critical mass" or "threshold level" of activity in rapidly advancing research fields. On the other hand, the Council for Scientific Policy gave strong endorsement to the system of dual support by which the UGC provides basic operating funds and equipment for the university departments which are supplemented by selective additional support from the research councils. The ratio between general and supplementary funding may change, and there may be need for further concentration of support in some fields, but the CSP argued that concern must also continue for those departments and institutions which are not selected for concentration. [59] The process of concentration is thus likely to be implemented gradually.

More fundamental issues were raised by the Rothschild Report, [60] issued in November 1971, and the subsequent Government White Paper, Framework for Government Research and Development, [61] published in July 1972. They indicate that basic changes are underway in the historic pattern of research support in Britain. The report by Lord Rothschild, head of the new Central Policy Review Staff in the Heath administration, [62] came as a shock to many in the scientific community. In blunt, unsparing language, he argued that a considerable volume of publicly supported research had no clear objective or use, and that in future government R&D must be related more closely to programmatic goals. He drew a sharp line between basic and applied research, and insisted that, as a general principle, applied R&D must be done on a "customer-contractor" basis. That is, research and development "with a practical application as its objective" must be demanded (and thus contracted for) by the potential user or "customer" of the end product. This meant that an increasing proportion of research should be financed through the government departments with major program responsibilities rather than through the semi-independent research councils. He suggested that approximately one-quarter of the funds currently allocated to the research councils could be transferred to related departments, which would then contract for needed research from the research council laboratories, the universities, or other bodies. [63] The departments or ministries, equipped with their own scientific staff, would then be in a position to commission applied research projects directly relevant to their program goals and administrative obligations. The research councils would retain their finances and responsibilities in supporting basic research and applied work of a more general nature, but would be brought into closer consultation with the departments in this realm as well.

Rothschild's proposals aroused bitter criticism and controversy in the press and scientific journals, [64] particularly insofar as they appeared to question the validity of much of the research being conducted under the auspices of scientists on the research councils. The Council for Scientific Policy, representing the research councils and what might be called the professional scientific establishment, presented its views in a document published along with the Rothschild Report. [65] The Dainton Report, as this statement is known, argued strongly that no clear demarcation can be made between "pure" and "applied" science, due to the increasingly inter- and multidisciplinary character of R&D activity. It suggested instead a more complex, functional distinction between "tactical," "strategic," and "basic" activities. [66] The group maintained that the growing interdependence of these activities requires open communication among scientists pursuing different levels and types of research, and that scientific interchange would be inhibited if research were further compartmentalized among different bureaucratic agencies.

The Rothschild and Dainton reports placed the issue of public responsibility and accountability in support of science in sharper focus than at any time in the postwar era. Who is to commission research, and for what purpose? To what extent can different types of R&D activity be separated according to their potential contribution to public policy and welfare? Should decisions on "practical" as well as fundamental research be made by relatively autonomous boards of professional scientists or by scientists and other experts involved in the administration of broader government programs? These and other questions now divide the scientific community, partly because financial support may be less certain in the future, but also because many object to the proposition that research must be justified by some direct contribution to government policy.

The Government made its decisions known in the White Paper of July 1972. Essentially, the Rothschild doctrines were to be implemented, with some modifications and concessions in the research council sector. A considerable share (though less than projected by Rothschild) of the budgets of the Agricultural Research Council, Medical Research Council, and Natural Environment Research Council was to be transferred from the science vote of the Department of Education and Science to related departments over the next three years. [67]

In each of these departments, a central scientific organization is being established, including usually a chief scientist with a small scientific staff, and one or more requirement boards or similar mechanism for contracting. These groups will determine departmental R&D priorities and contract with the research councils for the required work, [68] with the proviso that the councils may refuse a project if it does not appear feasible on scientific grounds or in terms of available resources. Once commissioned, the councils will undertake the detailed project management, but "Departments will need to be satisfied before committing funds that a project has been carefully planned and that arrangements exist for systematic surveillance and review."[69] This means, of course, that the research councils will be under scrutiny from the regular government departments.

Indeed, the White Paper announced a number of further changes in the research council structure to integrate them more closely in the work of the departments. The research councils now have departmental representatives as full members (rather than as assessors— as previously), and all appointments to the councils apparently require clearance from ministers in related departments. More importantly, the Council for Scientific Policy was replaced in late 1972 by an Advisory Board for the Research Councils, which includes the chairmen of the research councils and departmental officials. There are still independent members, but the majority are ex officio so that the new board is in a better position to discuss and coordinate policies.[70]

As a beneficial side effect, the government indicated that new regulations and training courses have been designed to facilitate the movement of scientists into high administrative positions in the departments, thus raising the scientific and technical competence of the entire bureaucracy. Taken as a whole, the White Paper asserts that the "new framework provides a partnership within which science will have more influence on the Government's central policy-making activities than before, and which will contribute more directly and more effectively to the task of making the best use of science and technology for the needs of the community as a whole."[71]

Industry and Technology

The problems encountered in the sphere of industrial research and development over the past decade have been the most difficult and, indeed, crucial for Britain's national growth. Moreover, as noted above, the Labour government took office in 1964 with major commitments in this area, having promised to revitalize British industry through technological modernization—or, as Harold Wilson once put it, to take British industry "by the scruff of its neck and drag it kicking and screaming into the twentieth century."[72] The Ministry of Technology was consequently established, although initially the new Department of Economic Affairs was given primary responsibility for economic "growth" policies, including general industrial development. The relationship between these two departments was never very clear, but the Ministry of Technology was clearly the junior partner under its first head, Mr. Frank Cousins, who resigned over the government's wage restraint policies in July of 1966.[73] However, Mr. George Brown, Secretary of State for Economic Affairs, also resigned over this issue, and thereafter DEA rapidly declined in significance.

86

Under Cousin's successor, Anthony Wedgwood Benn, the Ministry of Technology—or Mintech, as it was now dubbed—then emerged as the chief industrial department. It grew by leaps and bounds, first consolidating responsibility for several advanced technologies (computers, electronics, telecommunications, and machine tools) and then for all mechanical engineering industries; followed by a second major expansion in 1967, in which it incorporated the Ministry of Aviation with its far-flung defense research and procurement functions. This action culminated with a third major extension of powers in October 1969, when it absorbed most of the remaining industrial responsibilities of the moribund Department of Economic Affairs and the Board of Trade, plus responsibility for the nationalized industries of the Ministry of Power (coal, gas, and electricity) and the renationalized steel industry. [74] By the end of the Labour government, the ministry had grown into an enormous industrial empire—manager of most civil and military R&D, sponsor for some 85 percent of manufacturing industry, controller of the principal fuel and energy sources, and general industrial and regional development planner. Aside from America's Pentagon, it is doubtful that any governmental agency in the non-Communist world has amassed a comparable range of authority (or potential authority) over industrial-technological development. [75]

Mintech's operations were so varied, became so complex, and grew so fast that it never attained internal coherence or a clear sense of direction. However, Mr. Benn attempted to define its evolving purposes in numerous speeches and interviews, [76] and there is some additional evidence as to its underlying philosophy and goals. Its most general function was to promote industrial efficiency and international economic competitiveness by aiding technological innovation and restructuring certain industries into larger units. Although initially conceived as a means for strengthening and coordinating government research and development programs on the industrial side, its obligations soon extended far beyond R&D into basic investment, production, and marketing policies. Its increasingly commercial focus was symbolized by the ministry's official slogan, "technology for profit," which emphasized the readiness of Mintech to assist private companies in rationalizing their operations and in launching new products or processes with export potential in advanced industrial markets. In essence, this reflected a growing realization that R&D policies could not be separated from general industrial policy, and that economic growth depended on selective aid to those sectors of industry with greatest prospects for expansion. [77]

Insofar as it linked administration of most civil and virtually all defense R&D, including aerospace and nuclear energy, Mintech provided for the first time a central structure for reassessing priorities and reallocating resources between the military and civilian

87

sectors. As noted earlier, defense and other "big science" research was significantly curtailed in this period. While this reflected strategic governmental decisions beyond the scope of any one department, Mintech actively encouraged the conversion of defense research facilities to civilian industrial projects. The budgetary figures on this conversion[78] are somewhat conjectural since some defense work was apparently reclassified as civilian for accounting purposes, but there is no doubt about a substantial shift in priorities to the civilian side. On the other hand, the ministry was saddled with a number of aircraft projects and other commitments which required an increasing volume of government assistance to reach commercial development, notably the Concorde supersonic airliner being built with France. In other cases, Mintech actively sought contracts for ailing companies in order to keep them afloat in international competition; the ill-fated Rolls-Royce contract with Lockheed is an outstanding example.

These pressures, together with Mintech's other administrative obligations, made it difficult to advance any clearcut strategy for technological development. At its height in 1970, the ministry's budget totaled about £2.35 billion, mostly for defense procurement and investments in the nationalized power and steel industries. The R&D and related "industrial services" component of the budget was a relatively small fraction of the total, including some £200 million for defense R&D and about £180 million for civil research and general technological support programs. It was primarily under the latter categories that the ministry sought to promote industrial growth. Table 3.4 indicates expenditure patterns for 1966-70 in this area.

Although the combined spending under these headings increased substantially, nearly two-thirds of the increase was for aerospace support. This included large capital grants in the form of "launching aid" given to commercial aircraft developments such as Concorde.[79] Atomic energy research was significantly reduced, and some personnel redeployed on nonnuclear projects, but rising costs and scheduled reactor projects brought total spending in this field back to its 1966-67 level. Including new forms of industrial-technological support to such industries as shipbuilding and computers, the other categories of expenditure more than quadrupled over the period.

In addition, the ministry gave a great deal of advice and assistance not directly reflected in the budgetary figures. Mintech conducted or commissioned some fifty surveys of individual industries, to assess development potentials, and sought close working "partnership" with the management of large British and international corporations engaged in advanced technological competition.[80] The effects of such consultations cannot be assessed, but one of Mr. Benn's principal objectives was to develop a professional staff in the ministry with sufficient expertise to discuss the most intricate investment, production, and marketing problems with business and industrial executives.

TABLE 3.4

Major Categories of Technology Expenditure, 1966-70
(in thousands of pounds)

| | 1966-67 | 1967-68 | 1968-69[a] | 1969-70[b] |
|---|---|---|---|---|
| Industrial Services[c] | 9,324 | 11,574 | 18,969 | 22,063 |
| Atomic Energy[d] | 50,530 | 46,123 | 47,409 | 50,314 |
| Aerospace[e] | 57,168 | 76,216 | 102,829 | 110,101 |
| Other industrial support[f] | • • | • • | 18,700 | 20,600 |

[a]Provisional.

[b]Estimates.

[c]Includes general technological support activities, expenditure by the National Research Development Corporation, and grants to industrial research associations.

[d]Includes AEA civil research expenditure and capital expenditure for major reactor projects.

[e]Includes civil research in aviation laboratories and capital expenditure for aerospace projects and launching aid. In 1970, civil research was about one-fifth of the total.

[f]Includes assistance to shipbuilding industry; assistance for computer merger project and aluminum smelting scheme under Industrial Expansion Act, 1968; and allowance for new projects.

Source: Statistics of Science and Technology, 1970, Table 13, p. 35, and Public Expenditure 1968-69 to 1973-74, pp. 33-34 ("other industrial support" only).

In several industries, Mintech (along with the new Industrial Reorganization Corporation) became intimately involved in the details of corporate structure by promoting company mergers. In the big science field, the ministry carried out reorganizations of the nuclear power, aviation, and computer industries; it concentrated shipbuilding in several larger centers; and it supported other mergers in electrical engineering, automobiles, and ball-bearings. The professed object was to create larger, more efficient and market-oriented companies capable of competing on a European and world scale (the most outstanding example being, perhaps, the creation of International Computers Ltd. in 1968).[81]

The ministry also tried to reorient its own R&D towards industrial growth and maintained a panoply of technical advisory services on everything from low-cost automation to metrication. In cooperation with the nationalized industries and other departments, it attempted

89

to employ government purchasing power to force technological changes and raise technical standards generally. It is doubtful that the government's role as customer was exploited to anywhere near its potential, but in some fields (notably computers) purchase of British-made goods over cheaper foreign imports helped to subsidize crucial development sectors. In a few cases, the government went further and purchased shares in private companies, though scarcely on a scale commensurate with preelection promises to establish public ownership of science-based industries.

The overall thrust of Mintech policy was to curtail R&D in government establishments in favor of extramural research under contract. It came to be seen as a major error of postwar science policy that Britain had not followed the general American pattern of contracting research out to private industry in more fields of development. Wedgwood Benn was much impressed with American contract research firms and institutes (such as Battelle, Arthur D. Little, Rand, and General Dynamics); he stated that Mintech would like to contract out as much as possible of the ministry's research work. Although the government remained fearful of an American-style military-industrial-technological complex through defense contracting—and had no wish to emulate this aspect of the model—it was felt that R&D of ultimate benefit to civil industry ought to be carried out as closely as possible to commercial production processes. On the other hand, it was also suggested that government research establishments necessary in the public interest might take on an increasing share of private contract research for industrial firms along the lines of American research corporations. With this in mind, Mr. Benn proposed a far-reaching reorganization of government research facilities in early 1970.[82]

Under this plan, the civil research laboratories and facilities of the U.K. Atomic Energy Authority, the Ministry of Technology's principal industrial research establishments, and the National Research Development Corporation were to be joined in a new statutory body outside the civil service—a British Research and Development Corporation. On-going nuclear reactor work and other government programs would continue to provide the bulk of BRDC finances, but the corporation would engage in a growing proportion of work on contract for both other government agencies and private industrial firms. The corporation was to operate under supervision of a board appointed by Mintech, it would, however, have been free to undertake on its own initiative work or investments on which it expected to recover its costs. It would thus have been able to "engage in joint ventures with industry, sharing costs and risks," and, if successful, the government's direct subsidy to industrial research might eventually be reduced.

The guiding principle of the proposed reorganization was that, "Experience in this country and abroad suggests that no Government

90

department can decide centrally what research programmes are best designed to serve the needs of industry. As a general rule, only the 'customer' knows what he wants, and by his readiness to pay for it makes the 'supplier' aware of his requirements."[83] This, in extreme form, was the lesson of the Labour government's efforts to promote a technological revolution in industry. Put another way, Wedgwood Benn came to the conclusion that policies for technology could not be separated from those towards industry generally, and that although it was crucial to maintain a "powerful scientific capability at the heart of industrial policy" if government was to "interact intelligently with industry,"[84] the burden of innovation and competitiveness must rest ultimately with industry itself. The Ministry of Technology was well on the way to becoming a "Ministry of Industry," foreshadowing some of the changes under the subsequent Conservative government.

The Conservatives had been highly critical of Mintech, as well as other agencies such as the Industrial Reorganization Corporation (IRC) which Labour had created to promote industrial reform, despite the fact that these experiments had aroused considerable interest and attention abroad. They had argued strongly for "disengagement" of government from the economy and return to traditional market incentives. It thus came as no surprise when the Heath government dissolved Mintech and IRC shortly after coming to power in 1970 and replaced them with a Department of Trade and Industry (DTI) built around the old Board of Trade and the government's civil aerospace functions. Although continuing Mintech's basic industrial research activities and some its technical and advisory services, DTI indicated that it would critically review all state industrial research programs with a view toward turning as much R&D as feasible over to private enterprise.

However, the logic of Britain's economic difficulties soon led to renewed efforts in DTI to spur technological advances in fields of growing international competition. Following the Rothschild recommendations, six requirements boards were established in DTI to contract for R&D in private industry and otherwise to support promising industrial innovations. The principal departure from the structure proposed by Benn is that the contracting agencies now operate within the context of functional departmental divisions, rather than under an autonomous R&D corporation, although each of the requirements boards has its own budget and reports directly to Parliament on its activities. Thus a balance seems to have been struck between the need for both operational flexibility and public accountability while relating R&D support more closely to ongoing departmental responsibilities.

It should also be pointed out that military and aviation research were placed under a separate procurement executive in the Ministry of Defence, although DTI is responsible for civil aviation projects and has its own aerospace group and minister (who then contracts with the procurement executive for civilian aerospace R&D). Thus

91

responsibilities for civil and military R&D are again divided, although much of the work is shared between DTI and Defence. [85]

## European Industrial and Scientific Cooperation

With some exceptions (notably large space ventures), Great Britain followed what Gilpin has called a "broad-front" strategy into the 1960s; that is, attempting to compete with the U.S. and other nations across the entire range of scientific and technological developments. [86] The strategy followed by Japan and, to a lesser extent, West Germany—that of "importation" or buying foreign technology through license and royalty agreements—had been followed to a lesser degree by Britain than any nation of comparable size; indeed, Britain has been a net exporter of technology by these standards. [87]

It has become apparent in recent years that Britain cannot continue to spread her scientific resources so broadly, and consequently an intermediate strategy of scientific and technological specialization or concentration of resources in areas of greatest competitive advantage has become increasingly attractive. Mintech in fact attempted to concentrate support in key expansionary sectors and seek collaborative agreements with foreign companies and governments in other areas. However, policies of this kind are inevitably limited by a host of other diplomatic and strategic considerations, and the effort to find a new balance between domestic and international commitments has been a tortuous one.

British policies in this field have suffered from conflicting interests in American and European cooperation, as well as the general financial constraints mentioned earlier. The Labour government remained heavily dependent on American goodwill and cooperation during the economic crisis leading to devaluation, and in defense matters as well. On the other hand, as part of the second attempt to enter the European Common Market—eventually the European Economic Community, EEC—in 1966-67, Prime Minister Wilson took up the cudgels against the "technology gap" and proposed a "European Technological Community" to counter American influence. When General DeGaulle again exercised the veto, relations with Europe soured and commitments to international scientific organizations were reduced during 1968-69. Several joint aviation developments with France and other countries were continued and some new projects explored, but intergovernmental collaboration in science and technology had made relatively little progress by the early 1970s.

In part, this reflected foreign policy shifts, as well as the Labour government's growing caution over international projects of dubious commercial benefit. Concorde and other "prestige" projects were subjected to increasing scrutiny and criticism as the economic situation deteriorated. In one of the more dramatic budgetary cuts of 1968, the government decided, against the advice of its scientific advisory councils, that Britain would not participate in construction of the large nuclear particle accelerator proposed by Centre Europeene pour la Recherche Nucleaive (CERN) in Geneva.[88] Despite widespread recognition of CERN as the most successful cooperative scientific venture in Europe, and general acknowledgement that access to an accelerator of this size was necessary if European scientists were to remain in the forefront of nuclear physics research in the 1980s, a tangible economic case could not be made for the project. Although this decision has since been reversed,[89] it was indicative of the mood prevailing in British governmental circles. In April 1968, on similar grounds, the government stated that it would make no further contributions to the European Launcher Development Organization (ELDO) following completion of current projects: later support was increased for the European Space Research Organization (ESRO), contingent upon adoption of applications satellite programs of greater commercial potential.

Between the decision to seek entry to the Common Market in November 1966, and its failure a year later, Wilson took the lead in proposing European industrial and technological collaboration. Four days after the decision for application was announced he stated that

> I would like to see . . . a drive to create a new technological community to pool with Europe the enormous technological inventiveness of Britain and other European countries, to enable Europe on a competitive basis to become more self-reliant and neither dependent on imports nor dominated from outside, but basing itself on the creation of competitive indigenous European industries.
>
> I can think of nothing that could make a greater reality of the whole European concept and in the field of technological cooperation no one has more to contribute than Britain.[90]

At the Parliamentary Assembly of the Council of Europe in Strasbourg in January 1967, Wilson attacked "industrial helotry" by the United States, and argued that "We have to see that the European industry of tomorrow does not become dependent on an outside technology, with all that can mean in terms of industrial power and independence."[91] In subsequent speeches throughout the spring and summer, he repeatedly stated that one of the primary reasons for entering the EEC was to establish an industrial and technological base of sufficient scale to compete with the U.S.

As prospects for EEC admission dimmed, Wilson separated the issue of European industrial-technological development from formal British entry to the market. In a major address shortly before the devaluation and collapse of the application, the prime minister

93

warned that the technology gap was growing, and he outlined an impressive seven point program for European technological collaboration--whatever the outcome of the EEC negotiations.[92] He now called for a multinational European Institute of Technology, to "examine, case by case, industry by industry, the means to greater European cooperation, and to work with governments in achieving it. " In a categorical pledge, he asserted that Britain was "prepared to go as far and as fast—and indeed perhaps further and faster than—any country in Europe in preparing technological cooperation and integration that can give a new impetus to a European economic union. "

These statements are quoted at length not because they succeeded in generating new European policies (the details seem never to have been worked out) but because they remain relevant after Britain's successful entry to the enlarged European Community in 1972-73. The Labour government attempted to lay the groundwork for greater industrial cooperation through technological collaboration. The Ministry of Technology continued to emphasize that international cooperation must go beyond scattered R&D projects to industrial application and marketing, through international corporate mergers and agreements as well as intergovernmental arrangements.[93] As one example, the ministry concluded negotiations in late 1969 on formation of a private Anglo-Dutch-German consortium for production and sale of gas centrifuges used to produce enriched uranium fuel. The enormous potential market for such equipment, and for British uranium fuels in general, epitomized the type of commercial-industrial opportunities which the Labour government hoped to exploit.

Britain still has much to offer the European Community in both science and technology. The U. K. 's gross expenditure on R&D has until recently been over half that of the EEC countries combined, and in nuclear power, computers, aeroengines, and many other fields of basic and applied research Britain leads Europe.[94] Larger markets are necessary if production runs in aircraft and other expensive goods are to reach profitable volume. On the other hand, the Labour government was undoubtedly correct in viewing the problem of industrial collaboration and competition more broadly than in terms of formal economic association. As Wedgwood Benn frequently stated, success ultimately depended upon international linkages at the company level. Mintech thus sought to develop confidential relationships with individual firms both at home and abroad. Consultations were held with many foreign companies, and "quasi-diplomatic" relations opened with the principal multinational corporations with operations in Britain. Meanwhile, possibilities for industrial cooperation continued to be explored through a variety of other channels, including the Council of Europe, Western European Union, European Space Conference, and the Science Committee of the EEC Parliament.

These efforts may have contributed to the agreement of the nine members of the enlarged Common Market—announced in October 1972—

to pursue common policies in the area of science and technology. The European Commission and Council of Ministers have since formulated guidelines for the coordination of national R&D programs and for cooperation across a broad field of basic and applied research; they have established a "Europe Plus 30" group to engage in long-term assessment of research needs.[95] At the same time, possibilities continue to be explored for both bilateral and EEC collaboration with the U.S. in post-Apollo space ventures and other programs. It should be noted that, in the case of Britain, only about seven percent of government R&D funds have been spent on overseas projects in recent years; this proportion could be expanded considerably as R&D increasingly conducted on the international level.

But the fundamental issues remain: in which fields of science and technology can a nation of Britain's size and resources afford to pursue independent or competitive strategies, and in which must it seek to pool recources with other countries or reduce commitments below the threshold of current advances and thus become more reliant on foreign research and technology transfers? Present trends are towards greater selectivity and prudence in support of the national R&D effort, but there are as yet few indications of the scientific and technical goals to be singled out for national concentration.

## MANAGEMENT, CONTROL, AND PUBLIC ACCOUNTABILITY

A good deal of organizational change and controversy over the proper structure of government for science policy was manifested during the past two decades in Britain. There has also been growing pressure for public accountability. Until the early 1960s relatively little concern existed over the organization and functions of government support programs, but escalating costs and mounting disputes over the effectiveness of government R&D programs gradually eroded public confidence in the role of the state in promoting national development through scientific and technical advance.

While this problem is not unique to Britain, the economic strains of the middle and late 1960s contributed powerfully to the current mood of retrenchment and reassessment. Already, R&D priorities have shifted substantially, but as yet there does not appear to be any consensus over the goals and functions of science policy in the 1970s. Issues such as the level of scientific support in relation to economic growth, the degree of public and private responsibility for research and innovation, the degree of centralization and coordination in national scientific policies, and the relationship between scientific support and other governmental programs remain essentially unsolved.

These problems reflect, of course, underlying differences of opinion over the relationship of science to society, as well as over

95

the proper role of government. In Britain, science has traditionally been supported as a cultural good in itself, without expectation of direct economic and social benefits, although from the turn of the century a certain amount of general applied research has been conducted in government laboratories. Since World War II, the government has vastly expanded support for mission-oriented R&D in defense, aviation, nuclear energy, and other fields, but basic research has continued to receive aid through the research councils and universities as an end in itself. In recent years, economic, social, and educational objectives have been emphasized more strongly, but the scientific community has resented pressures in this direction.

Thus, while science is beginning to be seen more as a technical or social "overhead" (that is, the costs are justified as a necessary adjunct to advancing technology or as a social service in supplying manpower and skills needed for general social and economic progress), there is little agreement on the extent to which any one rationale is to shape the emerging research system. [96] In applied science and technology, the objectives would appear clearer, but in fact a good deal of controversy exists at present over the basic terminology and concepts to be used in classifying different types of scientific activity. The role of the state would presumably vary according to the immediacy of different R&D activities to its various program goals or usages, but distinctions—for example, between "strategic" and "tactical" research—are not likely to settle the issue. [97]

In lieu of agreement on such fundamentals, partisan doctrines and managerial strategies have increasingly influenced British science policies. Prior to the 1964 election, a considerable gap had developed between Labour and Conservative party thinking on scientific matters, reflecting general differences in political philosophy. The Labour party favored greatly enlarged governmental responsibilities for R&D of economic consequence, as well as greater coordination and direction in science policy generally. The result was a lengthy and acrimonious debate over proper departmental responsibilities; this ultimately led to greater concentration of authority in the Department of Education and Science and the now-defunct Ministry of Technology.

Whether central "direction" was greatly increased by these measures is open to question: certainly government involvement in R&D decisions reached an unprecedented level in peacetime. Although the Labour government largely abandoned its initial plans for state-controlled technological development, the concentration of responsibilities in the Ministry of Technology continued to grow. This trend was reversed by the Conservatives, who seemed intent on dispersing scientific and technical obligations more widely in government and eliminating those which are better performed in the private sector.

Scientific Advice and Management

The frequency and extent of administrative changes and attendant turnover in ministerial personnel since 1964 has not been conducive to coherent policy direction. Indeed, in some areas—notably industrial research and development—organizational discontinuity has reached a dangerous level. To this must be added growing confusion over the role which scientists are to play in decision-making. In the past, professional scientific advice has been given through the research councils and other counciliar organs such as the Advisory Council on Scientific Policy and the restructured Council for Scientific Policy and their various subcommittees and study groups.[98] The Labour government maintained this system and added further advisory councils (the Advisory Council on Technology in Mintech and the Central Advisory Council for Science and Technology) as well as a full-time Chief Scientific Adviser (Sir Solly Zuckerman).[99] Although the advisory (rather than executive) status of such bodies must be emphasized, their role as peer representatives of the scientific community has lately been called into question. The "customer-contractor" relationship called for by Lord Rothschild at least raises doubts about science policy direction by corporate scientific peer groups.

The problem of accountability has always been difficult in scientific matters due to the criteria applied by scientific advisers and to the ambiguous nature of the results. The expert judgments of scientists are not readily intelligible to the layman, and their advice may be conflicting or may be rejected by those with executive authority; the results of decisions are not easy to evaluate, since research may not culminate in any measurable product. However, by the early 1960s there was increasing concern in Britain over cost escalation, excess profit-making, and general lack of control in defense R&D projects.[100] Although management and accounting procedures have been tightened considerably since then,[101] the problems raised in R&D management have lately merged with those in public administration generally. There has been a broader movement in British government over the past decade towards forward public expenditure planning, functional cost accounting, and what is generally known as program budgeting (that is, allocation of funds by program or function rather than spending authority and item).[102]

The movement for administrative reform was given further impetus by the report of the Fulton Committee on the civil service in 1968.[103] This committee, appointed by the prime minister, challenged many traditional attitudes of the civil service and called for sweeping reforms in the organization and procedures of public administration.

97

Among other things, Lord Fulton attacked the notion of administration by cultivated "amateurs" or "all-rounders" and recommended more professional training for civil servants; recommended abolition of the established civil service classes to facilitate more flexible utilization of specialist personnel; and called for reorganization of administration into "accountable units" of management. This implied not only a reorganization of the bureaucracy according to program objectives and managerial responsibilities, but also "hiving off" of administrative tasks better performed by organizations outside the traditional civil service departments.

It has been suggested by many that the size and complexity of modern government may increasingly require delegation of authority to responsible private or quasi-public bodies.[104] Although the restructuring of the civil service is proceeding slowly under the new Civil Service Department established by the Fulton reforms, the Heath Government was committed to the major administrative doctrines that have emerged in recent years. Budget planning and programming, functional cost accounting, clarification of managerial responsibilities, and decentralization of functions to new management units within or outside the departmental structure all represent new managerial strategies designed to improve efficiency and economy in government.[105]

What is important for science policy is that those managerial techniques borrowed essentially from the business world are likely to play an increasing part in scientific organization and decision-making. The Rothschild reforms are indicative of the cost-effectiveness methods that are likely to be applied in scientific support programs generally. However, they solve neither the inherent difficulties of measuring scientific output nor the broader problems of accountability to society at large. In Britain, as elsewhere, one finds growing public concern over the social and ecological implications of science and technology. The government's manifest preoccupation with commercial exploration of technology has aroused in many scientists and intellectuals a profound conviction that material objectives are distorting scientific priorities and further endangering the quality of life. Younger scientists, in particular, are increasingly uneasy about the role of the state in scientific affairs.


Parliament and Science Policy


Parliamentary accountability has also become more important in recent years, as science policy has become something of a test case for reasserting prerogatives of deliberation and control which have increasingly slipped to the executive and bureaucracy. The development of a parliamentary constituency for science policy is one of the most interesting and promising aspects of the British experience. Since there are no standing legislative committees in the House of Commons comparable to those of the U.S. Congress and some other parliamentary bodies, it has been particularly difficult to cultivate specialized expertise in different fields of policy. Policymaking has long been regarded as a prerogative of the Cabinet and party leaders, with parliamentary backbenchers and opposition forces playing a subordinate role in debating and publicizing the actions of government (that is, the executive).[106] Facilities for independent investigation and research have been minimal in Westminster until recent years.

In the field of science policy, Parliament was denied access to information on many of the crucial postwar developments in defense and atomic energy, and further inhibited by the concentration of authority in quasi-military departments (Ministry of Supply, later Aviation), independent statutory corporations (U.K. Atomic Energy Authority, National Research Development Corporation), and other semiautonomous bodies (the research councils and University Grants Committee). A forum for discussion between M.P.'s and representatives of the scientific and industrial community was established in the Parliamentary and Scientific Committee but, as an unofficial parliamentary body, this informal grouping could do little more than keep communications lines open between the various interests affected by current policy developments and occasionally prod the government.

However, the controversy over science policy during 1962-64 generated a movement to improve the mechanisms for parliamentary scrutiny in this field.[107] A specialized Select Committee on Science and Technology was established in late 1966, one of the first of a series of new policy committees introduced by the Labour government. By general consensus, the science committee has been one of the most successful of these experiments, and its life has been renewed by subsequent governments.[108]

It was given a broad mandate "to consider Science and Technology and report thereon," with powers to send for persons, papers, and records, hold public hearings, employ specialist assistance, and travel abroad to carry out investigations.

Though hampered somewhat by shortage of staff and facilities, the science committee has investigated a number of important subjects including the nuclear power industry, defense research, and computer development. Its fact-finding mission into the operations of government programs has been more significant than its policy influence, but its informational role is critical in a system plagued by secrecy. Moreover, the committee has recently addressed itself to broader issues such as the implications of population growth in Britain and reorganization of the science policy establishment (in light of the Rothschild Report). In the latter case, its lack of equanimity in proposing organizational changes aroused considerable debate in executive and scientific circles, [109] and in other matters it has not hesitated to challenge the technical basis of decisions made by the government. [110]

The committee has thus provided an alternative means of gathering scientific advice and intelligence in government. As such, it opens a limited but significant forum for scientists who have heretofore been excluded from the higher councils of science advising in the research councils and administration. Since the latter have been relatively closed circuits of prestigious individuals, and there have been few public "adversary" proceedings in science policy formulation, the committee's relations with the broader scientific community are especially important. [111] It may be hoped that as new issues push to the fore—environment and energy questions, to cite only the most obvious—the committee will further enhance the potentials for long-range scientific and technological assessment in Parliament.

NOTES

1. See R. B. McCallum and Alison Readman, The British General Election of 1945 (London: Oxford University Press, 1947), p. 44.

2. House of Commons Debates (Nov. 30, 1945), vol. 416, col. 1857.

3. See, for example, Don K. Price, Government and Science (New York: Oxford University Press, 1962), chap. 2.

4. Private industry was, of course, brought in at the procurement stage and generally came to play a larger role in contract R&D. But, in general, Britain got the worst of both worlds—a high and expanding defense budget, with limited benefit to industry through research experience and spillover to the civilian sector.

5. Scientific Manpower—Report of a Committee appointed by the Lord President of the Council (Barlow Report), Cmd. 6824, 1946. University enrollment surpassed the prewar level of about 50,000 and reached 80,000 in the early 1950s.

6. Solly Zuckerman, "Scientists in the Arena," in Ciba Foundation Symposium, Decision Making in National Science Policy (Boston: Little-Brown, 1968), pp. 8-9. Emphasis added.

7. According to official statistics, government support for civil R&D increased from about £6 million in 1945-46 to £30 million in 1950-51. But most of the increase was in aviation and nuclear energy research of potential civil application.

8. See A Programme for Nuclear Power, Cmd. 9389, 1955, which outlined the first ten-year program. A second ten-year program was approved in 1964.

9. The comparative economics of nuclear power generation have remained a controversial subject in Britain as elsewhere, and Britain

100

may have had particularly good reasons for proceeding more rapidly than other nations. In the 1950s, and particularly after nationalization of the Suez Canal, there were acute fears that Middle Eastern oil supplies might be cut off. Then, too, the discovery of alternate supplies such as the North Sea natural gas deposits could not be foreseen. Yet the strain on national scientific and technological resources was obvious, and there is no doubt that the prestige of the atomic energy program was an important factor, much as it was in France later.

10. It is estimated that in 1958-59 about £20 million of the ministry's R&D was of "civil application." Total defense R&D expenditure at this time was over £200 million, while government spending for all civil research amounted to around £80 million.

11. For a personal exposition of Lord Hailsham's philosophy, see his Science and Politics (London: Faber and Faber, 1963).

12. Research council grants to the univertities and CATS totaled about £10 million by 1963.

13. See C.F. Carter and B.R. Williams, Science in Industry: Policy for Progress (London: Oxford University Press, 1959).

14. Hailsham, op. cit., p. 19. He also warned against "militarization" and "commercialization" of science, should governmental controls increase. These concerns have ironically been taken over by the political left in recent years.

15. Ibid. Cf. My Science and Technology in British Politics, (Oxford: Persamon Press, 1968) pp. 67-73 and chap. 4 generally, for a fuller treatment of Hailsham.

16. I have covered this in detail in chap. 5 of Science and Technology in British Politics. I do not imply, as Hilary and Steven Rose have charged, that this was the only reason for the Labour party's renewed concern over science. Cf. Rose and Rose, Science and Society (Harmondsworth: Penguin Books, 1969), p. 98.

17. Labour Party, Signposts for the Sixties London, 1961. This theme was originally raised at the 1959 party conference (following the electoral defeat) and set out in the 1960 conference statement, Labour in the Sixties.

18. See Wilson's speech on "Labour and the Scientific Revolution", delivered at the 1963 party conference.

19. Higher Education (Robbins Report), 6 vols., Cmd. 2154.

20. The recommendations will be considered later in this essay.

21. Committee of Enquiry into the Organisation of Civil Science (Trend Report), Oct. 1963, Cmd. 2171.

22. The most important change, transfer of responsibility for the University Grants Committee from the Treasury to the Minister for Science, had already taken place in 1963. As the new Secretary of State, Hailsham merely added further domains to his supervisory realm without altering his basic principles of decentralized and largely autonomous scientific administration.

101

23. The New Britain, The Labour party's Manifesto for the 1964 General Election, pp. 9-10.

24. A new Social Science Research Council was also created, but it was not yet considered part of the science policy establishment.

25. Jean-Jacques Servan-Schreiber, Le Defi Americain (Paris: Denoel, 1967, trans. The American Challenge).

26. This is a major theme of Michael Shanks in The Innovators: The Economics of Technology (Harmondsworth: Penguin Books, 1967).

27. See, for examples, "White-Hot Revolution?" five articles in New Scientist (Sept. 26, 1968): 644-653.

28. Lewis A. Gunn, "Government, Technology and Planning," in J. N. Wolfe, ed., The Impact of Technology (forthcoming).

29. It should be noted that estimates for 1970-71 include overseas expenditures, whereas the figures for the previous years do not. Thus, an additional £33 million was spent overseas in 1967-68. For more recent expenditure figures, see Department of Education and Science and Ministry of Technology, Statistics of Science and Technology, published annually by HMSO.

30. See C. Freeman, C. H. G. Oldham, C. M. Cooper, T. C. Sinclair, and B. G. Achilladelis, "Discussion Paper: The Goals of R&D in the 1970s," Science Studies, vol. 1 (October 1971): nos. 3-4, table 1, p. 363.

31. Ibid., table 2, p. 371.

32. Moreover, the proportion of defense R&D has again risen in Britain. The estimates for 1972-73 indicated that defense expenditures would increase to £335 million, or 43 percent of the total government R&D budget of £780 million. For the complete 1972-73 R&D estimates, see Third Report of the Council for Scientific Policy, Cmd. 5117 (1972): 2.

33. United Nations Educational, Scientific, and Cultural Organization. World Summary of Statistics on Science and Technology (Paris, 1970), table 4, and Organization for Economic Cooperation and Development, International Statistical Year for Research and Development. Volume I: The Overall Level and Structure of R&D Efforts in OECD Member Countries (Paris, 1967), table 2, p. 14.

34. See OECD, Gaps in Technology: Analytical Report (Paris, 1970): table 9, p. 32, and table 10, p. 33.

35. Ibid., table 13, p. 38.

36. It might be said that the only comparable concern with manpower supply has been in the government's own recruitment of personnel for military service. Even there, science and technology obviously played a critical role.

37. Two factors were responsible for the increasing demand: the "bulge," or high postwar birth rate which brought an exceptionally large number of students to university age by the early 1960s; and the "trend," or tendency of students to remain in school longer and thus to complete university entry qualifications.

102

38. Higher Education (Robbins Report), vol. I., par. 31.

39. This is not entirely true, as some recommendations were made pertaining to curriculum and teaching methods, as well as the status and accountability of the various higher educational institutions. One important recommendation which was implemented in 1964 was raising the ten Colleges of Advanced Technology to full university status. The full list of 178 recommendations is given ibid., pp. 277-291. For a recent assessment, see "Robbins Plus 10," New Scientist (Nov. 1, 1973): 344-346.

40. Ibid., pp. 71-73, 204-207.

41. Ibid., 163-66. The proportion of students reading science (26 percent) and technology (19 percent) in the universities in 1962-63 was to increase to 28 percent for each subject by 1980-81.

42. David Webster and Adam Westaby, "Social Sciences Explosion," Times (London), Dec. 4, 1970. While the number of first university degrees awarded in pure science increased 113 percent and in technology 105 percent (excluding former Colleges of Advanced Technology) between 1957-58 and 1967-68, the number in the social sciences rose 190 percent.

43. C.F. Carter, "Unrealistic Assumptions in Higher Education Forecase," Times (London), Oct. 28, 1970, p.12.

44. Council for Scientific Policy, Enquiry into the Flow of Candidates in Science and Technology into Higher Education (Dainton Report), Cmd. 3541 (1968).

45. Committee on Manpower Resources for Science and Technology, The Flow into Employment of Scientists, Engineers and Technologists (Swann Report), Cmd. 3760, p. 1, 1968. The committee stated: "In 1965 over 72 percent of the new graduates gaining first class honours in science either continued their studies or took employment in research; and over half (58 percent) of those who gained higher degrees in science were either already in posts in higher education, took up appointments there, or went abroad for employment. In contrast, only 6 percent of the first class honours graduates in science entered schools or took up teacher training, and only 10 percent entered industry. A somewhat different pattern was found for graduates in technology (notably in the higher proportions entering industry) but again there was a marked tendency to seek employment involving research in nonindustrial sectors. Of new graduates gaining first class honours degrees in technology in 1965, 45 percent continued their studies or took employment in higher education and research, 41 percent entered industry, and 1 percent entered schools or further education establishments, or took a course in teacher training. More than one-third (37 percent) of higher degree students in technology continued in higher education and research or went abroad. . . ."

46. Committee on Manpower Resources for Science and Technology, The Brain Drain (Jones Report), Cmd. 3417 (1967): 8-10. It was calculated that the percentage of the new supply of British and

103

Commonwealth engineering and technology graduates going abroad for a year or more had increased from 24 percent in 1961 to 42 percent in 1966, nearly half of them to North America.

47. See M. C. McCarthy, The Employment of Highly Specialized Graduates: A Comparative Study in the United Kingdom and the United States of America, Science Policy Studies No. 3, Department of Education and Science, 1968.

48. See report of the Department of Trade and Industry, Persons with Qualifications in Engineering, Technology and Science, 1959-1968 (Studies in Technological Manpower No. 3, 1971), which indicates secular trends towards unemployment rates among qualified scientists and engineers comparable to those in the economy generally.

49. See ACSP, Annual Report, 1963-64, p. 4; DSIR, Annual Report (1962: 9; and "Problems of Choice and Priorities in Science and Technology, " Nature (March 13, 1965): 1039-41.

50. CSP, Report on Science Policy Cmd. 3007 (1966): para. 6.

51. CSP, Second Report on Science Policy, Cmd. 3420 (1967): esp. paras. 22-50. The council now stated that, "We do not believe that any one specific project or programme of basic research should require justification by reference to any measurable economic or humanitarian benefits. Science is interdependent and one cannot opt solely for the lines which pay off in the short term."

52. In fact, the council did not appoint a working group to develop criteria for determining scientific priorities until 1970. See Third Report of the Council for Scientific Policy, Cmd. 5117 (1972): paras. 15-16 and appendix C.

53. See Table 3.1 above. Excluding the Social Science Research Council (which did not come under the science vote until 1972-73), the growth rate in real terms for research council funds declined to about 6 percent in 1969-71 and 4 percent for 1971-73. Ibid., appendix B.

54. For some international comparisons, see Caryl P. Haskins, "Science and Policy for a New Decade," Foreign Affairs, vol. 49 (January 1971): esp. 263-66.

55. The research council budget is scheduled to decrease by some 2 percent in 1974-75. For the latest figures, see "How Britain's R and D Suffers," New Scientist (Jan. 10, 1974): 50-51.

56. See Third Report, para. 7 and appendix B.

57. See SRC, Report of the Council for the Year 1969-70, pp. 1-3, for a summary of these changes.

58. The new policy is outlined in a special SRC publication, Selectivity and Concentration in Research, 1970, which is partially reprinted in CSP, Report of a Study on the Support of Scientific Research in the Universities, Cmd. 4798, 1971, 53-54.

59. CSP, ibid., esp. chap. 8. This report provides the most up-to-date description of the present system of research support in the universities, and the problems which are emerging as the

universities expand and scientific funding declines. See also the report on a conference held by CSP at Strathclyde University on January 5-7, 1972, Problems Facing University Science.

60. "The Organization and Management of Government R. and D.," in A Framework for Government Research and Development (Green Paper), Cmd. 4814.

61. Cmd. 5046.

62. On the new "central capability unit" or Central Policy Review Staff, see the White Paper on The Reorganization of Central Government, Cmd. 4506, and accompanying articles published in Times (London), Oct. 16, 1970. Lord Rothschild, a former Cambridge biophysicist, Royal Society Fellow, chairman of the Agricultural Research Council, and, most recently, research director at Royal Dutch Shell, was named to head the unit about two weeks later.

63. The overall figure of 25 percent of the research council budgets to be transferred to related departments was misleading since the proportion was to vary from about one-fourth of MRC funds to three-fourths of the ARC's, with the SRC and SSRC excluded entirely as they support basic research in the universities. Rothschild's projections for redistribution of funds are given on pp. 9-13 of his report, but they have since been modified.

64. See the articles in New Scientist (Dec. 2, 1971), and Minerva (April 1972), and the correspondence columns of Nature and Times (London). Cf. also L.A. Gunn, "Government Research and Development," Political Quarterly, 43 (April-June 1972).

65. "The Future of the Research Council System," Report of a CSP Working Group under the chairmanship of Sir Frederick Dainton, in A Framework for Government Research and Development.

66. Definitions of these terms are given on pp. 3-4 of the Dainton Report. They argued that much of what Rothschild considered "applied research" falls into an intermediate range of strategic activity which has potential application but no clear objective at the time it is being performed.

67. Specifically, a fixed sum is to be transferred which rises from £10 million in 1973-74 to £20 million in 1975-76 at 1971-72 prices. Of the total in 1975-76, £10 million will come from the ARC budget, £5.5 million from MRC, and £4.5 million from NERC. It is not stated how these figures were arrived at, but the maximum amount to be transferred (£20 million) represents only about 17 percent of the total research council budget for 1971-72, as opposed to the 25 percent projected by Rothschild on grounds that this represented the allocable portion of "applied" research.

68. The White Paper states that "No conditions will be placed on the use of money transferred to customer Departments, but the expectation is that it will be spent to commission research work by the Research Councils." (Para. 51.) The departments thus are

presumably free to contract with other bodies but are likely to do so mainly with the research councils.

69. Ibid. para. 53.

70. The membership will include the chairman or secretary of each of the five research councils, the chairman of the University Grants Committee, senior scientists from departments with a major interest in the work of the research councils, a representative of the Chief Scientific Adviser to the Government, and independent members drawn from the universities, industry and the Royal Society. The Board will advise the Secretary of State for Education and Science on the allocation of the science budget among the research councils and other bodies and promote closer liaison between the councils and users of their research. A geologist, Prof. Fred Steward, was chosen to head it in 1973; see New Scientist (October 4, 1973): 31-32 for his views.

71. Ibid., para. 61.

72. Solly Zuckerman, Beyond the Ivory Tower (London: Weidenfield and Nicolson, 1970), p. 127.

73. It was a major weakness in Labour's preelection planning that the relationship between technological development and economic planning was never clarified, and the choice of Mr. Cousins, a militant trade unionist, as Minister of Technology was an obvious political maneuver which got the ministry off to a slow start.

74. Details of the 1967 reorganization are set out in Times (London), Feb. 15, 1967. Cf. also Financial Times, Aug. 3, 1967, and Times (London), January 17, 1969, for major articles on the ministry. The final expansion and role of Mintech is covered in Financial Times, Nov. 17, 1969, and Sunday Times, June 21, 1970. The ministry published a sketchy review of its activities in The Ministry of Technology, 1964-1969, but more complete reports on its work were never published due to its dismemberment by the Conservative government after the 1970 elections.

75. Japan's Ministry of International Trade and Industry might be the other exception.

76. In addition to the articles cited in the previous note, see Financial Times, Sept. 29, 1966; Times (London), Jan. 22, 1967; Observer, Feb. 19, 1967; Financial Times, Jan. 15, 1968; Times (London), Mar. 29, 1968.

77. This orientation in turn reflected general disillusionment with Labour's original efforts at comprehensive sectoral planning and wage-price controls through the Department of Economic Affairs; cf. The National Plan for 1965-70 published in 1965. A huge balance of payments deficit, in part inherited from the Conservatives, and continuing speculation against the pound resulted in the wage-price freeze and other austerity measures of July 1966, and ultimately in the devaluation crisis of November 1967. As its general policies

106

failed, the government placed greater emphasis on Mintech's efforts to stimulate key sectors of industry and trade.

78. See table 3.1 above.

79. Although the ministry was not overly sanguine about economic prospects in this field, aviation has provided a significant share of British exports, and it was thought necessary to protect Britain's large aircraft industry at a time when excess production capacities throughout the Western world had rendered international competition for airline contracts especially intense (a situation since dramatized by the collapse of Rolls-Royce in 1970 and Lockheed's demands for public assistance). In the case of Concorde, the government was bound by international agreements to continue—despite escalating costs. It should be noted that the Labour government cancelled several major military aircraft projects shortly after assuming office, notably the TSR-2 counterpart to the American F-111.

80. Some details are given by a former junior minister in Jeremy Bray, Decision in Government (London: Gollancz, 1970), pp. 155-68.

81. ICL combined International Computers and Tabulators (ICT), English Electric, and Plessey interests into what is now by far the largest European-owned computer company. The Ministry of Technology provided some £13 million in R&D grants to the new company and purchased 10 percent of the company's shares. For details see Industrial Investment, the Computer Merger Project, Cmd. 3660, 1968.

82. The proposal was outlined in the Green Paper, Industrial Research and Development in Government Laboratories: A New Organisation for the Seventies (Jan. 1970). Cf. Timothy Johnson, "Mintech March to the Open Market," Sunday Times, Jan. 18, 1970.

83. Ibid., p. 11.

84. Anthony Wedgwood Benn, "Mintech: Key Decisions Needed," Times (London), Sept. 18, 1970.

85. The new arrangements are explained in Government Organisation for Defence Procurement and Civil Aerospace, Cmd. 4641, 1971. According to the recent White Paper, Framework for Government Research and Development, DTI would contract for £109 million in civil aerospace R&D in 1972-73, about the same as in the last year of the Labour government's administration.

86. Robert Gilpin, "Technological Strategies and National Purpose," Science (August 31, 1970): 442.

87. Comparative figures on patent, royalty, and license earnings and expenditures are given in OECD, Gaps in Technology, pp. 199-206. While the U.K. has generally earned a surplus on such exchanges, Germany and France have spent nearly three times as much on foreign royalties as they have earned on their own sales.

88. The advice of the Science Research Council and of a special scientific panel to evaluate the project was published in The Proposed 300 GeV Accelerator, Cmd. 3503, 1968.

89. Times (London), December 5, 1970. The project has been revised to provide for lower initial generating levels and a smaller financial contribution from Britain.

90. Ibid., Nov. 15, 1966.

91. Ibid., Jan. 24, 1967.

92. Reported in full, ibid., Nov. 14, 1967.

93. See "The Logic of Benn's European Concept," ibid., Feb. 15, 1968.

94. For general discussions, see Roger Williams, European Technology (London: Croom Helm, 1973); Christopher Layton, European Advanced Technology: A Programme for Integration (London: Allen & Unwin, 1969); and Eric Moonman, ed., Science and Technology in Europe (Harmondsworth: Penguin, 1968).

95. See "Science and Technology: the 'Nine' Move Toward a Common Research Policy," European Community (June 1974): 17-21.

96. I have drawn here on some of the concepts set out by Harvey Brooks in "Models for Science Planning," Public Administration Review, 31 (May-June 1971): 364-374.

97. As mentioned earlier, the Dainton Committee distinguished between tactical, strategic, and basic science, and the Parliamentary Select Committee on Science and Technology has suggested a further distinction between applied, oriented strategic, basic strategic, and basic R&D. See Nature (May 12, 1972): 63-64.

98. As well, of course, as through informal consultations with individual scientists and bodies such as the Royal Society.

99. Solly Zuckerman's role was never clarified, but apparently he functioned as the British equivalent of the (then) President's Scientific Adviser in the U.S. He chaired the Central Advisory Council on Science and Technology and various interdepartmental committees, but remained an enigmatic figure behind the scenes. Subsequent, Chief Scientific Advisers have enjoyed considerably less status; see "Exit the Mandarins?," New Scientist (August 29, 1974): 371.

100. See Office of the Minister for Science, Report of the Committee on the Management and Control of Research and Development (Zuckerman Report), 1961. The Parliamentary Select Committees on Estimates and Public Accounts also rendered a number of critical reports on R&D management; see S.A. Walkland, "Science and Parliament: the Role of the Select Committees of the House of Commons," Parliamentary Affairs (Summer 1965).

101. See Martin Edmunds, "Government Contracting in Industry: Some Observations on the Ferranti and Bristol Siddeley Contracts," and Roger Williams, "Accountability in Britain's Nuclear Energy Program," in Bruce L.R. Smith and D.C. Hague, eds., The Dilemma of Accountability in Modern Government: Independence versus Control (New York: St. Martin's Press, 1971).

102. This was the subject of a major report of the House of Commons Select Committee on Procedure in 1969; see First Report,

Scrutiny of Public Expenditure and Administration, H. C. 410, especially the Treasury Memorandum reprinted on pp. 14-25.

103. The Civil Service, Cmd. 3638, 1968.

104. See Smith and Hague, op. cit., especially the introductory chapter by Smith. For an insider's views, see also David Howell, A New Style of Government, Conservative Political Centre, London, 1970. Howell became Parliamentary Secretary in the new C. S. Department.

105. Cf. The Reorganization of Central Government, Cmd. 4814, 1970, and, on the government's new program analysis and review system (PAR, modeled after the American PPB), Economist (Feb. 6, 1971): 69.

106. The best analysis and interpretation of parliamentary functions is still Bernard Crick's The Reform of Parliament (originally published in 1964). For more recent developments see A. H. Hanson and B. Crick, eds., The Commons in Transition (London: Fontana, 1970), which includes a chapter on science policy by S. A. Walkland.

107. See my Science and Technology in British Politics, op. cit., chap. 6; Austen Albu, "The Member of Parliament, the Executive and Scientific Policy," Minerva, 2 (Winter 1964); and N.J. Vig and S.A. Walkland, "Science Policy, Science Administration and Parliamentary Reform," Parliamentary Affairs, 19 (Summer 1966).

108. Roger Williams, "The Select Committee on Science and Technology," Public Administration, 46 (Autumn 1968); Walkland, "Parliament and Science Since 1945," in Hanson and Crick, op. cit.; Arthur Palmer, "The Select Committee on Science and Technology," in Alfred Morris, ed., The Growth of Parliamentary Scrutiny by Committee: A Symposium (Oxford: Pergamon, 1970); John P. Mackintosh, M. P., "Specialist Committees in the House of Commons: Have They Failed?" The Waverly Papers, Occasional Paper 1, Series 1, European Political Studies (University of Edinburgh, 1970), pp. 13-22; and Donald R. Shell, "Specialist Select Committees," Parliamentary Affairs, 23 (Autumn 1970): 380-404.

109. Cf. Nature (May 12, 1972): 61-64, and Roger Williams, "Towards the Scientific Ombudsman," New Scientist (July 6, 1972): 13-15.

110. See, for example, "R&D Assessment Hovers out of Reach," New Scientist (Sept. 13, 1973): 603-604.

111. This is still unexplored territory, but on recent political developments in the scientific community, see Stuart S. Blume, Toward a Political Sociology of Science (New York: The Free Press, 1974).

CHAPTER

# 4

## SCIENCE, TECHNOLOGY, AND FRENCH INDEPENDENCE
Robert G. Gilpin, Jr.

In the aftermath of the crushing French defeat in the Franco-Prussian War of 1870, Ernest Renan wrote his famous essay, La Reforme Intellectuelle et Morale. [1] This was no longer the Renan who had found in scientific truth an ally in his lifelong battle against the doctrines and superstitions of his two arch enemies, the Roman Catholic Church and the French political Right. The war had revealed another very different side to science. Following Sedan, Renan and his fellow Frenchmen realized to their sorrow that the Germans had won the war in their universities and industrial laboratories. Science was not only truth, but it was power, and in his essay Renan made a plea which many Frenchmen have made subsequently for the revitalization of French science and the enhancement of its place in national life.

This was a lesson that the French had learned and forgotten. Under the ancien regime, the revolution, and the First Empire, the French had formally recognized the importance of science in military affairs and commerce. In fact, the French were the first people to appreciate the practical utility of science, to found modern research institutions, and to incorporate science into their system of higher education. The Conservatoire des Arts et Metiers, the College of France, and the Ecole Polytechnique founded by the Convention and Napoleon in fact had become the models for scientific and educational reform throughout the Western world. [2]

### THE NAPOLEONIC FOUNDATIONS

To understand the successes of French science in the early part of the nineteenth century or its subsequent decline, one must appreciate the scientific and educational system firmly erected by Napoleon. Consolidating and building upon the reforms of the revolution, the

110

Napoleonic system continues now to dominate French science and education. While one cannot do justice to the system in a few paragraphs, its essence has a Cartesian logic and clarity. A marvel in theory and conception, it is a cause for despair in the realm of practice and execution.

The initial consequence of the revolution was to sweep aside all autonomous and corporate entities, including the Royal Academy of Sciences and the universities —which represented privilege and stood apart from the nation. After the fury of the revolution had subsided, many of these same institutions were reestablished under a new guise or new ones, including the Ecole Normale Superieure, were created. With the founding by Napoleon in 1808 of the university facultes, the the system was in its essence complete. What, then, were its most distinguishing characteristics?

The chief feature of the Napoleonic system remains its etatisme. Through such institutions as the College of France, the Museum of Natural History, and the facultes, science became a ward of the state. The University of France founded by Napoleon was in reality a ministry responsible for the administration of the individual facultes (science, medicine, letters, law, and pharmacy) which were the basic units of the system. Overarching the whole system of education at both the secondary (lycee) and higher levels and giving it a remarkable inflexibility were a series of uniform, national examinations of which the best known is the baccalaureat.

The second characteristic of the system is its geographical concentration in Paris. As a consequence of the levee en masse in defense of the revolution and empire, the best men of French science and technology were drawn to Paris. The foremost institutions of French science and education were established. Reinforced by the great attractions of Paris the city, one's career aspirations could only be fulfilled there. The Parisian elite controlled the College of France, the Ecole Normale, and the facultes, and its ideas came to dominate all French scientific life. As a consequence of this hold of the old and the established over the young and the unorthodox, French science became pervaded by a conservatism and resistance to new concepts and ideas.

The third trait of the Napoleonic system is excessive fragmentation of scientific and technical activities. Intellectual functions which should be united, or else carried out in close association, were separated into different sets of institutions. To oversimplify the situation, scientific research became the responsibility of the so-called grands etablissements scientifiques such as College of France and the Museum of Natural History. The teaching of science fell to the science facultes and a few of the prestigious grandes ecoles, notably the Ecole Normale and the Ecole Polytechnique. Technical education was the monopoly of the grandes ecoles.

Many evils have flowed from this extreme division of labor. Science, medicine, and engineering cannot easily fructify one another but have developed in separate compartments. Scientific advances have been slow in penetrating medical or engineering practice, and problems in the latter areas have not sufficiently stimulated the direction of French scientific research. Moreover, scientific fields which are intellectually close and important for one another are frequently institutionally separate; they are even subject to the authority of different government ministries. And, lastly, the exaggerated separation of research and teaching may not only be an inefficient use of scarce resources, but it deprives both the scientific researcher and the prospective scientist of the stimulating benefits of the student-teacher relationship. These were difficulties, however, which would show up later in the century.

In the early decades of the nineteenth century, the concentration and unified direction of the national scientific effort fostered by the Napoleonic system made France for a time the foremost scientific and technical power on the European continent, if not in the world. But the system lacked one essential ingredient, namely, a capacity to adapt itself to changing conditions. It could not easily, for example, accomodate the new scientific disciplines which were spawned incessantly throughout the century. It could not meet the challenge posed in the latter part of the nineteenth century by the increasing relevance of scientific theory to technological and medical practice. As a consequence, the system became ever more inappropriate for the type of industrial society scientific and technological advance were helping to bring into existence.

While French scientific and educational institutions grew sclerotic, across the Rhine the Germans began their advance in basic and applied research, by mid-century, Germany had surpassed France as the leading scientific nation of the world. France continued strong in technology but, as the century progressed, German technology and industry became supreme on the European continent. Long before their defeat in 1870, France had become what Stanley Hoffmann has characterized as a stagnant society. [3] Largely agricultural, with a declining birthrate, underindustrialized, and expending energy on the acquisition of an overseas empire, France would twice more be overrun by their more powerful German neighbors.

In founding the Ecole Pratique des Hautes Etudes (1868), Frenchmen first took official cognizance of their declining scientific position. Following defeat and the subsequent inauguration of the Third Republic, a period of scientific, educational, and technical reform began. Impetus for reform was the interpretation of the defeat provided by Renan, Louis Pasteur, and others. [4] Another source was the desire of the Third Republic, especially in its reforms of elementary education, to return to the republican and equalitarian ideals of the revolution. The ideals of the Left and the exigencies of power were united in the

112

effort prior to World War I to improve the quality of French education, science, and technology, but to little avail.

In response to near defeat in World War I, the rhetoric of reform was heard once more in the air. A symposium, L'Avenir de la France, held immediately after the war, gave prominence to the view that science must play a greater part in national life. [5] But French political energies were devoted to keeping Germany down rather than to improving French institutions. Bled white by the war, the response of France was to rebuild the prewar status quo.

With the Great Depression, followed by the Popular Front government in 1936, a new commitment to reform emerged. Drawing upon the rationalist, humanistic faith of the earlier Renan, and impressed by the apparent Soviet achievement in harnessing science for human benefit, Socialist scientists like Jean Perrin and Paul Langevin actively pressured for reform. [6] From these efforts came a new and important research organization, the National Center for Scientific Research (CNRS) established in 1939. But it had hardly been founded when once again French defeat revealed the industrial and technological superiority of Germany.

## INSTITUTION BUILDING AND REFORM AFTER WORLD WAR II

The sources of the profound transformation of French science and technology that has taken place since the end of World War II are many. In part, they were found in the legacy of Vichy and the resistance. Bitter enemies though they were, the intellectual leaders of both sensed the need for a drastic reform of French institutions and the creation of more efficient, industrialized France. The experiences of Frenchmen during the war and the highly technical character of the war provided another impetus for reform. Participation in Anglo-American research programs revealed to French scientists just how far behind France was in her scientific capabilities and her ability to use science for military and other purposes. Finally, the loss of empire over the postwar decade, and the decision to participate in a united Europe as a counterweight to the two dominant superpowers have forced France to undertake for the first time the serious task of uprooting the Napoleonic system.

The reform of French scientific and technical institutions which began in 1945 was the result of the collaboration of two very dissimilar allies: General Charles de Gaulle and Frederic Joliot-Curie. The one, a professional soldier, aristocrat, and man of the Right; the other, a Nobel Laureate in chemistry (1935), a hero of the resistance, and a communist. They shared, however, the conviction that the welfare and the very survival of France necessitated a vast regeneration of her scientific and technical capabilities. With the appointment of

113

Joliot by de Gaulle in 1946 as High Commissioner of Atomic Energy, one can date the real beginnings of French postwar scientific reform. As a consequence of this appointment, for the first time in French history an outstanding scientist was made a powerful official in the French government and, until his downfall in 1951, because of his communist associations, Joliot was in a position to exercise a strong influence over the development of French science and technology.

The importance of the establishment in 1946 of the Atomic Energy Commission (CEA) cannot be stressed too strongly. [7] The CNRS, which was revitalized at this time, greatly expanded the base of French science and was of immense importance, yet it fell within the traditional pattern of French scientific institutions. Although the CNRS provided research careers for scientists, supported laboratories, and gave financial aid to university research, it merely supplemented the Napoleonic grands etablissements, the facultes, and the grandes ecoles. The CEA, on the other hand, was an entirely unprecedented type of institution, which had been made necessary because atomic energy posed an unprecedented problem for France.

In the first place, the scale of atomic energy was beyond the capabilities of existing institutions and particularly the facultes; also, the security and defense aspects warranted an organization which gave the government more control than is desirable in academic affairs. The traditional ministerial form did not seem appropriate—given the high scientific and technical content of the subject; scientists them- selves, it was reasoned, should have a larger influence in the organi- zation, and greater flexibility should exist than is possible under a ministerial structure. Lastly, given the importance of atomic energy, the CEA was granted an extraordinarily broad mandate that extended from basic research to industrial and military applications. As a consequence, both directly and by example, the CEA was able to exercise a strong influence counter to the traditional patterns of French science.

From 1945 to the end of the Fourth Republic, in 1958, was a period largely of institution building and reform. [8] In addition to the revitalization of the CNRS and the founding of the CEA, numerous other research organizations were established in medical, agricultural, and industrial research. Higher education was reformed in order to increase the number of scientists and engineers. Although the initial steps were taken toward the development of a French atomic bomb, scientific and military affairs (in contrast to the Anglo-American powers and the Soviet Union) remained largely separate and hostile.

Though reforms had been made, they were not sufficient, and throughout the course of the Fourth Republic, France was aware of her scientific and technological backwardness in comparison to the United States, Great Britain, and the Soviet Union. What seemed increasingly necessary to a large segment of the scientific and tech- nical community was the creation of institutions to articulate a national

114

policy for scientific research and development. As early as 1952, the Education Commission of the Planning Commissariat had warned that the demand for scientists and engineers would soon exceed the supply. Subsequently, a Commission on Scientific and Technical Research called for a thorough reform of scientific institutions; this resulted in the appointment by Prime Minister Pierre Mendes-France in 1954 of an Under Secretary of State for Scientific Research and of a Supreme Research Council.

Though these institutions were of little consequence in a France racked by urgent political and economic problems, they did reflect the growing national concern over the status of French science. This concern received its most cogent expression in the convening at Caen in November 1956 of a national colloquium on problems of French science. Leaders from French political, scientific, and industrial affairs heard the Caen colloquium propose a twelve-point plan for the renovation of French science that included the following proposals: A ten-year development plan; the reform of graduate training and of higher education; and the establishment of mechanisms for developing national policies for scientific and technical research. 9

While the Caen colloquium had no immediate effect, it gave rise to the first organized scientific lobby in France, the Permanent Committee for Expansion of Scientific Research. Led by some of France's most distinguished scientists, the committee, or study association as it came to be called, kept alive the ideas articulated at Caen and propagandized for the cause of scientific and educational reform. As a result, by the time de Gaulle returned to power in the late spring of 1958, a program of reform had been formulated and a broad spectrum of public opinion had been prepared to support it.


SCIENCE POLICY AND NATIONAL GRANDEUR


The fate of French science under the Fifth Republic can only be understood in terms of de Gaulle's overall political strategy. Once the Algerian war was settled, de Gaulle's policies had three primary concerns, each of which had important implications for French science. First, in the wake of the collapse of empire, France had to be restored to a sense of self-confidence; his emphasis on grandeur was not mere vanity—it was based on his instinctive realization that nations, like people, must have a feeling of pride and worth. Second, the primary threat to French independence was held to be no longer the overt military or subversive threat of communism, but the economic penetration of France and Western Europe by large American corporations. Third, the keystone of French policy was German-French cooperation towards the goal of a strong independent Western Europe and, one day, the reuniting of Europe from the Atlantic to the Urals.

It was de Gaulle's hope that France would maintain the balance in the international system he envisaged. A nuclear-armed France would dominate nonnuclear Germany; together they would dominate Europe; on a global scale Europe would be a Third Force between the two superpowers. It was an ambitious concept, designed to restore France to her assumed rightful position in the international order. For its achievement, however, France needed industrial and military superiority over Germany. This in turn required the mobilization of French science and technology. To achieve this goal, one of de Gaulle's first acts upon his return to power was to institute the mechanism for a national policy for science and technology.

By a decree of November 28, 1958, the essentials of the present structure for science policy were established.[10] To coordinate policymaking and budgeting for science and technology, the government instituted an Interministerial Committee for Scientific and Technical Research (CIMRST) under the chairmanship of the prime minister or his deputy. Composed of the relevant cabinet ministers and twelve scientists (those who constitute CCRST—the Advisory Committee for Scientific and Technical Research), CIMRST was made responsible for "recommending all measures tending to develop scientific research," including the approval of the newly initiated annual science budget and the drafting of the science section of the French five-year plan.

Like its now-defunct American counterpart, the President's Scientific Advisory Committee, CCRST was composed of eminent scientists and technologists drawn from universities and industry. As a result, a committee of scientists was placed in a position to exercise a strong influence over a broad segment of French science.

In addition to the interministerial and scientific advisory committees, a permanent set of officials and institutions responsible for science policy was established. On the political side, the post of Minister for Science was created to be responsible for nonmilitary, atomic, and space research. On the scientific side, a General Delegate for Scientific and Technical Matters was appointed to assist the minister. Lastly, a secretariat, entitled the General Delegation for Scientific and Technical Research (DGRST), was created to assist in the work of the other bodies and to produce policy studies.

The achievements of this policy mechanism have been impressive, especially during its first years. The institution of a unified science budget permitted the government to obtain for the first time an overall view of its support of nonmilitary science, as well as to improve its allocation of funds for research. In addition, a number of important but underdeveloped fields, such as molecular biology and electronics, were given priority. The CNRS was encouraged to take a greater leadership role in scientific affairs, and important steps were taken to integrate science planning within the framework of the national five-year economic plan. Important research institutes were estab-

116

lished and, finally, on the initiative of the Science Advisory Committee, important reforms in military research and development were undertaken (see below).

As vital as these accomplishments were, their limitations should also be appreciated. In the first place, the science budget and national plan cover only a relatively small percentage of the total French expenditures for research and development; it excludes the three exceptionally important areas of space, atomic energy, and military research. Not even all of university or CNRS research is included. Only about 15 percent of the total French expenditure for science and technology is included. The science mechanism is largely an advisory and coordinating mechanism; the decision-making authority continues to reside in the ministries themselves. And, with respect to fundamental research, the locus of power rests with the professors in the universities and the directors of research in the CNRS.

These criticisms of the French mechanism for science policymaking focus attention upon the underlying weaknesses of scientific research and technological development in France. While this short analysis cannot deal adequately with all these problems, two areas deserve particular emphasis because of their strategic importance for the health of French science and technology. For this reason, the next sections of this discussion will be devoted to an evaluation of French effort to improve the two areas of basic research and technological development.

## HIGHER EDUCATION IN A SCIENTIFIC STATE

Under the Napoleonic system, basic research was made primarily the responsibility of the grands etablissements such as the College of France and the Museum of Natural History. With two or three exceptions—such as Ecole Normale and the Paris science faculty— relatively little important research was conducted in institutions of higher education. Their responsibility under the Napoleonic division of labor was to train teachers for secondary schools in the case of the facultes and engineers in the case of the grandes ecoles.

In addition to his initial division of labor, the ethos and structure of the Napoleonic system of higher education inhibited the conduct and advancement of scientific research. Because of their prestige, the grandes ecoles for their part have tended over the years to divert the most scientifically adept minds away from research into engineering and administration. As for the facultes, several factors have operated to hinder scientific research and education.

Initially, the system of higher education has been geared to the production of secondary school teachers with a broad education in

117

general culture. Little incentive or capability has existed for research within the facultes or the training of students in scientific research. For reasons which go deep into French psychology and the French commitment to egalitarianism, the whole system has been under the tyranny of the system of national uniform examinations. The primary emphasis in higher education has been upon the preparation of students for these examinations; one's success as a student has been determined by performance in these examinations rather than competence for original research. Under these conditions, too, there has been little incentive on the part of the Ministry of Education and the facultes to introduce into the curriculum new fields of study spun off by the advancement of scientific knowledge. Also, the chair system of faculte organization has placed power over university resources in the hands of the established and conservative older generation of scientists. In contrast to a departmental structure, where power is shared by several professors—and frequently by professors in the same specialization—under the chair system a single professor dominates the discipline; he not only determines who can qualify for an academic degree in his field, but he may control faculty appointments and research funds as well. As a result, younger men interested in new fields of research and committed to new ideas have found it difficult to break the hold of the past upon French science.

Prior to 1945, amazingly little transpired to change these essential features of higher education. [11] As we have seen, the first important change was the establishment of the CNRS, which broadened the foundation of basic research within the universities as well as establishing its own laboratories. The greatest force for change over the past several decades, however, has been the explosion of the student population. Under the impact of expanded numbers, the old structure has been stretched to its limits and beyond. The facilities and attitudes which were appropriate for an era of restricted and elite education no longer are appropriate for one moving in the direction of mass education.

In response to this challenge, France has had an impressive expansion of higher education. New facultes and campuses have been established, and older ones have been renovated. With this expansion of facilities, new career opportunities have been created; the number of faculty members has increased substantially, particularly at the assistant and associate professor levels. These changes in turn have loosened the hold of the past and have facilitated the efforts of those reformers who favor a greater emphasis upon scientific research within the university system.

Because of these developments, the so-called "events of May 1968" were vital to the future of higher education and scientific research in France. [12] A product of the growing conflict between the archaic university structure and emergent social conditions, the events of May seemed to offer to the reformers their golden opportunity to restructure the system. For this reason, any analysis of the present situation of French science and higher education must begin with the events of May and their consequences.

Any assessments of these events and their consequences depends very much upon one's view of what caused this violent upheaval. On this there is no lack of suggested explanations. Indeed, the fecund production of different and conflicting explanatory theories testifies to the absence of a real understanding of the events of May, and to the significance of the issue for any evaluation of the future of French higher education and of French society itself.

While they are not mutually exclusive, at least three categories of explanations or factors have been advanced. For lack of more descriptive terms, these three categories might be called the ideological, sociopsychological, and institutional explanations of the student uprisings in France. The ideological explanation is the one most frequently put forth by the "revolutionaries" themselves and by their sympathizers.[13] The mythology of the events of May is that the students—as well as the young professors or professional workers and the liberal professions who joined them—revolted against twentieth-century capitalistic society. The students, it is argued, were rejecting the university as an instrument of a repressive, technological society, while the workers' behavior reflected their alienation from the modern industrial structure. The liberal professions (such as law and medicine) whose younger members supported the revolt are seen to be responding to the loss of their traditional dignity under capitalism. Together, these groups sought—during a brief but glorious revolutionary moment—to overthrow the dehumanizing capitalistic system which dominates and controls their lives.

Undoubtedly, the ideological factor played a part in the student rebellion, especially among its more militant members. But its role can easily be exaggerated and misunderstood. As many of the injustices and problems against which the students rebelled have long existed, the question to be asked is "Why then?" More importantly the image of a capitalistic French society is misleading. If one puts aside the revolutionary rhetoric and examines the specific complaints and demands of students, workers, and liberal professions, they have little to do with capitalism, or even with industrialism. On the contrary, the characteristics of French society being criticized and attacked were not capitalistic but feudal and bureaucratic. The students and their allies were protesting against those features and institutions of French society described earlier as inimical to the emergence in France of modern industrial, educational, and scientific structures. These obstacles to modernization include the Napoleonic system of education; the overcentralization of authority; the rigidity of class and status relations; the grand patron system in education, science, and the liberal professions, and so on. For this reason, there is little basis to sustain the revolutionaries' own ideological explanation of the causes of the May revolution.

119

The sociopsychological explanations of the student revolt are advanced primarily by social scientists and rest upon the common features of student revolts in France and elsewhere.[14] While these explanations differ in details, all of them emphasize the conflict of generations as the underlying cause of the rebellions. The demand for "student power" was the rallying cry of the younger generation against the domination by the older generation. The university and its administrators from this perspective were not the instruments of an oppressive capitalistic class, but rather of the older generation which controls the lives of the younger generation and forces upon youth its standards of behavior.

But conflicts of generations have always existed. The question, therefore, is why they are more pronounced and universal in the contemporary world. In part, it is simply because affluent industrialized societies have produced a large population of disaffected youth, especially from the middle class. A general malaise pervaded their lives; many sought salvation and purpose in attacking the institutions of the older generation.

In addition to these sociological factors, there is the fact that social phenomena like rebellions, murder, and miniskirts are contagious. Through television, travel, and international student conferences, large segments of educated youth have come to identify with one another and to share a common cause against the domination of the ruling older generation. As a consequence of this generational consciousness of students throughout the world, student rebellions easily spread through contagion from Berkeley and Columbia to Nanterre and beyond.

In order for infection to take place, however, there must not only be the pathological agent, the host must be susceptible to the disease. To understand why France was especially susceptible to the student rebellion, and why it took such a virulent form, we pass to the institutional explanations for the events of May.[15] Many of the institutional factors which various writers have stressed, such as the archaic structure of the university system and the fantastic overcrowding of facilities, have already been mentioned; while one could add to this list, two factors in particular ought to stressed. The first was and continues to be the presence in the French university system of a large number of students whose career prospects are rather limited, given the present state of the French economy and of a relatively large "revolutionary" group due to the rapid expansion of the junior faculty ranks.

With the coming of mass higher education to France, the universities have become filled with many students who are receiving little preparation for effective or self-satisfying positions in French society. These students are not, as the ideologists would have us believe, victims of a dehumanized technocracy but of an economy whose demands for the products of higher education lags far behind the supply. In a society traditionally organized in terms of a small, highly talented elite and the large mass of the population, France has done far too

120

little to create satisfying careers for the tens of thousands of ordinary men and women passing through the contemporary French university. Contrary to the charges of the ideologists, the universities have not done nearly enough to equip these students with the technical skills increasingly required by French society today. Far too many students are in literary fields, the social sciences and the pure sciences; at this stage of its development, French society has a limited capacity to absorb the products of these studies. As a consequence, the French universities have been and are educating a large number of unemploy- able and hence potentially disaffected students.

The expansion of the number of graduate students and of the lower ranks of the faculty had the unanticipated consequence of transforming this group into a rebellious "class." As has been frequently observed in other circumstances, it is not necessarily the lowest status group which is most dissatisfied and revolutionary, but it is those individuals at the secondary and tertiary levels. This phenomenon of the revolu- tionary potential of rising expectations has affected the lower ranks of the faculty. While they have made enormous advances over the past decades, they are painfully aware of their continuing inferior status relative to the professeurs titulaires des chaires and of the great discrepancy between their great numbers and the small number of higher positions open to them. Consequently, as their numerical strength increased, so did their intolerance of their status. As Marx foresaw with respect to the concentration of workers in factories, the quantitative increase and concentration of the number of individuals in the junior faculty ranks—and similarly within the student body itself—has developed a class consciousness in them. The result was that large segments of both groups became a "revolutionary" group within the French university system.

The events of May which developed out of these sets of ideo- logical, sociopsychological, and institutional factors dealt a severe blow to the French university system. In the first place, it shattered the traditional authority of the university without substituting anything in its place; both the ministry and the professors, each of whom once reigned supreme in their respective spheres, were weakened. The university became fragmented into at least three conflicting groups; in addition to the political moderates (including conservatives) and the old left (including adherents to the French Communist party), was added a vociferous and powerful new left, the enrages. Entry of the enrages into the university system had the profound and disconcerting effect of politicizing the university—that is, the entry of external political issues and decisions by doctrinaire politics. Whereas the moderates and the old left accepted the traditional function of the university—the primacy of the objective search for truth—the new left, intoxicated by the rallying cry of "student power" and revolution sees the university merely as an instrument of capitalist domination and a background for class conflict.

121

In the light of these developments, there is little basis to hope that higher education in France, at least in the universities, will be effectively reformed to meet the challenges expected of it. As in the past, the burden of meeting French scientific and technological needs, in so far as they are met, will fall on the grandes ecoles and the highly competent elite they continue to form.

## RESEARCH AND DEVELOPMENT FOR INDUSTRY AND DEFENSE

The key to the Gaullist strategy of industrial and military supremacy in Western Europe was the French plan for the modernization of her armed forces. [16] In conjunction with her ambitious space program, the development of a nuclear striking force and the associated advanced technologies would have two very important effects. France could leapfrog more traditional industries and establish herself as the European leader in advanced technologies: computers, supersonic aircraft, telecommunications satellites, and atomic energy. The effort itself to develop space technology and to modernize weaponry would bring about a transformation of France's industrial structure and the role of the state in the economy.

In the view of President de Gaulle and his advisors, America's rise to scientific and technological preeminence had been due primarily to its space and military programs. Contrary to the view of many Americans that these programs divert scarce resources from more productive programs, the prevailing French view has been that these programs are essential for industrial modernization, at least during its initial stage. Under the guise of national security, and principally through the use of research and development contracts to universities and private industry, because of their immense scale these programs can provide a democratic society with the necessary leverage for reforming scientific, educational, and economic institutions.

For the leadership of the Fifth Republic, the choice appeared to be not between a costly military program and more commercially relevant programs but between modernization and stagnation. [17] The structure of French industry and the attitudes of her industrialists were not appropriate for the type of economic transformation which was necessary if France was to meet the challenge of the Common Market and foreign competition. The economy was composed of too many small family firms, too long protected by an external tariff and the empire. These firms had to be merged into one or two large-scale enterprises, industrial research and development had to be stimulated, and a more enterprising attitude among French businessmen encouraged. The space and military programs gave the government a vital weapon with which to achieve these objectives.

The implications of this idea were enormous for the role of the state in the economy and in higher education. Prior to this effort in

122

space research and nuclear weapons development, the military establishment had had little role in the economy and scientific research. With some major exceptions, almost all military research, development, and production had been conducted under the so-called arsenal system. While this method of weapons development was appropriate for an earlier age, it had serious drawbacks for an era where weaponry was increasingly dependent upon scientific and technological advance. From this perspective, the awarding of contracts to private industry and universities has several important advantages; it not only broadens the base of industrial support, but military contracts can subsidize and stimulate technological developments of potential commercial importance. Similarly, the awarding of contracts or research grants to institutions of higher education give the military access to the French scientific community and to research in the more advanced branches of science.

In essence, what the Fifth Republic has sought to achieve is the creation in France of a military-industrial-university complex patterned on the American model. Such a goal actually had motivated early postwar thinking on the evolution of science policy in France. As one of the founders of the Atomic Energy Commission observed, World War I had proved that in the contemporary era "there must be an active cooperation among the state . . . industry . . . the universities . . . and the defense establishments."[18] But it was only with de Gaulle's return to power in 1958 that the necessary steps were taken to advance this goal.

The primary consequence of this reorientation of military R&D was the establishment of the Directorate of Research and Testing (DRME).[19] Under the leadership of eminent scientists and technologists, its mission is to give research grants and contracts to private industry and universities. In contrast to other military research agencies which tend to work on short-range problems, the DRME's responsibility is to support research on the frontiers of science and technology. As such, the DRME is in a strategic position to influence greatly the direction of fundamental research and technological development in France. Moreover—following a pattern long established in the United States and Great Britain—through the DRME, university and industrial scientists have become intimately associated with the French military effort.

Although the primary emphasis of public policy has been on these advanced technologies with military applications, the growth of foreign and particularly German industrial competition due to the actualization of the EEC has made the French realize in recent years their weakness across the broad spectrum of industrial technology. To remedy this situation, the advancement of industrial research and development has become a primary concern of French policy. In the past, the French government has sought to strengthen French industry by forcing corporate mergers and the development of powerful French companies in each industrial sector. In addition, the French government has moved in the direction of subsidizing industrial research and development, although it is still too early to know the ultimate form and magnitude of this endeavor.

## LIMITS TO TECHNOLOGICAL INDEPENDENCE

In facing increased international economic competition, the French find themselves in a relatively weak position. In order to decrease their dependence upon the United States and to balance German industrial power, the French have sought to establish their technological self-sufficiency, or at least to establish a French "presence," in all those domains of science and technology believed to be important for military power and economic competition: atomic energy, computers, electronics, high performance aircraft, space technology, and so forth. Where France was unable by itself to develop the necessary technologies such as rocket launchers and telecommunications satellites, the French have taken the lead in promoting European technological cooperation (see below). In short, the French sought to compete against the two superpowers across the broad front of science and advanced technology.

However, threats to this policy existed in certain fundamental but generally unappreciated weaknesses of the French scientific and technological situation. When the student and worker uprisings convulsed France in the spring of 1968, these weaknesses were exposed and the French scientific-technological effort was thrown into a state of confusion from which it has yet to emerge.

A fundamental threat to the French strategy of scientific and technological independence lay in the scarcity of the resources necessary to progress across too broad a front of research and development. Resources were virtually wasted in duplication of American or other foreign efforts rather than concentration on potentially important new scientific and technical fields.

Programs operated on an extremely narrow margin, one too narrow to withstand serious financial or technical setbacks. As a result, therefore, of the inflationary spiral set off by workers' wage demands and of the government's subsequent stabilization program, many of these projects and programs were abandoned completely or severely set back. The retrenchment that took place affected the overall level of support for science and technology, as well as the fate of important programs. Projects in high-energy physics, aviation, space research, computers, biomedical sciences, and nuclear weapons development were cancelled or seriously retarded. The optimistic growth projections of the Fifth Plan (1966-70) were shattered. [20] The consequences for French scientific ambitions have been severe.

124

The crisis of French science and technology provoked by the resulting austerity program was compounded by a general disappointment in the fruits of the national R&D effort. Aside from the remarkable successes of Marcel Dassault in high-performance aircraft (Mystere, Mirage), there are few indigenous innovations in advanced technology to which the French can point with pride. Large developmental projects upon which the French have placed so much hope have been set back drastically. The atomic power program based on natural uranium reactors has suffered. The huge investment of funds in space has led to no significant scientific or commercial results; the preponderance of these funds went into the establishment of large ground facilities such as the Guyana base, whose utility has yet to be proven. The French color television system (SECAM) has failed to be adopted outside France except for markets such as the Soviet bloc and the underdeveloped countries. And as for computer development, the French are beginning to realize that the task of making an indigenous computer is going to be many times more difficult than they had initially anticipated. While Concorde remains as a technical achievement upon which the French can fasten their pride, its eventual commercial success is far from assured. 21

These setbacks illustrate a danger in the strategy of scientific and technological independence chosen by France—that is, the tendency toward the premature translation of research programs into the development and production stages. In order to create independent French technologies rather than to depend upon proven foreign technologies, France undertook a number of grave risks which now appear to have been unwise. Technological innovation is an extremely hazardous business at best, and for a relatively small country the risks involved in costly, advanced technologies can be extremely great indeed.

The United States has had two important advantages over France with respect to successful innovation, first, in the superiority of American resources in scientific manpower and capital, and second, in its managerial superiority. The French are usually confined to one option fairly early in the R&D cycle. Thus, the U.S. —with its greater resources—can pursue several lines of inquiry until a particular technology appears to be superior; the shift to prototype development and production can then be undertaken with a greater assurance of success. Of course, this more cautious strategy has not always been applied in the area of armaments. Here the United States, locked in its arms race with the Soviet Union, has wasted immense resources upon fruitless projects such as the nuclear-powered aircraft, controlled fusion, and missile development. Again, however, America's wealth has given it a large margin for error.

Furthermore, management superiority has been a vital element in America's technological strategy. As Christopher Layton has pointed

125

out in seeking to explain why "Europe's innovations have often been overtaken by American rivals," American firms tend to emphasize basic and applied research until development and exploration appear to be ripe. [22] Then there takes place a concentration of effort which, in the area of advanced technology, involves the cooperation of private industry, the government and, frequently, the university. It is this capacity for concerted effort rather than any specific managerial techniques which accounts for America's relatively shorter lead-time (compared with that in France) between new knowledge and technological exploitation.

The contrasting positions of the United States and France with respect to the translation of scientific knowledge into technology may be summarized in terms of two lead-times which relate to the chain of events between new knowledge and new technology. The first is that between new knowledge and the invention or technological conception to which it gives rise; the second is the lead-time between this invention and its perfection into a practical innovation. In general, with respect to advanced technologies, while the first lead-time has been decreasing over the past several decades, the second lead-time has been lengthening. In other words, new scientific knowledge may be giving rise at an accelerated rate to new technical concepts, but the development of these concepts into practical commercial or military technologies is taking longer than in the past.

Given the shortened lead-time between science and technology, there is increased probability today that new knowledge will make an an invention obsolete at a relatively early stage of its development. For this reason, the decision whether to go from the research to the development or to the production phase is always plagued by the danger that further research will make one's concept obsolete. On the other hand, to delay until more knowledge is available and thereby to decrease the risk of rapid obsolescence may mean falling behind one's competition. This dilemma is inherent in all modern technological development. But the problem is compounded if one has in addition a long lead-time between the conception of a new technology and its practical development. In this case, there may not only be a tendency to go from research to development at too early a point in the state of the art, but there is a longer period of time during which new scientific advances may make a particular technological project obsolete.

The relationship of these two lead-times has operated to the disadvantage of France's technology strategy. In order to maximize their independence from the United States, the French have gone from the research stage to that of development and even production relatively early in the evolution of the state of the art. While this is a risky business in any event, the French have also lacked the managerial competence to perfect and exploit these technologies rapidly prior to their eventual obsolescence due to scientific and technological advances. This situation is responsible for a number of French technological defeats.

126

Perhaps the best illustration of these criticisms of France's technology strategy comes from the area of nuclear power development. In the early 1950s, France decided to base its nuclear power industry on natural uranium. Technical as well as historical reasons existed for this decision, but primarily it was based on political considerations. First, a nuclear power industry based on natural uranium would be independent of the U. S. for its supply of fuel. Second, the "plutonium way," as it was called, would provide the fissionable material for a future nuclear weapons program. Thus, at a rather early date in the evolution of nuclear power technology, France in a very real sense cast its other possible options aside and concentrated its efforts on the development of the so-called graphite gas, natural uranium reactor.

In contrast, the U. S. pursued a more cautious approach. If one may be permitted to mix metaphors, rather than put all its eggs in one basket, the United States let many flowers bloom and held off until much later its decision with respect to which type or types of reactors to exploit for commercial purposes. As the reasons for these contrasting policies tell one a great deal about the differing contexts of French and American technological policies in the specific case and in general, it may be worthwhile to analyze them.

The United States (unlike France) had an indigenous supply of enriched uranium due to its nuclear weapons program; therefore, both the natural and enriched uranium options were readily available to it. France saw in nuclear power the opportunity to overcome immediately the historic shortage of fossil fuels which in the past had stunted French industrialization; United States, on the other hand, possesses great resources of oil and coal. Finally, and perhaps of greatest importance, French nuclear power development was dominated by the Atomic Energy Commission (CEA), whose leadership (largely due to its participation during the war in the Canadian phase of the atomic bomb project) was committed to a particular type of reactor; the one customer in France for nuclear power reactors, the nationalized Electricite de France (EDF), in turn had to accept what its one supplier had to supply. In the United States, on the other hand, the Atomic Energy Commission enjoyed no such unchallenged position in the councils of government; nor did any such unanimity exist on the best type of reactor to develop. Congress, fossil fuel interests, and the several laboratories of the commission waged a battle for one type or another. On the consumer side, private industry brought its own ideas and interest into the debate over reactor development. As a consequence, the United States postponed until much later than France its decision on the types of reactors to be developed for commercial purposes.

Whereas French nuclear power policy was motivated largely by political considerations, commercial criteria in the last analysis dominated American policy. The choice of two types of light water, enriched, uranium-fueled reactors for America's first-generation nuclear power plants was based on their lower cost relative to other types of reactor systems and fossil fuel plants. Once these decisions were made, American industry in cooperation with government quickly brought these types of reactors from the development stage to the production line.

In contrast to the seemingly disorganized but ultimately successful American nuclear policy, France's apparently more logical policy has had a much less happy outcome. Despite its technical success, the graphite gas natural uranium reactor—because of its much greater costs—is simply not competitive with the smaller enriched-uranium type of reactors. For this reason, by 1969 the French government had capitulated to the policy of "buying American." Future nuclear power stations in France will be American in design and will be fueled by enriched uranium bought from the U.S. Thus, having made the wrong decision much too early in the development of the first generation of power reactors, France can only hope that its candidate in future competition will be more successful. However, across a broad spectrum of French science and technology, the CEA and atomic energy research have had a beneficial and modernizing influence. In all such cases where scientific and institutional reform is a byproduct of massive technological efforts, one must ask whether or not the benefits were worth the cost.

## THE CHOICE OF A TECHNOLOGICAL STRATEGY

In order to assess France's future prospects with respect to technological development, it is necessary to appreciate that any nation can follow essentially three strategies in developing its science, technology, and industry.[23] The first or broad strategy is to develop science and technology across as wide a spectrum as possible. In general, the purpose of this strategy is largely political: prestige, political independence and, most of all, national power. Only the Soviet Union and the United States have followed this strategy with success; Great Britain until the early 1960s and France until more recently tried but failed.

The second strategy is to specialize in a limited range of scientific and technological areas. Usually, activities from basic research through production are spanned, and the basic purpose of this strategy is commercial. Among the nations that have been most successful in following this strategy are Sweden, Switzerland, and the Netherlands.

The third strategy is that of importation or imitation. While specialization is also involved, relatively little research is undertaken, and emphasis is placed on the importation of foreign technologies. One's own R&D effort is concentrated largely on improving these imported technologies. Japan and Canada are the two countries that

128

have exploited this strategy but from quite significantly different perspectives. Whereas Japan has imported foreign technology (primarily American) through the purchasing of licenses, Canada through its tariff policy has encouraged direct foreign investment.

The strategy employed by a nation reflects its national ambitions and circumstances. As these factors change, so will the nature of the strategy itself. One must appreciate, too, that when one speaks of a national strategy, the point is largely one of emphasis. No nation's technological and scientific policies can be wholly described by one strategy or another. This understood, the French situation may perhaps be appreciated if we compare it to the three successful practitioners of the second, or specialization, strategy.

The nations like Sweden, Switzerland, and the Netherlands which have successfully pursued the strategy of specialization have three distinct characteristics. They are distinguished by an exceptionally high degree of entrepreneurship. Each has a small number of highly competent, technologically based firms; additionally, these firms—Philips, Brown Boveri, or Volvo—have a global perspective with respect to their markets. Lastly, the economy is subject to a high centralization of decision-making authority; this may involve a close relationship between the political and industrial elites as in the Netherlands, or in effect a clear division of political and business authority as in Sweden, where the politicians run the welfare state, and the bankers and industrialists run the economy and finance the state through high taxes.

In each of these highly successful practioners of the second strategy, industrial and economic decision-making is concentrated. A high degree of cooperation and consensus exists among government (particularly the high civil service), industry, and the banking community. In practice, this means a national capacity for determining priorities, for shifting resources rapidly into areas of higher priority, and for eliminating areas of lower priority. In these countries, science policy is not so much a conscious area of governmental policy, it reflects the close professional and personal ties among high civil servants, educational leaders, and industrialists. In effect, these societies are managed, and science policy is made by a rather narrow elite. [24]

It is a paradox that those European countries which give greatest stress to formal planning for science and the creation of powerful, coordinating mechanisms are precisely those countries which lack this highly informal and effective network of personal ties among the elite. France, of course, is the outstanding example with its five-year indicative economic plan and its science minister. Rather than being signs of strength, these measures are symptoms of weakness. It is precisely because of the profound divisions within the French elite and the fragmentation of French institutions that these formal mechanisms are deemed necessary. France does not have the close coordination among civil servants, industrialists, and bankers one finds in Sweden, Switzerland, or Germany. Industrialists and professors are set apart by deep ideological cleavages and differences in educational backgrounds. The effort to overcome these divisions by formal structures has not solved these problems.

In contrast to Sweden, Switzerland, and the other followers of the second strategy, France's technological policy was directed primarily toward political and military goals; the emphasis was on independence. In consequence, as we have seen, the French government invested heavily in technologies already developed in the United States such as computers, or in technologies of questionable commercial value such as natural uranium reactors. In one area only have French technological efforts been highly successful: high-performance aircraft—Marcel Dassault's Mysteres and Mirages have captured world markets. Here one has entrepreneurship of a high order and a close attention to technological possibilities and the demands of the market. Only in this area do we find a French equivalent to the Swedish, Swiss, and Dutch successes in high technology industries.

While France is relatively weak with respect to the characteristics necessary for the successful pursuit of the specialization strategy, this fact does not foreclose the strengthening of French science and technology. For this reason, one must ask what lessons are provided for France by the experiences of these other countries.

The first lesson is to beware of establishing high-level coordination ministries or ministers as the solution to problems of technological strategy. While these mechanisms can help, the basic problems, as this chapter has sought to show, are found at the levels of entrepreneurship and of relationships among the elites. These are problems which coordinating ministers and mechanisms cannot easily resolve and may actually exacerbate. The very talk of creating such ministers is a clue to more fundamental problems which must be attacked, and the establishment of high-level mechanisms may actually blind one to this deeper reality.

The second lesson is the danger of supporting projects for reasons of prestige and independence rather than for social and commercial utility. From this perspective, there is considerable merit in the observation of those critics who argue that government entrepreneurship almost by definition tends to support noneconomic projects.[25] If, these individuals reason, the projects were of potential economic significance, they would have been undertaken by private enterprise. Both the Concorde and the supersonic transport (SST) can be cited as examples.

There may very well be examples, on the other hand, where a particular technological development is highly desired for reasons of public welfare, and the scale of the investment is such that government support is required. Or demand may not be sufficient to stimulate private development even though a public need may exist for the technology. Such, one might argue, is the case of pollution control and mass transportation technologies or labor-intensive technologies for the underdeveloped countries. What the experience of other countries seems to suggest, however, is that in addition to incentives and other bureaucratic devices, the most beneficial role which government can play is that of providing a guaranteed market. In advanced technology, the existence or nonexistence of a public market has been a crucial variable in determining the role of technological development. The very scale of the American public market in Western Europe has been far more important than subsidization of research and development in explaining the "technological gap."

Lastly, France must learn to keep its technological ambitions and resources in balance. This means specialization in those areas where France has a comparative advantage and keeping a close eye on market conditions. It also means acceptance of a high degree of technological dependence upon other nations. Gradually, since the events of May 1968 and the revival of German economic power, France has taken this direction. In response to the failures of her own technologies and her fears of German preeminence in Europe, France is looking more and more to American, British, and Soviet technology as a means to balance German economic hegemony.

In conclusion, we come back to where we began. Science policy in France has been first and foremost a product of France's international position. From the founding of the Royal Academy of Sciences in 1666 to the reforms of recent decades, the primary concern of French leadership has been France's economic and military position relative to the other major powers. The home of the Enlightenment and the belief in science as a great liberating force, France under the revolution and Napoleon was also the first nation to mobilize science for the sake of power. Whereas in the past the challenge was primarily a military one, today it is essentially economic and calls for a profound restructuring of French scientific, educational, and technical institutions.

## NOTES

1. Ernest Renan, La Reforme intellectuelle et morale (Paris: 1872).

2. See my France in the Age of the Scientific State (Princeton: Princeton University Press, 1962), chap. 4, for a more extended treatment of this earlier period.

3. In Search of France (Cambridge: Harvard University Press, 1963), chap. 1.

4. For Pasteur's views, see Rene Dubois, Pasteur and Modern Science (New York: Doubleday, 1960), pp. 144-55.

5. See Henry Guerlac, "Science and French National Strength," in Edward Earle, ed., Modern France (Princeton: Princeton University Press, 1951), p. 88.

131

6. For this period see David Caute, Communism and the French Intellectuals, 1914-1960 (New York: Macmillan, 1964), pp. 308-309.

7. On the founding of the CEA, see Lawrence Scheinman, Atomic Energy Policy in France under the Fourth Republic (Princeton: Princeton University Press, 1965), and Bertrand Goldschmidt, The Atomic Adventure, trans. Peter Beer (Elmsford: Pergamon Press, 1964).

8. This period is well covered by Pierre Piganiol and Louis Villecourt, Pour une politique scientifique (Paris: Flammarion, 1963).

9. The recommendations and proceedings of the Colloque are reported in Les Cahiers de la Republique, no. 5 (Jan.-Feb. 1957).

10. Piganiol and Villecourt, op. cit., p. 140. Also, see OECD, Reviews of National Science Policy—France, 1966, for a discussion of subsequent reforms.

11. A good discussion of French higher education reform is Jean-Claude Passeron, La Reforme de L'Universite (Paris: Calmann-Levy, 1966).

12. The literature on the "events of May" is overwhelming. A sympathetic treatment is that of Alain Touraine, Le Mouvement de mai ou le communisme utopique (Paris: Editions du Seuil, 1968). More critical is Raymond Aron, Le Revolution introuvable (Paris: Fayard, 1968).

13. See, for example, the writings of Alain Touraine.

14. See, for example, the writings of Seymour Lipset.

15. See my France in the Age of the Scientific State, op. cit., chap. 4.

16. Edgar Furniss, De Gaulle and the French Army, (The Twentieth Century Fund, 1964), chaps. 7-9. See also Gilpin, op. cit., chap. 9.

17. See Raymond Aron, The Great Debate, trans. Ernst Powel (New York: Doubleday, 1965).

18. Lew Kowarski, "Psychology and the Structure of Large-Scale Physical Research," Bulletin of the Atomic Scientists, vol. v, nos. 6-7 (June-July, 1949): 187.

19. For the discussion of these reforms, see Ministere des Armes, L'Orientation Nouvelle de la Recherche de Defense, Feb. 1963.

20. See Rapport sur les problemes poses par l'adaptation du $V^e$ Plan, Commissariat general au Plan, 1968.

21. For a summary, see Nicolas Vichney, "La recherche scientifique est a l'heure d'une revision dechirante," Le Monde, July 8, 1969.

22. Christopher Layton, European Advanced Technology (London: Allen and Unwin, 1969), p. 236.

23. Robert Gilpin, "Technological Strategies and National Purpose," Science (July 17, 1970): 441-449.

24. See Ingemar Dorfer, Chapter 6 in this volume.

25. George Eads and Richard Nelson, "Governmental Support of Advanced Technology—Power Reactors and the SST," Public Policy (Summer 1971): 407-427.

In less than a century, Japan has transformed itself from a weak, isolated, and nearly colonized nation at the periphery of the Western industrial world, to third largest industrial producer; Japan is also a candidate (according to some) for the ranks of superpowers. This feat has been achieved in the absence of domestic supplies of many vital raw materials; with a base of arable land dramatically less than that of leading nations; on savings and investment almost wholly internally generated; and with practically none of the advantages of centuries of interaction shared by the nations of the North Atlantic basin. This is only a partial and suggestive listing of contrasts, but it is important to begin with a reminder that, to most observers, Japan's rise has appeared little short of miraculous.

Most analysis of the Japanese success has attributed it to one or more conventional factors, such as the high rate of savings, the spoils of conquest, or the habit of obedience. Relatively little attention had been paid to the contribution of modern science and technology, though it is to some extent implicit in the development of modern industry, education, and military power. While it is not suggested here that science and technology are the "master variables" that synthesize existing explanations of economic growth or national power, [1] they are significant for a number of reasons hitherto unexplored in a specific and connected way. Furthermore, as Japan's status increases along with her determination to play a greater part in world affairs, the significance of science and technology will increase correspondingly.

Historically, the growth of modern industry and of scientific and technical professions in Japan was not—as in Europe and North America—an indigenous process. Rather, they were grafted on to Japanese society, mainly through the policies of a central government that had, in addition to an overall strategy for national development, a moral authority of unusual scope and effectiveness. The preeminent position of government constitutes a key historical factor, one that

133

may help explain continuing differences between Japanese policies and mechanisms for their promotion, and those of other advanced industrial nations.

Underlying the role of government, Japanese progress in almost all respects has been fueled by an enormous determination to achieve equality with the West. Beginning with the effort to revise the treaties forcibly negotiated by Western nations (the first of which resulted from Commodore Perry's ultimatum in 1853), Japanese national purpose has not deviated in many important respects from this overriding goal. Japan is now on the verge of effective material equality with much of Western Europe, and lags very little behind North America by most quantitative measures. Yet to political and academic leaders, Japan's access to the deepest wellsprings of material advancement appears to remain elusive. The creativity that spurs modern science, closely intertwined with technological innovation, seems yet another obstacle to Japan's realization of full equality with the West.

Despite this perception of the continuing race to catch up, many Japanese, along with critics and admirers of contemporary Japan, con-cede that it is becoming a scientific state in the same sense as the nations of Europe and North America. [2] While cultural and linguistic differences continue to set Japan apart, a number of organizational arrangements and national objectives are quite comparable to those of other industrial nations. Moreover, intensive competition and cooperation with the industrialized world as a whole demand the emergence of such symmetries.

The study of Japanese scientific and technological achievement logically begins with the founding of the modern Japanese state—the Meiji restoration of 1868. Broad new policies introduced in the dozen years from 1868 to 1880 have been remarkably constant down to the post-World War II period. While the period of military domination from 1931 to 1945 was in some respects a digression, it was also a culmination. It fulfilled a movement toward centralization in policy for and control of research and development that has had lasting effects.

Following World War II, the main current in national policy for science and technology was recovery from both wartime destruction and a decade of isolation from international scientific relations. For a brief interlude the occupation force was suspicious, and exercized tight controls. After 1949, however, Japan was rapidly transformed into the westernmost outpost of communist containment. The result for Japanese scientific and technical capabilities was to put the nation once again in a race to catch up, though largely in nonmilitary economic and prestige fields.

THE LEGACY OF THE MEIJI RESTORATION

Many factors distinguish the mid-nineteenth century situation of Japan from the mid-twentieth. The first of these is the political

134

climate. In the 1860s and 1870s the tide of western colonialism was rising. Japanese leaders, insulated after two and a half centuries of seclusion, still were aware of the presence—and growing pressure— of Russia to the north, England to the south, and the United States to the east. The significance of the Opium War—when in 1842 England imposed her will on China—was not lost on the Japanese. A considerable difference of opinion developed within Japan over how to respond to these western pressures. The drive for the "opening" of Japan was compounded of an external struggle against the colonial nations and an internal struggle over national policy. The initial treaty with the United States in 1854 was followed in 1868 by a political upheaval that brought the end of 250 years of the Shogunal form of government.

World politics are only one dimension of Japan's situation in the mid-nineteenth century. The intellectual climate was also considerably different from that of a century later. The principle of free movement of scholars was then the practice. They crossed national boundaries in time of war or peace, conversed with each other in Latin, and organized the first global effort of observation and experiment: the International Polar Year of 1878-80. European and American scientists, who had little knowledge about Japan, responded quickly and generously to Japanese requests to assist in the establishment of schools, universities, and technical agencies of government.

This relatively unrestricted intellectual climate extended also to technology and commerce. The laissez-faire spirit of governments in Europe and North America assisted the movement of ideas, goods, and the men who bore thm. Especially by Americans, Japan was seen as a new member of the world community, tentatively stepping on the first rung of the ladder that led to material prosperity.[3] It was a Christian duty to assist her, and not incidentally the practical benefits of developing commerce were linked with the spiritual rewards of spreading the Christian faith.

In this general setting, Japan faced the related problems of maintaining national independence in a world of colonial competition, and of promoting industrialization in a fashion consistent with her cultural heritage. As for independence, it was unquestionably fortuitous that the Meiji Restoration was accomplished with little civil disorder. A phenomenon elsewhere related to civil disturbance—antiforeignism— was kept to a minimum, thus obviating the interventions that invariably followed to protect western residents and treaty rights.

At the same time, a "modernizing" revolution in Japanese society was achieved in a relatively short time and with little violence. But why did Japanese experience differ from that of other Asian nations whose modernization in the late nineteenth and early twentieth centuries has been both bloody and long? The underlying reasons are found in the nature of Tokugawa society from which modern Japan emerged. For a student of the role of science in this process, the explanation also lies in the choices made by the government leaders, and the effects of these choices on the emerging structure of modern science and technology.

Social and Psychological Factors in Modernization

One of the key choices was the emphasis on human factors in preference to others such as physical endowment or the role of institutions.[4] This focuses the issue of modernization on beliefs and attitudes. To describe Japan as a Confucian nation is not the same kind of categorization as to say that the United States is Christian. Still, there is a useful analogy between the influence of neo-Confucianism during the period of Tokugawa rule (1602-1868), and the influence of Protestantism in Europe and North America.

Among the tenets of Confucian belief, the most crucial for Japanese society was the idea of hierarchy and its practice in social relations. Changes of government, which are highly disruptive and may ultimately destroy other nations, have had little effect in Japan on the established relations of classes or—more important—on public attitudes toward civil authority.

Another fundamental distinction between the Protestant and the neo-Confucian orientation is found in the emphasis on achievement. In the neo-Confucian sense, achievement is unrelated to social mobility. Rather, it stresses fulfillment of duties determined by the social hierarchy: agricultural productivity for the farmer, production of goods by the artisan, and maintenance of public order by officials of the state.

Confucianism is clearly analogous to Protestantism at the point where the religious ethic intersects the economic order, through teachings on the public utility of private gain. The duty of thrift and the moral rewards of hard work, joined in their aggregate benefit to the community, illustrate this comparison. In Japan, the neo-Confucian perspective was reinforced in the leaders by the home-grown ethic of Bushido, the "way of the warrior," that taught practice and self-improvement, denial of the body for purification of the spirit, and intense personal loyalty to the leader. This reinforcement of a social code—Confucianism—with an individual ethic—Bushido—influenced the general mass of Japanese through its romantic associations.[5]

The elite samurai class was important as the propagator and defender of values that influenced the general population. But the samurai also reflected attitudes particular to their leadership role. Among these, the ones bearing most directly on the response to the West were martial valor and national pride. A neo-Confucian writer of the early seventeenth century, Yamaga Soko, exemplifies this attitude in the following passage:

136

No less deserving of mention is Japan's pursuit of the way of martial valor. The three kingdoms of Han were conquered and made to bring tribute to the court. Korea was subjugated and its royal castle made to surrender. Japanese military headquarters was established on foreign soil and Japanese military prestige was supreme over the four seas from the earliest times down to the present day. Our valor in war inspired fear in foreigners. As for invasion from abroad, foreigners never conquered us or even occupied or forced cession of our land. [6]

An element of the samurai class succeeded in directing this pride and valor away from domestic vigilantism and foreign adventurism into commercial, educational, bureaucratic, and scientific achievement in the Meiji state. With relatively minor exceptions, the chauvanistic side of the leading elite did not reappear until the end of the nineteenth century. Even then, it emerged in a form familiar and palatable to the western nations, who applauded the prowess of Japanese infantry at Port Arthur and praised the tactical brilliance of the battle in the Straits of Tsushima, during the war with Russia. [7]

Attitudes of the general public and the leaders were reinforced by institutional factors, giving them social reality along with historical continuity. In the realm of political affairs, the governmental bureaucracy had been national in scope and bureaucratically organized since 1602. This stable and prestigious bureaucracy was dominated from the beginning of the Meiji period by an oligarchy of middle-ranking samurai from the former feudal domains of Satsuma and Choshu—the so-called "Sat-Cho Clique." Such a system was consistent with the Confucian principle of hierarchy, proved to be an acceptable informal instrument of government and, fortunately, put able and ambitious men in positions of authority.

## Economic and Political Factors in Modernization

In the economic sphere, Japan had a highly developed money economy, market and distribution systems, and craft production sector at the time of the Meiji restoration. Perhaps more important, Japan's agricultural system was technologically advanced when modernization began, especially as regards experimentation with seeds and fertilizers.

The development of education was a significant element in Japan's response to internal forces and competition with the industrializing western nations. Literacy was already widespread by 1868 and among the samurai was practically universal. [8] Institutions approximating public primary schools in a modern educational system were numerous and accessible.

137

Another factor supporting Japan's readiness for the influx of western knowledge was urbanization. Tokyo and Kyoto in the mid-nineteenth century had populations in excess of one million each. These and other cities such as Yokohama, Osaka, and Nagoya were long-established centers of commerce, trade, culture, and learning. Industrialization was introduced to Japan in the context of an existing urban culture. Together with the factors of public and elite attitudes, and the character of the economic and educational systems, it facilitated the reception of western knowledge during the crucial early years of the Meiji period.

Japan was obviously favored in particular ways for the rapid introduction of western science and technology. The habit of learning was embedded in the traditional culture, the prestige of learning was very high, and numerous institutions for the dissemination of knowledge were in existence. [9] In external relations, experience with foreigners (the Chinese and especially the Dutch in the period following the closure of Japan from 1640 onwards) had two important results. Western medical knowledge was sought by a growing band of industrious scholars identified with "Rangaku" or Dutch studies. This later led to studies of military science, astronomy, geography, and politics, though always in a semiclandestine fashion and in numbers hardly comparable to those of students of the official Confucian doctrine.

The second result was to establish the authority of government to control the kind and amount of foreign knowledge entering the country. Successive liberalizations of Tokugawa regulations rendered this a positive rather than a negative instrument of policy by the 1850s. The point, however, is the power and priority of government in controlling—and later promoting—knowledge received from abroad.

The Meiji political leaders recognized that mastery of the principles of natural science and their application to industrial technology gave the West its overwhelming material superiority. Yet their philosophy was not one of uncritical and unselective absorption of western knowledge. The formula of a Tokugawa scholar and governmental advisor, Sakuma Shozan, sums up the attitude: "Western science, Eastern ethics." [10] With their conservative background and reformist aims, the leaders sought to pry the techniques of the western nations from their setting in western social and political thought.

Some years before the establishment of a parliamentary form of government in 1889, the government was reorganized as a modern bureaucracy. Departments—later Ministries—of Industry and Education were set up in 1870 and 1871 respectively. The Ministry of Industry had the main responsibility for the importation of western technology. An engineering school was established to select future national leaders and inculcate them with a basically technical outlook. Within the school—which subsequently became the Engineering Faculty of Tokyo Imperial University—an engineering institute was organized. It employed foreign teachers, and involved a six-year course of study combining general, theoretical, and applied engineering in a single program. Many of the graduates of this course later became industrialists and high-level bureaucrats.

The Ministry of Education had the initial task of organizing a national system of primary and secondary education, to carry out the aim of the Fundamental Code of Education of 1872 that "There shall, in future, be no community with an illiterate family, nor a family with an illiterate person."[11] The new elementary curriculum consisted of a western-style "three R's" course, plus Japanese history, physical education, and moral instruction. Organization of secondary education lagged considerably. Not until the passage of a vocational education law in 1894 and the expansion of the two-stream system of education (that is, vocational and academic) did secondary education begin to flourish.

Not only engineering education, but higher education generally underwent major changes. In the Tokugawa period, it had been the prerogative of the samurai to pursue higher studies. Now it became accessible to young men of talent whatever their origin. From training for leaders, higher education became training for leadership. For the first thirty years of the Meiji period there was only one university: the Imperial University in Tokyo. Then, as now, it functioned as a funnel, directing talented and ambitious young men into careers that usually led to membership in the ruling elite.

Within this framework, the introduction of western scientific and technical knowledge took two forms in the early Meiji years. Foreign experts were invited to work in Japanese ministries and to teach at the Imperial University and other government schools, and government employees and students were sent abroad.

It has been estimated that by the mid-1870s, some 5,000 foreigners had been employed, mostly under contract to the national government but some in private positions. The cost for salaries alone was nearly 4 percent of the total budget from 1868 to 1872. The figure gradually declined to something more than 1 percent by 1882. These salaries were very large by Japanese standards, often 10 to 12 times the average earned by civil servants of equal rank.

During the entire Meiji period (1868-1912), the government supported study abroad of more than 700 university students. More than half of these students went to Germany. In addition, nearly 1,000 government officials went abroad on study missions between 1868 and 1881, and the number subsequently increased. The largest number went to England. As in the case of students, the subjects investigated were law, medicine, and applied science in Germany, engineering in England, pure science in France, and agricultural science in the United States.[12]

The major objective of these educational policies was to promote industrialization. In 1870, for example, about 70 percent of western experts invited to Japan by the government were in fields of industry.

139

Half the salaries paid to foreigners in the early Meiji years were to industrial advisers. The government itself took the lead in establishing steel mills, railroads, mines, shipyards, textile factories, and other industries that form the foundation of a modern industrial state.

The first phase of this policy began to come to an end in the late 1870s. The combination of large government expenditures for salaries to foreigners and overextension in other areas led to the decision to sell off most government-founded industrial enterprises in 1880 (though the purchasers often were men who had been trained in the Imperial University and had several years of service in government departments). In addition, Tokyo University was beginning to produce trained teachers and civil servants capable of replacing foreigners, and foreign trainees were completing their courses of study abroad.

Outside the crucial areas of industry and education, the Meiji leaders pursued policies for the introduction of western science and technology in all departments and activities of the newly organized government. Scientific and technical service agencies were established rapidly between 1870 and 1890.[13] Many of these activities, such as coastal charting and buoyage, geological surveying, and the writing of technical standards, were initially the responsibility of foreign advisers.

The introduction of foreign knowledge was so rapid and its effect on the modernization of Japan so ramified throughout the society that it is unlikely that government was more than one ingredient in the process—though a catalytic one. A student of business entrepreneurship in Japan has written that "The most important resource for development is the will to succeed."[14] This will must be widely manifested if a nation is to transform both its style and level of living. At the same time, the attention of society must remain focused on goals which may be too general and too distant for the multitude. Another writer has characterized the role of the government as follows:

> The case of Japan is . . . perhaps unique in Asia, in that political and social leadership throughout this period of transition was exercized by certain dominant groups who remained firmly in the saddle and were technologically progressive. These groups maintained their ascendancy, accommodated their differences, and pursued their aims through a variety of social institutions and controls. Of these the political hierarchy was only one, although perhaps the most important.[15]

The situation faced by Japan in the mid-nineteenth century was not easier than that of developing nations today, but the global context was very different and the preparedness of the Japanese much greater. Though Japan may be said to have succeeded, there were costs that

140

became apparent only when the political system established by the Meiji leaders came under the strain of worldwide economic depression and an outburst of nationalist fervor in the 1920s and 1930s. Because the governing oligarchy was determined to suppress the political liberalization implicit in western-style modernization until Japan had caught up technologically with the leading industrial nations, those costs were eventually paid not only by Japan but in some degree by all the nations involved in the global war.

## CONSOLIDATION IN WAR AND OCCUPATION

The modernization of the governmental apparatus for science and technology policy, in Japan as in Europe and North America, received a powerful stimulus during World War II. In Japan, however, the military leaders began the series of moves in Manchuria in 1931 that culminated in conflict throughout the Pacific. These sprang from an authoritarian domestic regime, hence the connection of science and technology with national priorities initially had a much more sinister connotation.

### Wartime Political Organization

The establishment of a cabinet-level resources bureau in 1927 did not have particular significance until the organization, also in the cabinet, of a planning board in 1937. Later that year, the two were combined in a planning authority that "centralized all policies with the object of building up military power, and later undertook the control of mobilization plans based on the National Mobilization Law enacted in April 1938."[16]

Control over scientific research was delegated to a Division of Science, set up in 1939. This was further expanded after the outbreak of war with the United States, so that a two-tier system composed of a policy-making Scientific and Technological Deliberative Council, and an administrative Department of Technology, were putatively in existence by 1941. The facts are significant because no other industrial nation prior to the end of World War II had achieved a similar degree of centralized administration of the entire national effort in scientific research and development. Yet one should not forget that "The main objective of this scientific mobilization was the organization of national research power in the most effective manner for converting scientific technique into military power."[17]

Scientists and engineers were also organized by field into neighborhood associations to provide for mutual oversight and

141

stimulation in research endeavors. These associations were tied into a vertical chain of command leading at the peak to a nationwide Scientific Mobilization Association, nominally headed by Prince Konoye. As the domestic situation deteriorated with the worsening of Japan's position in the war, efforts were made to increase unity and to exploit loyalty as a spur to scientific productivity: " . . . a Research Mobilization Committee was set up within the National Research Council; a liaison committee was stationed at each university; and all research had to be organized in line with the objectives of the war."[18]

There is no evidence that this system worked effectively. Organizational schemes could not substitute for vital materials, and these were simply not available to the research community. But the lessons of failure were evident to the Japanese, for in the last analysis

. . . scientific mobilization was not a worthless process. The experience acquired, the systems set up and continued in post-war years, the realization of the necessity to reinforce Japan's scientific power and to renovate the academic system, all served as a background to the development of science in Japan after World War II.[19]

The Role of the U. S. Occupation

The significance of the experience was, however, largely lost on the U. S. occupation authorities. They set about creating new, democratic structures that would represent a clean break with Japan's past. Occupation science policies had the objective of reestablishing Japan's capacity to engage exclusively in peaceful scientific research and development activities. Thus, four experimental cyclotrons were dismantled and destroyed, aeronautical and electronic research were prohibited, and military research institutes were disbanded.

Two institutional innovations were sponsored by the occupation. Both probably delayed somewhat the convergence of structures and objectives of national science policy that was implicit in wartime measures. The Natural Resources Section of the Supreme Command of the Allied Powers (SCAP) instituted a complete survey of domestic resources and encouraged the establishment in 1947 of a Resources Committee in the Economic Stabilization Board (later the Economic Planning Agency) to centralize planning and policymaking on resource allocation for reconstruction and rapid recovery of economic self-sufficiency. In 1949, this body—under SCAP's urging—became a separate resources council with a full-time chairman responsible to the prime minister. This move was made in disregard of the convention that advisory councils are almost exclusively representative of special

142

interests, with highly political functions and very little coordinative capacity or policy initiative.

SCAP's second and more significant error was its attempt to reorganize the Japanese scientific and academic community. This effort was supplemented by the dispatch of two high-ranking scientific missions from the U. S. National Academy of Sciences. The first, in 1947, was headed by Roger Adams and the second, in 1948, by Detlev Bronk. Their reports supported a plan providing for an elected Science Council of Japan, designed to balance regional, disciplinary, and institutional interests—in short, to reduce the influence of the imperial universities, especially Tokyo, and that of the metropolitan centers.

This organization was to function as a deliberative body for science, and as a source of advice to the prime minister, to whose office it was attached for funding and administrative support. [20] Almost from the beginning it was dominated by left-leaning intellectuals, making it anathema to a conservative government. At the same time, internal politics of the Science Council reflected disparate views of natural scientists, engineers, social scientists, and humanists, so that no concerted policy advice was forthcoming.

Throughout this period, the climate of world politics was changing, with the result that U. S. policy moved more quickly toward the re-instatement of Japanese independence. In the affairs of science, the new policy was symbolized by the authorization of a Japanese delegation to attend the Pacific Science Congress, held in New Zealand in February 1949. Japan's return to the ranks of peaceful nations was underscored by the award of a Nobel Prize in physics, the same year, to Yukawa Hideki. [21]

ORGANIZATION AND RESOURCES OF JAPANESE SCIENCE POLICY

In Japan as elsewhere, the financial and human resources for science and technology have increased rapidly in the postwar period. To state briefly the story of Japan's phenomenal economic success: industrial production between 1956 and 1963 (a typical period) grew about twice as fast as in Italy, three times as fast as in West Germany and France, and at seven times the U. S. rate. [22] It was thus that Japan quickly became the world's third-ranking industrial power.

While it is not possible to state that research and development provided the engine of this growth, R&D expenditures did grow nearly twice as fast as the economy, and R&D manpower expanded faster than any other segment of the service sector. By 1968, Japan was spending 1. 5 percent of gross national product on R&D (a sum of $2, 133 million), [23] and employing scientists and engineers in a ratio of 1. 5 per thousand population (an aggregate number of 157, 000). [24]

Considered in comparison with other industrial nations, the Japanese R&D effort is modest but impressive. The Japanese "research ratio" (R&D expenditure as a percentage of gross national product) has grown at about the average rate of other industrial nations, while the ratio of scientists and engineers to total population is exceeded only by the United States and the Soviet Union. (See Statistical Appendix, Table 3.1).

If these data confirm the quantitative similarity of Japan's research and development effort with that of other industrial nations, other factors underline unique qualitative characteristics. When R&D expenditure is broken down to show the sectors of funding and of performance, it is clear that only in Japan does private industry both supply funds for and carry out nearly two-thirds of all national research and development activities. Elsewhere, the proportion varies, with industry supplying half (as in the United States) to five-sixths (as in West Germany), and government providing the difference. [25]

Another special characteristic of the Japanese R&D effort is the large number of college and university graduates with degrees in humanities, education, and social science in contrast to the small number in natural science and engineering. An equally notable fact is the recent rapid increase in the proportion of engineering graduates, both in absolute terms and in comparison to natural science.

Policy Advisory Bodies

The development of new organizations and procedures for the allocation of R&D resources had been significantly influenced by these fundamental characteristics. Japan's policy-advisory and planning bodies resemble those of nations in Western Europe and North America partly because the overall scale of the R&D effort and its relation to national goals is similar. But they differ in key respects—as allocation procedures differ—because of the very powerful position of private enterprise, and because of the balance of disciplines in the scientific and academic community. These are not the only sources of divergence, but in science policy affairs they are crucial.

Japanese organization for science policymaking is a typical two-tier system, in which the coordinative and policy-advisory (or staff) activities are distinguished from administration and execution of defined missions (line). The central policy-advisory organ is the Council for Science and Technology (CST) a cabinet-level body made up of the prime minister (ex officio) and four other cabinet ministers (education, finance, economic planning, science and technology) plus the president of the Japan Science Council (JSC) and five men appointed by the prime minister. The statutory membership of the president of

144

FIGURE 5.1

Science Policy-Advisory System

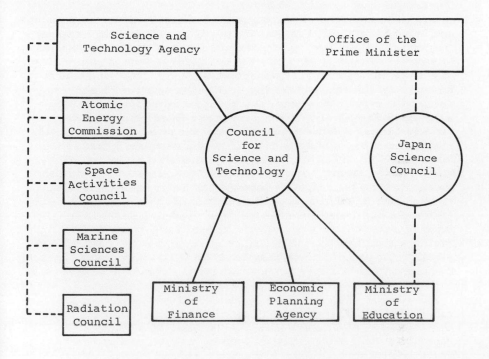

Note: The Economic Planning Agency (EPA) is formally established as a subsidiary of the Office of the Prime Minister. However, it is physically located in the Ministry of Finance, and in functional terms its contribution to science policymaking is closely identified with that Ministry. The Science and Technology Agency is also a formal subsidiary of the Office of the Prime Minister. It plays a somewhat more independent role in science policymaking since, unlike the EPA, it has a large constituency in the laboratories, public corporations, and special legal persons under its administrative or budgetary control.

145

the JSC, in addition to the existence of a large, complex subcommittee for coordination between the two councils, underlines the importance of this aspect of the CSTs functions. Other subcommittees provide for long-range planning and short-term investigations of various problem areas, principally within the government's own programs but to some extent in the nation as a whole.

Several other specialized advisory councils —for space, atomic energy, marine science, and radiation—are brought into working relationship with the CST through cross-membership of one or more of their appointed members and key cabinet officers. The role of the Science and Technology Agency (STA) is equally important in this regard. As an administrative subsidiary of the office of the prime minister, the STA connects the two tiers of the system. Through functionally organized bureaus, it links the administration of major government research and development programs with their policy-advisory organs, and in its very important planning bureau provides the administrative backup for the cabinet-level Council for Science and Technology. The STA is administratively equivalent to the Defense Agency. It has its own cabinet-level director-general, a substantial staff of civil servants, and a number of subsidiary units under its control. Though it disburses directly less than 15 percent of the government R&D budget, the STA has "coordinative" control over about 40 percent of the total amount. It does so by preparing the total (noneducational) research budget of the government, and by submitting as part of its own budget certain "bloc" allocations (for atomic energy R&D, for example) which it redistributes to other departments and agencies carrying out parts of key programs.

### Administrative and Coordinating Bodies

The various ministries and their attached agencies undertake routine research such as development of standards, testing, extension services, and other normal governmental activities. These are carried out in more than seventy laboratories and research stations, a large number of which are under the Ministry of Agriculture. Public health, industrial services, weather reporting, and similar technical missions are distributed more or less predictably to the appropriate ministries. In terms of financial allocations, four departments account for 80 percent of the R&D budget: Agriculture, Education, International Trade and Industry, and the Science and Technology Agency.

Every department has an internal scientific and technical advisory mechanism. Some incorporate interest groups (notably in International Trade and Industry). Others reflect the degree of technical complexity of the department's mission (such as the medical side of health and welfare programs).

146

With respect to the management of large-scale research and development activities, Japanese R&D administration begins to depart from the conventional model. While there are some significant exceptions in the industrial sector, management of these programs generally lies with the STA. Several large-scale research and development activities under STA control have been organized in a comparatively flexible and undogmatic way. The bloc budget approach to atomic energy provides one salient example, but other organizational innovations are significant. For example, six new national laboratories were created between 1955 and 1966 in areas lacking any concentrated efforts in either fundamental or applied research. [26]

The use of quasi-governmental public corporations is especially significant. Two were chartered in 1956, with leaders brought from private industry: the Japan Atomic Energy Research Institute and the Nuclear Fuel Corporation. The following year, the Japan Information Center for Science and Technology was set up (with industrial backing) to centralize the collecting, translating, and abstracting of foreign scientific and technical publications.

In 1958, the Institute of Physical and Chemical Research (IPCR) — a public corporation first chartered in 1916—was revived from its prostrate postoccupation status, to provide a center for projects outside the purview of clearly defined departmental research missions. [27] One section of the IPCR was delegated to seek and develop promising ideas generated by university researchers or in laboratories of firms with limited capital and research facilities. This activity was spun off, following the British experience with NRDC, and in 1961 a Research Development Corporation was independently organized. A Nuclear Ship Development Corporation was set up in 1964, and it successfully guided development of Japan's nuclear-powered Antarctic research vessel.

Although the formula for support varies from case to case, these quasi-governmental corporate organizations have several common characteristics. They are all jointly capitalized by industry and government, and current expenses are financed by both as well as by operating income. All are free of civil service regulations on hiring and remuneration (though they are under the general budgetary surveillance of the STA), and they are legally empowered to enter contracts as private corporations.

Another innovative means of supporting research has been the use of public foundations. Two such examples are the Japan Society for the Promotion of Science, and the Japan Science Foundation. Both have mixed public and private functions, a fact reflected in the character of their boards of directors and in their programs. Neither performs research. Their activities involve promoting communication among academic, business, and political leaders and arranging for international cooperation and exchange activities in fields of research and applied technology. [28]

147

Competitive standing among industrial nations in terms of the proportion of GNP devoted to R&D activities has been particularly important to the Japanese. In the decade of the 1960s, "research ratios" were a challenge to the effectiveness of their system of collecting and reporting economic data, of which they are justifiably proud. Furthermore, Japan gained favorable public attention in the early 1960s when she first sought membership in the club of rich nations, the Organization for Economic Cooperation and Development (OECD) following widespread praise for her "economic miracle, " the perennially high growth rate. These facts partially explain why the first report on Japan's overall position with respect to science and technology, published in 1960, gave such prominence to her position among industrial nations in terms of various criteria of comparison. [29]

Investment in R&D provides a uniquely authoritative indicator, since it brings into consideration the quality of "creativity." The appearance of concern with Japanese originality in science and technology, first in the White Papers of the early 1960s and then as a priority issue in the second general report of the CST in 1966, [30] underscores an element of dependence on foreign standards (perhaps in another sense "international" standards) to confirm a national image of worth.

## Bureaucratic Competition and the Budget

Bureaucratic concern about the resources available for research could be explained as merely a function of the relatively low per-capita level of Japanese expenditures compared with other industrial nations. For example, in 1962 Japan spent about $8 per head as against $15 in Belgium, $20 in Germany, $34 in the U.K., and $94 in the U.S. [31] Except for the United States, these countries have all been increasing their expenditures faster than Japan. The overall Japanese research effort in 1968—$2,133 million—roughly equals the U.S. effort in basic research alone.

While these features of the international environment suggest reasons why the Japanese have sought to expand the total national investment in R&D, they do not tell us much about the internal distribution of resources among competing groups and objectives. The balance of evidence indicates that strong traditions of departmental autonomy, based on a pattern of status hierarchy among departments and a rather rigid budgetary process, are the major factors determining the amount and character of R&D investment.

In discussing the organization of science policymaking the term "quasi-ministry" was used to describe the Science and Technology Agency because its status as an agency of the prime minister's office does not square with the extent of its activities and the size of its budget. Indeterminate status helps keep the STA in a constant struggle with the more powerful ministries, not just for a share of the research and development budget, but for the authority it desires in terms of programs under its general control. This—among other factors—has encouraged existing interdepartmental rivalries. Competition (between the Ministry of Education and the STA in space research, and between the STA and International Trade and Industry in electronic research) follows from the recognition that at a time when technology is receiving increased attention from politicians and public alike, successful programs can result in increased status in the administrative hierarchy. [32]

Competition in the budgetary process is more formalized but has similar sources. Agency and ministry budgets are submitted annually to the Finance Ministry for preliminary trimming, at which time the tugging and hauling over programs and spending levels occurs. Ultimately, political decisions (that is, cabinet decisions) settle outstanding questions. The budget that goes to the lower house for approval is rarely tampered with: hearings are pro forma, since most of the significant negotiation has taken place in the setting of inter- departmental competition.

Thus an intense struggle over the budget compounds the competition for status in the bureaucratic hierarchy. Political interest that do not have representation in this competitive context do not have much opportunity to influence the budgetary process. Since the civil service is in an important sense nonpolitical, the entire process is largely private, being conducted in the arcane metaphor of programs and budgetary allocation procedures.

### Coordination of R&D Activities

Despite these conflicts, coordination of R&D activities with economic planning stands as a signal achievement of postwar science policymaking in Japan. The machinery of coordination is comprised of a planning organ headed by a cabinet officer. The Economic Planning Agency is empowered to establish guidelines for public and private investment in the five- to ten-year range. In some ways, it is anal- ogous to the U.S. Bureau of Management and Budget and the Council of Economic Advisers combined, though it does not provide a day-to- day critique of business conditions and government monetary and fiscal policies. Control is exercised through the formulation of sectoral policies.

## FIGURE 5.2

### Research Budget and Administration System

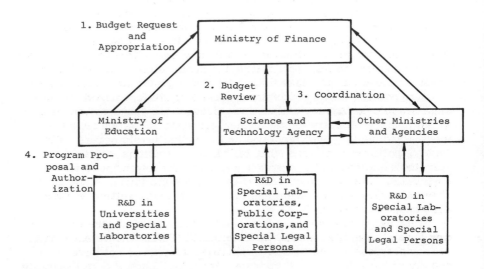

Note: A budgetary authorization takes the following sequence of steps:

1. Ministries and agencies submit budget requests to Ministry of Finance, including items for research and development;
2. Research and development items are "packaged" for review by STA;
3. Particular items for coordinated research or bloc funding are negotiated jointly by STA and ministry/agency concerned;
4. R&D activities are authorized in the laboratories, public corporations, and special legal persons under the aegis of particular ministries and agencies.

The progress of a budget proposal may be followed by reading the chart in the order 4, 3, 1, 2, substituting in 4 the word "proposed" for the word "authorized." The final step is authorization by the Ministry of Finance following receipt of the STA's review.

Two examples of sectoral policy that have been significant for R&D activities are energy and industrial technology. The absence of domestic supplies of fossil fuels for industrial and other purposes led to a determination to emphasize atomic energy. The second general report on atomic energy policy proposed a 20-year development period. For the latter half (1965-75), when Japan would have acquired and developed the requisite technical capabilities, the planners foresaw the installation of large-scale generating facilities.[33]

Observers have long suspected that the introduction of foreign industrial technology is carefully regulated. As with the long-term energy picture, planners faced the prospect of a period of dependency before Japan could become, if not self-sufficient technologically, at least capable of world leadership in selected fields. The complex of administrative and financial controls on know-how agreements between Japanese and foreign (70 percent American) firms was a somewhat evolutionary process, designed not simply to avoid foreign control but also to strengthen the technological base in particular industries.

Neither of these sectoral policies was science policy in the sense of "policy for science," but both had significant research components. In energy, the emphasis was on long-term domestic capability in the design and construction of nuclear generating plants. In industrial technology, the emphasis was on a broad, self-supporting system of technological innovation. Thus, the planning component in R&D activities was made subordinate to planning in the industrial sector. Yet this was not a self-contained process in which objectives in basic science, engineering, and other applied fields were separately prepared as inputs to the economic planning process. Rather, R&D was shaped to help meet economic objectives.

The evolution of this approach began in the immediate postwar period, but economic planning did not converge with research and development planning until much later. In 1959, when the Economic Deliberation Council (whose staff support comes from the EPA) was preparing the first 10-year economic plan, the Council for Science and Technology was also preparing a 10-year plan for science and technology. While the staff work was performed separately for each council, one finds on the technical subcommittees of the two councils a considerable amount of overlapping membership. This fact suggest the means used initially to bring science policy considerations into the economic planning process.

The 10-year plan published in 1960 (called the Double-Income Plan because of its stated goal of doubling national income within the decade) gave focus to the heretofor diffuse relationship of R&D to national goals. In the framework of measures to maintain a high economic growth rate, it called for the increase of research investments from about 1 percent of national income to 2 percent by 1970.[34] In addition, a number of the working papers prepared by members of

151

the Economic Deliberation Council called attention to factors such as technically qualified manpower in the long-run economic picture.

The Double-Income Plan was in many respects a political document, an expression of one administration and, to a considerable extent, of one man, Ikeda Hayato, prime minister from 1960 to 1964. With his resignation and the accession to leadership of Sato Eisaku, economic planning took a somewhat different direction. Long-term plans by nature cannot respond to exigencies, and an interim plan for 1964-68 was formulated. Here, science and technology received renewed emphasis, though manpower development took precedence over R&D investment. Support for domestic research activity was justified on the grounds that "those who develop their own technology or merchandise win in international competition."[35]

The Medium-Term Plan was superseded by still another in 1967, reflecting the interaction of the Japanese economy with other industrial nations, and the emergence of domestic political issues such as urbanization and environmental pollution. This plan reinforced the trend to incorporate research and development activity into overall economic objectives. It called for raising R&D funds to 2.5 percent of national income by 1971.[36] It also brought out the need for sharp increases in the level of government expenditures on R&D, which are the lowest among major industrial nations.[37]

Industrial R&D Objectives

A salient fact about Japanese research and development programs has been the extent to which organizational and funding efforts over the past generation have been concentrated in a few fields. Since over 60 percent of the entire national research effort has been funded (and carried out) by private industry, it is important to explore how the efforts of government and industry have supported and complemented each other.

The dominant objective for industry has been international competitive strength. Government has assisted this by promoting research and development in particular fields, such as electrical machinery and chemicals.[38] Lacking the familiar American method of the grant-contract system (transfers of funds for such purposes have been less than 1 percent annually of government research outlays) Japanese efforts have concentrated on tax measures and approval procedures governing "know-how" agreements with foreign firms.

These mechanisms have favored the large scale, technologically sophisticated firms. They have emphasized selection of technology not only on technical grounds but also in relation to political and contractual considerations (for example, length of time and geographic extent of market restrictions). They have helped to retard and in some

152

cases avoid the influx of capital and management from technologically superior nations such as the U.S. threat to Europe during the 1960s. The complementarity of governmental and industrial approaches is best illustrated in the atomic energy program. It is also clearly demonstrated, though on a smaller scale, in fields such as aeronautical and information science.

Japanese scientists were well integrated into the global network of nuclear research by 1939, as illustrated by the award of two Nobel Prizes in theoretical physics. After the end of the U.S. occupation and its "peace and democracy" policies for science, the government took the lead in reestablishing nuclear research. A new law passed in 1956 emphasized development for exclusively peaceful purposes. A decision was quickly taken—with support from the industrial community—to import a British reactor in order to gain experience. The reactor was plagued with difficulties and became operational only in 1965. However, the second decade of atomic energy development promises a substantial market for domestic generating equipment, this in large measure justifies the original decision.

Aeronautical research was also prohibited by the occupation, partly due to the excellence of Japanese fighter aircraft in the Pacific war. The first new research institute set up by the government after the end of the occupation was for aeronautical development (it was later renamed "aerospace"). Under a program of governmental guidance and support of research, governmental choice of design, and a governmental decision to use the British Rolls-Royce engine, Mitsubishi in 1963 brought out the YS-11 as a replacement for aging DC-3's. It has been moderately successful in the world market.

In information science, Japan (like Europe) got a late start, failing to anticipate the rapid expansion of computer applications. The earliest indication of government involvement was the appearance of an item in the STA budget in 1960 for research on computers, electronic communications, and electronic technology in medicine. Relatively slow movement in computer research probably has been rooted in competition between the Science and Technology Agency and the Ministry of International Trade and Industry. For several years there was no agreement on the division of responsibility for support of domestic research, or criteria for approval of a know-how agreement or joint venture that would bring computer technology into Japan. To help build a domestic market, the government organized a computer leasing firm to make available easier terms than would have been possible through private industry alone.

An activity that sheds some light on failures in contrast with successes is Japan's space research program. Competition between the STA and the Ministry of Education seems to have been the root of the problem. A university organization of a new kind was established at Tokyo University in 1964. This "joint research institute" provided for coordination among public and private university

153

researchers in the field of space and aeronautical research. Based on an existing aeronautical research program that had made possible Japan's contribution to the International Geophysical Year, the new institute manifested the desires of academic researchers and their education ministry supporters to mount a space program on their own. Coordinative attempts by the STA were rebuffed. [39] As a consequence, academic researchers announced in 1965 their intention to orbit an experimental satellite, but they did not succeed until 1970. The small size of the payload and the absence of any but the most primitive guidance system cast doubt on the economic significance of the academic space research program.

Despite these and other difficulties, [40] an overview of Japanese efforts in programmatic research and development activity permits the conclusion that these exceptions only test the rule. Most have exemplified two basic elements of success: a coordinated, planned approach, and the priority of commercial criteria.

### THE DYNAMICS OF POLICYMAKING

While there is not yet a generally accepted view of the policy-making process in Japan, if we are to understand who influences science policy and for what purpose, we must proceed on the basis of some hypotheses. [41] Two formulations seem particularly useful in describing the play of forces in Japan. The concept of pressure or interest groups has been used by western scholars, and adopted by a representative Japanese analyst with a reasonable degree of success. [42]

A less generally recognized approach emphasizes accommodation of opposing views. As one writer presents it in contrast with the interest-group approach:

> Western political theory holds that the party winning a clear majority in a general election has a mandate to govern without interference for a set period. Japanese theory seems to contain the doctrine that the power of the party or parties in office should be limited by considerations of respect for and accommodation of the views of the opposition. [43]

Some studies in the field of law underline a preference in Japanese culture for accommodation ("adjustment" is the sense of the Japanese word <u>matomari</u>) as opposed to the adversary process familiar to western nations. [44] This preference for accommodation in policymaking must be qualified with a word of warning: it is neither an absolute nor a universal characteristic of Japanese society. In other spheres, such as interparty political conflict and generational differences of view, much occurs that is better explained in terms of open confrontation.

## Conflict and Adjustment in Science Policy

Proceeding from these related hypotheses—the existence of interest group conflicts and a preference for accommodation rather then adversary relations—it is possible to identify the groups that are prominent in science policy affairs and the ways in which they interact to adjust their differences on policy matters. Some typical contemporary policy issues will illuminate the discussion.

Of the many and varied groups that have some concern with science policy issues, only three are continuously and significantly involved in the outcome. These are the scientific and academic community, the bureaucracy, and the industrial community. Each group contains admixtures of the other, such as engineers in industry, industrialists in government agencies, and ex-bureaucrats in the private sector.[45] Furthermore, the distinctiveness of each group becomes blurred as one's focus of interest shifts upward to senior members of each hierarchy. But these facts do not diminish important ongoing characteristics of group perspectives and modes of operation in the policy-making process.

It has already been noted that the body established by the U. S. occupation to provide advice to the executive branch and a representative forum for the scientific and academic community—the Science Council of Japan—was largely ineffective. The Council for Science and Technology was set up in 1958 to perform the main advisory functions, though it is weakened because it does not effectively utilize the special knowledge or interests of the scientific and academic community. This situation represents the single most serious shortcoming in the Japanese system for science policymaking. It is therefore important to understand how it came about.

The problem is certainly related to the fact that modern science and technology were imported into Japan and grafted to a deeply-rooted traditional system of teaching and research. The claims to universality of the concepts transmitted from the West tended to establish an alternative focus of loyalty, in conflict with the traditional focus on the state and the imperial family.

The field of engineering provides an important exception. Alone among the imported disciplines, engineering had immediate practical significance. For this reason, engineering education was initially conducted in the Department of Industry. But as the national university system developed into a training school for leaders, it was the law students, not the engineers, who came to dominate the civil bureaucracy. The preferred career for scientists was the university faculty

155

or research institute. Engineers, in contrast, became the most adapt-
able of the university graduates, moving into industry, the bureaucracy,
and the universities.

This simplified sketch helps explain the position of scientists and
engineers on the political spectrum and in the policy advisory process
in postwar Japan. In the affairs of the Science Council, engineers
have been outvoted by an alliance of natural and social scientists
who are leftist-influenced and wholly uncompromising on issues such
as Japanese research policy and the U.S. security treaty. Engineers
have been increasingly isolated as the membership of the Science
Council has shifted heavily toward university faculty while the division
in which engineers are represented has changed only slightly in that
direction. [46]

In the hands of a majority of academic natural and social scientists,
the Science Council has embarrassed and thwarted the government in
several ways. It has taken intransigent public positions on sensitive
political issues, such as radiation from American nuclear submarines
operating from U.S. bases in Japan. [47] Further, it has offered imprac-
tical and self-serving advice on the investment of resources in science,
such as its suggestion for a public foundation run by scientists to
dispense 10 percent of the research budget, [48] and its renewed demand
for a 40 BEV protron synchrotron in the wake of Tomonaga's Nobel Prize
in physics. Finally, an effort to publish a "White Paper" on science
and technology resulted in diverse suggestions by numerous contributors, rather than a comprehensive set of priorities. [49]

The Council for Science and Technology is a somewhat more adapt-
able mechanism. As described earlier, it is a group of advisers including cabinet ministers and others selected for their "learning and experience," a common euphomism for individuals who are team players
with a long record of service. Expert knowledge based on contributions
to research is not a major consideration.

As an "inside" advisory council, the CST operates largely through
subcommittees for long-range planning, priorities in research, manpower
development, scientific and technical information, and liaison with the
Science Council. This last function, which involves the largest and
most varied subcommittee, reflects the degree to which the Science
Council is deemed politically obstructive by the government.


The Politics of Bureaucratic Adjustment


The contrasting styles of the two advisory council suggest why
accommodation rather than adversary relations characterizes the
science policy-making process in Japan. The distance between public
conflict of aims and private coordination of a highly effective system
is bridged by a special kind of "scientific statesman." He is less

156

likely than in other industrial nations to be generally recognized for the major role he plays, and he may not even be a scientist in the narrow sense. Two of the most influential scientific statesmen of the past decade have been engineers (Kaneshige Kankuro and Kaya Seiji), and the specialized councils (including councils on space, marine science, and atomic energy) involve industrialists and economists as well.

On the other hand, scientists widely known for their views on the freedom of research, such as nuclear physicist Sakata Shoichi and two-term president of the Science Council Tomonaga Shin-ichiro, have little observable influence on the course of national policy. On rare occasions, such as the burst of national pride when Tomonaga received the Nobel Prize in 1965, the government will respond with a handout for the scientific community. [50]

An important measure of the effectiveness of scientific statesmen is accommodation of conflicts over the research budget. In spite of a somewhat arbitrary separation of "academic" from "governmental" basic research, a surprising degree of coordination was achieved between Tokyo University and the STA's National Space Development Center. A similar tendency of the Ministry of International Trade and Industry's (MITI) Agency of Industrial Science and Technology to pursue research on industrial innovation to the exclusion of other agencies or academic programs has been moderated by the continued efforts of scientific statesmen.

Three departments of government represent the major competing interests of the bureaucracy in national science policy. The Science and Technology Agency, whose Planning Bureau acts as secretariat to the CST, seeks to establish greater direct control over the R&D budget. However, the Ministry of Education commands an independent advisory organ, recently restructured to act more effectively on requests for research grants. [51] Research and development activities in national universities and their associated laboratories total 45-50 percent of the government R&D budget, and there has been a running battle over the effort of the STA to extend its "coordinative" power to those parts of the university budget related to research also carried on in STA laboratories. MITI, which funds relatively little research, has important powers of approval over the introduction of foreign know-how, tax incentives for research and development, and a number of more subtle financial and administrative devices. [52] Some of this authority is shared with the STA, the Bank of Japan, and other agencies, but the crucial powers of initiative and delay reside with MITI.

Each ministry and agency has relatively clear responsibilities with regard to the R&D it supports, and there is remarkably little overlap among the client groups whose interests they serve. For example, the STA has staked out priorities in space research, atomic energy, and domestic resource management. These correlate with a number of national laboratories and a small and quite specialized group of private

157

firms. The Ministry of Education tends to see itself as master of the national system of education and basic research, hence it identifies the national interest with the development of highly qualified manpower and the support of pure science.[53] The Ministry of International Trade and Industry is the spokesman in the bureaucracy for wealthy and powerful industrial interests, and thus portray's the nations needs in terms of industrial competitive strength based on modern technology. Yet each view of national needs and the role of research and development in meeting them is in some degree competitive with the others. This competition is reflected most directly in the research budget-making process already described.

In sum, there is no single set of criteria for policy on which all bureaucratic participants agree. Policymaking is a slow and laborious process, involving constant "liaison conferences" (renraku kaigi) for the discussion and adjustment of views. The following description of the adjustment process makes rather clear its costs and complexities:[54]

A typical decision-making meeting opens with a statement of the problem by the group's senior member. Each member then exposes a slight portion of his thinking, never coming out with a full-blown, thoroughly persuasive presentation. After this, he sits back to listen to the same sort of exposition from the others. . . . The discussion goes on at great length, each person slowly and carefully presenting his opinion, gradually sensing out the feelings of other people, making a pitch subtly, following it without pressing if he finds it acceptable, quietly backing off and adjusting his views to those of others if he finds himself not in tune with the evolving consensus. When the leader of the group believes that all are in basic agreement with a minimally acceptable decision, he sums up the thinking of the group, asks whether all are agreed, and looks around to receive their consenting nods. Nothing is crammed down anyone's throat. If, by chance, a consensus does not emerge and a deadlock seems likely, the group leader does not press for a decision, does not ask for a vote, does not rule that no consensus seems possible and thus embarrass people. Instead, he suggests that perhaps more time is needed to think about the problem, and sets a date for another meeting. . . . by the time the next meeting is called, the differences most likely will have been straightened out and the process can move forward to a final decision. In all of this, the most important principle is not to stand on principle but to reach agreement. All else is subordinate to this point.

The industrial community plays the least specific role in the making of science policy. Indeed, only one member of the Council for Science and Technology is from industry, and none of the interindustry organizations have given more than occasional and superficial attention to the subject of national science policy. Rather, the impact of the industrial community is reflected in the fact that economic planning dominates the planning of science policy.

There is one major channel of direct industry influence on policy and planning. That is, the membership of industry representatives on key policy advisory bodies. These include the Economic Deliberation Council (advisory to the Economic Planning Agency), the Foreign Investment Council (advisory to the Ministry of Finance), and the Industrial Structure Council (advisory to the Ministry of International Trade and Industry). Each of these councils works directly with the respective minister's secretariat, which often secures personal access to a cabinet officer. Each commands great prestige in bureaucratic circles and draws its membership from among the senior and most highly respected members of the business community. Academics are also represented, principally on the Economic Deliberation Council, but they are drawn exclusively from the ranks of "insiders."

As in the case of demarcations between departmental functions, these advisory bodies have specialized activities and develop specialized views. The Economic Deliberation Council seeks a comprehensive view of the direction of national development, but this view is necessarily limited by considerations such as the economic growth rate and the labor market. The Foreign Investment Council has acted as a "court of last resort" on know-how contracts and issues such as tariff decontrol which involve the absorption of foreign capital and technology. The industrial Structure Council has helped formulate the policy by which postwar Japanese investment was shifted into such high-technology sectors as petrochemicals, electrical machinery, automobiles, precision tools, large-scale construction equipment, and recently aero-space and computer electronics.

There is no satisfactory current description of how these councils work with government, or how they coordinate either within or among themselves to produce a unified view of policy. It has become fashionable to explain this phenomenon through use of the rubric "Japan, Inc.,"[55] but this oversimplifies the complexities of the system of conflict and accommodation. It fails to draw attention to gaps in the system, such as the business-academic divergence of view, and it ignores the time consumed in reaching policy decisions. The following chart, though it is also vastly simplified, provides an overview of the dynamics of policymaking.

Among the three major groups who determine science policy, the position of government is dominant. This is true for historical reasons (some of which antedate the Meiji Restoration) and for reasons

## FIGURE 5.3

### Advice and Accommodation in Science Policymaking

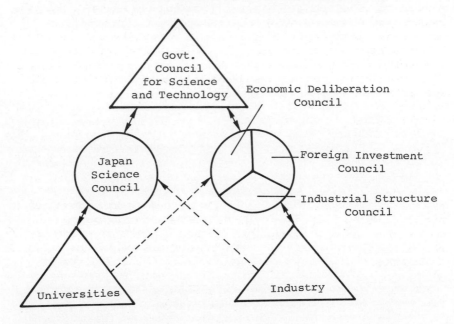

connected with the social psychology of the advisory process in Japan. It is especially borne out by the confrontation of political ideology, which arrays the conservative industrial community against the leftist-liberal scientific and academic community in continuous hostility. Only in the context of policy-advisory councils do representatives of the two interests meet on relatively neutral ground. This underlines the role of the councils as instruments for the accommodation of conflicting views.

The benefits of the process of accommodation have been discussed. The costs are primarily those of time. The lament of a century has been that Japan must "catch up" with the advanced industrial nations, yet new measures of the unclosed gap are constantly emerging. Japanese politicians are fond of cautioning that "Japan must not be the last one on the bus," yet the policy-making process is organized so that the bus is bound to be nearly full by the time a decision is crystallized.

In specific areas of research and advanced technology, Japan's postwar lag can be attributed to the effects of war and occupation. Atomic energy, aerospace, and computers are major examples. In less exotic industrial research and development, however, Japan was protected from the effects of her lateness and slowness by the particular character of the postwar situation: Europe's destruction, and the willingness of the United States to become the major source of knowhow, both through private contracts and public efforts to promote industrial reconstruction and national security. In these circumstances, Japanese leaders were able to pursue at leisure and without competition the national objectives of protecting a domestic market, building up national industrial capabilities, and seeking a viable strategy in a world market dominated by American (and some European) public and private undertakings. Now, Japan's competitors are fully cognizant of the challenge. The relatively benign attitudes of the 1950s and 1960s are not likely to recur.

## SCIENCE POLICY AND NATIONAL OBJECTIVES

Whether a national science policy is centralized or pluralistic, and whether the national strategy in research and advanced technology can be subjected to an overall pattern, the fact remains that real choices over any substantial period of time suggest the character of long-term national objectives. In the case of Japan, three such choices stand out.

### Manpower Development

First, a serious (and historically rooted) commitment exists to the development of highly qualified manpower, with special attention to the scientifically talented. Thus far, the expansion in the 1960s of university places in engineering and science has not elicited an equivalent response from the university generation. Nevertheless, the pool of qualified scientists and engineers has increased substantially, and employment in related occupations such as research administrators, laboratory technicians, and clerical and maintenance personnel has expanded even faster.

Since R&D manpower broadly defined is increasing faster than gross national investment in R&D, and is less affected by fluctuations in the rate of economic growth, Japan will continue to exhibit low levels of investment per researcher. This will be compensated by the growing strength of the yen in international trade (the domestic purchasing power of which continues to be understated by about one-third) and by substantial foreign exchange reserves which attest to the attractiveness of Japan's high-technology export goods.

161

## Industrial Technology

Second, there is a general recognition that production and marketing capability in high-technology goods is an essential element of domestic economic development, national security, and international competitiveness. Despite very low production of commercial aircraft (five per month) and the high costs and low initial returns from commercial nuclear power reactors and liquid-fueled guided rockets, national policy will continue to give them priority. [56] In each of these high-technology areas, the Japanese are unwilling to give up even a qualified independence.

Increasing demand for electric power (and products that use it) underlines the case for domestic reactor technology. Short lead-times to the establishment of a credible nuclear deterrent are the eventual fruit of a domestic nuclear fuel industry and a satellite-launching capability. The aerospace complex of technologies is increasingly diversified, opening up lucrative markets for items such as short-haul aircraft and satellite ground receiving equipment. Reorganization of the International Telecommunications Satellite Consortium (INTELSAT) has created the possibility of substantial participation in hardware contracts by Japanese firms.

## International Relations

Third, Japan is committed for the forseeable future to intensive scientific and technological relations with the United States. Statements to the contrary are not supported by other bilateral relations of comparable volume. The Japan-U.S. cooperative Science Program, which provides for the annual expenditure of about $1 million by each partner, far surpasses any similar binational cooperative scientific venture. [57] Japanese scientists, engineers, policymakers, and politicians journey to the United States for short or long periods, in numbers exceeding those traveling to any other country. The 1969 agreement on transfer of space technology to Japan[58] underlines the situation already extant with regard to enriched uranium for reactor use, in the field of military aircraft and rockets, in intercontinental passenger aircraft, in petroleum products, and in large-scale computers, to name the principal areas. There is, to be sure, a concommitant U.S. dependence on Japanese technology, for example in large ocean-going bulk carriers and tankers, special steels, optical instruments, and solid-state semiconductors. But dependence is a two-way street. Japan relies on U.S. purchases in these fields to maintain the economic scale of domestic production.

162

Choices Ahead

There are some choices that the Japanese significantly have not made with respect to the national research and development effort. With a "peace Constitution," popular fears of radioactivity, and acquiescence in the initial stages of the nuclear nonproliferation treaty, Japan is not opting for a large-scale military R&D effort. Until approval of the new 3-year defense plan, military expenditures were the lowest among industrial nations (about 0.8 percent of GNP)[59], and military R&D has averaged about 10 percent of that, most of it devoted to costs of adapting or testing U.S. equipment. The resistance of academic scientists to working on the Japanese Antarctic project which the military were supplying, and their stubborn determination to maintain an academic space research program distinct even from potential economic benefits, reinforce the nonmilitary character and prospects of the national effort.

With the major exception of medicine, Japanese R&D efforts related to public welfare have been very small. Budget figures are some indication of priorities. In fiscal 1967 (ending March 31, 1968,) the Science and Technology Agency allocated about $1.1 million—from a budget of over $80 million—for a range of projects covering the fields of fire prevention, environmental pollution, population, land use planning, and food preservation.[60] This is a rough, but not inaccurate measure of real choices, whatever the verbal commitments. Atomic energy, space, and other research directed at expanding the range and strength of heavy industrial and high technology capabilities take the lion's share.

These observations may provide some clues to the matter that perplexes both Japanese and foreign observers. As one of the most astute of those observers has put it: "What role will this new Japanese giant carve out for itself? How will it use its vast new economic strength?"[61] Prime Minister Sato put the situation in these words: "It is entirely a new case that a country such as Japan, possessing great economic strength, has no significant military power and yet makes its presence felt throughout the world."[62] These questions define the issues of the coming years, but they do not provide many hints of what the answers will be. At the very least, we may deduce from the record of postwar science policy that any new course in national affairs will emerge from lengthy and interlocking domestic processes of consultation and accommodation on each issue, and that developments in the fields of science and technology will play a significant part in the outcome.

163

# NOTES

1. Harold and Margaret Sprout, Foundations of International Relations (Princeton: Van Nostrand, 1962), p. 8.

2. Robert Gilpin, France in the Age of the Scientific State (Princeton: Princeton University Press, 1968), p. 4.

3. Akira Iriye, Across the Pacific (New York: Harcourt, Brace & World, 1967), pp. 26-28.

4. Johannes Hirschmeier, Entrepreneurship in Meiji Japan (Cambridge: Harvard University Press, 1964), pp. 288-289.

5. Note in this connection, the effect of the classical suicide of the novelist Yukio Mishima in 1971.

6. Yamaga Soko, An Autobiography in Exile, in Ryusaku Tsunoda et. al., eds., Sources of Japanese Tradition, vol. I (New York: Columbia University Press, 1958), p. 396.

7. Reginald Hargreaves, Red Sun Rising: The Siege at Port Arthur (Philadelphia: Lippincott, 1962), p. 15 et passim.

8. Passin reports estimates of 40-50 percent and 15 percent female literacy as of the end of the Tokugawa period. Chapter 9 "Japan," in James S. Coleman, ed., Education and Political Development (Princeton: Princeton University Press, 1965), p. 276 and n. 13.

9. See Herbert Passin, Society and Education in Japan (New York: Columbia Teachers College, 1965), chap. 2, pp. 13-49.

10. Tsunoda et. al., op. cit., vol. II, p. 96.

11. Passin, op. cit., p. 211.

12. Sources of data in the preceding paragraphs include: Passin, op. cit., pp. 94-95; Watanabe Minoru, "Japanese Students Abroad and the Acquisition of Scientific and Technical Knowledge," Journal of World History, vol. IX (1965): no. 2, 254-293; Nakamura Takeshi, "The Contribution of Foreigners," ibid., pp. 294-319; and Pahm-Van-Thuan, La Construction du Japon Moderne (Lausanne: Centre de Recherches Europeennes, 1966), pp. 159-80.

13. Major agencies were: Navy Hydrographic Office (1870): Hygienic Laboratory (1874); Central Meteorological Observatory (1875); Geological Survey (1878); Army Land Survey Office (1884); Patent Bureau (1885); Statistics Bureau (1888); and Tokyo Astronomical Observatory (1885).

14. Hirschmeier, op. cit., p. 288.

15 William W. Lockwood, The Economic Development of Japan (Princeton: Princeton University Press, 1964), p. 589.

16. Hirosige Tetu, "The Role of the Government in the Development of Science," Journal of World History, vol. IX (1965): no 2, 332.

17. Ibid., p. 334.

18. Ibid., p. 335.

19. Ibid., p. 335.

20. The facts are summarized in Harry C. Kelly, "A Survey of Japanese Science," Scientific Monthly, vol. 68 (January 1949): 49-50.

21. The views of a scientist on the occupation period and its conclusion can be found in Hideomi Tuge, Historical Development of Science and Technology in Japan (Tokyo: Kokusai Bunka Shinkokai, 1961).

22. William W. Lockwood, "Japan's New Capitalism," in Lockwood, ed., The State and Economic Enterprise in Japan (Princeton: Princeton University Press, 1965, p. 457, n. 8.

23. Japan, Science and Technology Agency, Kagaku Gijutsu Hakusho [Science and Technology White Paper] (Tokyo, March 1970): 424, table 2-2.

24. Ibid., p. 429, table 2-5.

25. Ibid., p. 223, chart 2-5.

26. They were: the National Aerospace Laboratory (1955); the National Research Institute for Metals (1956); the National Institute for Radiological Sciences (1957); the National Research Center for Disaster Prevention (1963); the National Center for Space Development (1963); and the Research Institute for Inorganic Materials (1966).

27. Established by the government in 1916, it took patents on its discoveries and developed several of them into profit-making business firms.

28. Japanese participation in the US-Japan Cooperative Science Program is organized through the Japan Society for the Promotion of Science.

29. Japan, Office of the Prime Minister, Council for Science and Technology. Shimon Dai Ichi-go: "Ju-nen Go o Mokuhyo to Suru Kagaku Gijutsu Shinko no Sogoteki Kihonteki Hosaku ni Tsuite" ni Tai suru Toshin [Inquiry No. 1: Report on Basic Comprehensive Measures for the Promotion of Science and Technology in the Next Ten Years] (Tokyo, October 4, 1960).

30. Japan, Office of the Prime Minister, Council for Science and Technology. Kagaku Gijutsu Shinko no Sogoteki Kihon Hosaku ni Kan suru Iken [Opinion Concerning Comprehensive Basic Policy for the Promotion of Science and Technology] (Tokyo, August 31, 1966).

31. OECD, Organization for Economic Cooperation and Development, Reviews of National Science Policy—Japan, (Paris, 1968), p. 65, table 4: p. 72, table 12.

32. Payoffs might include appointment of a more prestigious person as minister, enhanced desirability in the eyes of civil service applicants, preferment in the assignment of new office space, and so forth.

33. Japan, Atomic Energy Commission. Long-Range Program on Development and Utilization of Atomic Energy (Tokyo, February 8, 1961), pp. 15-18, English version.

34. Organization for Economic Cooperation and Development, Reviews of National Science Policy—Japan, op. cit., p. 216.

35. Japan, Economic Planning Agency, Medium-Term Economic Plan, 1964-1968 (Tokyo, January 1965), p. 50.

36. The STA reports that as of 1971, the 2 percent level had still to be achieved.

37. As of 1967, Japanese government R&D funds were 30 percent of total national R&D expenditure, compared with 63 percent in the U.S., 50 percent in the U.K., 41 percent in West Germany, and 54 percent in France. See Statistical Appendix, table 1.5. Organization for Economic Cooperation and Development, International Survey of the Resources Devoted to R&D in 1967 by OECD Member Countries: Statistical Tables and Notes, Vol.5 (Paris, 1970), p. 24, table T.1.1.(B).

38. These two fields regularly account for about half of research expenditure by industry.

39. As a result, the STA went ahead with its own program, in cooperation with the Defense Agency, the ministries of Transportation, and Posts and Telecommunications, for development of launchers designed to provide a capability to orbit communications, navigation, and geodesic satellites. This was expanded, and in 1969 the National Space Development Agency (NASDA) was established under STA auspices.

40. For example, the slow pace of marine science research, and the limited scale of projects such as MHD power generation.

41. See, for example, Fred N. Kerlinger, "Decision-making in Japan," Social Forces, vol. 30 (October 1951): 36-41; Milton J. Esman, "Japanese Administration—A Comparative View," Public Administration Review, vol. 7 (Spring 1947): 100-112; Tsuji Kiyoaki, "Decision-making in the Japanese Government," in R.E. Ward, ed., Political Development in Modern Japan (Princeton: Princeton University Press, 1968), pp. 457-475; and Nobutaka Ike, Japanese Politics (New York: Knopf, 1957), pp. 263-276.

There are also some studies of particular decisions, such as Robert Butow, Japan's Decision to Surrender (Stanford: Stanford University Press, 1954), and Tojo and the Coming of the War (Princeton: Princeton University Press, 1961); and James W. Morley, The Japanese Thrust into Siberia (New York: Columbia University Press, 1957).

42. Ishida Takeshi, "Pressure Groups in Japan," Journal of Social and Political Ideas in Japan, vol. II (December 1964): no. 3, 108-111.

43. J.A.A. Stockwin, "Foreign Policy Perspectives of the Japanese Left: Confrontation or Consensus?" Pacific Affairs, vol. 42 (Winter 1969-70: no. 4, 439-440.

44. Arthur T. Van Mehren, ed., Law in Japan: The Legal Order in a Changing Society (Cambridge: Harvard University Press, 1963), especially Kohji Tanabe, "The Process of Litigation: An Experiment with the Adversary System," pp. 75-93.

45. A common pattern of behavior is that high government officials take "early retirement" at fifty, and accept executive positions in private industry.

46. The Science Council as a whole was 75 percent university professors in 1963, compared to 94 percent after the triennial election of 1967. Division 5 (Engineering) by contrast was 53 percent professors in 1963 compared with 60 percent in 1967. Data from Science Council of Japan, Annual Report, 1963 (Tokyo, 1965), and Annual Report, 1967-68 (Tokyo, 1969).

47. Typical examples may be found in the Annual Reports of the Science Council of Japan. Of special interest is Sakata Shoichi et. al., "A Statement by Scientists Concerning the Call of Nuclear Submarines at Japanese Ports," Journal of Social and Political Ideas in Japan, vol. 2 (August 1964): no. 2, 103-104.

48. Fukushima Yoshio, "Japan's Five-Year Science Plan," New Scientist, vol. 32 (October 27, 1966): no. 518, 180.

49. Japan Science Council, Kiso Kagaku Hakusho [Basic Science White Paper] (Tokyo, April 1959).

50. On the occasion of the Nobel award, the Asahi Evening News remarked editorially that "The Government—like the press— seems to be competing with itself in congratulating Prof. Tomonaga. Education Minister Nakamura held a joint press conference with Prof. Tomonaga and said, 'Prime Minister Sato is also thinking of establishing some commemorative project. On this occasion, I would like to work for the construction of a building for the Japan Science Council.'" Asahi Evening News, Wednesday, October 27, 1965. The new building was completed in the spring of 1970.

51. In late 1967, a dispute erupted between the Science Council and the Ministry of Education over the manner of awarding grants. The Science Council refused to continue to recommend appointees for the screening committee, whereupon the ministry reconstituted the Science Deliberation Council with its own appointees. In the summer of 1968, continuing conflict led to the refusal of grants of 2.5 million yen by particle physicists, and of 5.8 million yen by cosmic ray researchers. See Yomiumi Shimbun, August 21, 24, 1968.

52. MITI's instruments of R&D policy are described in Reviews of National Science Policy—Japan, op. cit., pp. 151-59, and in Nicholas Jecquier, Le Defi Industriel Japonais, (Lausanne: Centre de Recherches Europeennes, 1970), pp. 119-38.

53. A rather striking example of this identification is the publication Japan's Growth and Education (Ministry of Education, 1963). It is also strongly expressed in the 1964 White Paper on education. See John E. Blewett, S.J., ed. and trans. Higher Education in Postwar Japan (Tokyo: Sophia University Press, 1965).

54. Richard Halloran, Japan, Images and Realities (New York: Knopf, 1969), pp. 92-93.

55. Typical examples are James Abegglen, ed., Business Strategies for Japan (Tokyo: Sophia University Press and Encyclopedia Britannica, 1970), and Herman Kahn, The Emerging Japanese Superstate: Challenge and Response (Englewood Cliffs: Prentice-Hall, 1970).

56. These technologies and government measures for their support are described in some detail in P. B. Stone, Japan Surges Ahead (New York: Praeger, 1969), especially chaps. 4, 11, 12, and 13.

57. This should not be confused with the predominantly technological character of the Anglo-French Concorde project.

58. Robert Gilpin, "Technological Strategies and National Purpose, pose," Science, vol. 169 (July 31, 1970): 447-448, makes a similar if more critical appraisal of U. S. -Japan relations, taking his departure from the space agreement.

59. Institute for Strategic Studies, The Military Balance, 1971-72 (London, 1971), p. 61, table 3.

60. Science and Technology Agency, Kagaku Gijutsu-cho Nenpo 13 [Science and Technology Agency Annual Report 13] (Tokyo, December 1, 1969), pp. 61-62, table 34: pp. 14-15, table 3.

61. James W. Morley, "Growth for What? The Issue of the 70's" in Gerald L. Curtis, ed., Japanese-American Relations in the 1970's (Washington, D. C.: Columbia Books, Inc., 1970), p. 48.

62. New York Times, "Sato Warns Japan on 'Great-Powerism, '" April 9, 1970, p. 10.

CHAPTER

# 6

## SCIENCE AND
## TECHNOLOGY POLICY
## IN SWEDEN
Ingemar N. H. Dorfer

Sweden forms a perfect example of what science and technology
wisely used and rationally allocated can do, and its dilemma mirrors
the problems facing small nations trying not to fall too far behind in
the race of the giants and at the same time defending their integrity.
As opposed to many other nations Sweden is not trying to change its
position—moving up like Japan, turning inward like the United States,
or keeping up appearances like France. Huddling on the fringe of the
center of action throughout this century, Sweden will now finally be
forced to make some hard choices. Through self-imposed ground rules
the choice will be starker than, say, for Holland or Italy. In brief
the problem will emerge as a result of the tension created in the 1970s
between what might be called international (that is, European) integration on the one hand and socialism in one country on the other.

In this chapter we shall explore how the remarkable continuity
in Swedish scientific and technological politics over this century is
breaking, and how the challenge of the 1970s has led to a polarization of science policy as well as other policies. In essence, the
question is—what do you do for an encore once you have achieved the
welfare state? What if the values of that post-welfare state clash
with the political mores of the larger political community upon which
you are dependent for your prosperity and with which you have to
associate closely?

A time lag in Swedish political development is being disclosed.
The technological underpinning of the Swedish welfare state since
World War II has been big science supporting high politics. Only
recently has science policy become welfare oriented, catching up

---

This study was supported by a grant from the Swedish Board for
Technical Development. The findings and conclusions are entirely
the author's own.

169

with the public mood at the time when the nation's main problem is European integration.

The break in continuity is obvious in the two structures that support the Swedish effort. A traditionally self-contained university system, largely isolated from the demands of a modernizing society, is being captured by the government and molded into the social democratic image. The technological community, on the other hand, dependent on and interacting with the outside world has not been so easily overwhelmed and is in conflict with the ideological demands put forth.

## HISTORICAL SETTING

It cannot be repeated too often that until recently Sweden was a land of farmers. Until the 1890s, the country was preindustrial, until World War II it was agrarian. Indeed, the remarkable transition of an agricultural country to a postindustrial society in one generation (the stage of full-blown industrialism was rapidly passed) may explain many aspects of the present signs of tension in Swedish society.

Sweden had, then, the advantage of backwardness. The breakthrough of industrialism came in the 1880s with the refinement processes of the staple goods wood and iron; in the 1890s the specialization began that has been pursued ever since: special steelmaking, electrical engineering, various kinds of machinery built on the innovative genius of a few men—Dahlen and his lighthouses (AGA), Ericsson and his telephones (LME), Winqvist and his ball bearings (SKF). According to Gilpin, Germany was the first state to apply the method of science on the field of industry and business. [1] In the field of chemistry, Sweden lacked Germany's natural resources and market, but in electrical engineering, Swedish firms quickly followed in the footsteps of Siemens and AEG. Germany, of course, was the state with which Sweden had the most intensive contacts at the time—the Swedish university system and officers corps were based on the German model, and many of the technicians and engineers had their training from Germany.

While the emphases on German technique and organization remained with Sweden throughout the interwar period, by World War I an interesting polarization arose within the establishment regarding foreign relations. While Sweden as always remained neutral, it was the conservative bureaucratic class, represented by the Hammarskjold family, that was pro-German; the emerging liberal and big business interests, symbolized by the Wallenberg dynasty, saw England as their spiritual home. [2] When the labor movement (embarking upon the path of bersteinian revisionism) literally lost its contacts in Germany throughout the 1930s, it turned inward—the isolationist impulse that

170

we now are calling socialism in one country. Big business, on the other hand, has always been cosmopolitan. In this fact lies the tension when choices have to be made in science, technology, and policies towards Europe. Still, the pattern established at the turn of the century has, until the 1970s, been remarkably consistent, given the infusion into that pattern of a well-organized, enlightened, and strong labor movement capable of ruling.

Through the establishment of the three commercial banks: Stockholms Enskilda Bank, Svenska Handelsbanken and Skandinaviska Banken, and their connection with various corporations, funding of promising and innovative ideas has often been quick and efficient. Of the three mentioned, the Stockholms Enskilda Bank stands out. Controlled by the Wallenberg family, it played an important role in the 1890s by funding the electrical engineering company ASEA and the first big electrical power distribution projects in the nation.[3] In recent years, its R&D corporation, AB Incentive, has carried the tradition further. From the beginning, industrial and technological development was thus tied to banking, a relationship that in Sweden exactly fitted Schumpeter's description as the headquarters of the capitalist system from where orders go out to its individual divisions.[4]

The banking system was not the only source of continuity for Swedish technology throughout the century. The technostructure of the nation, of which the banking system is a vital part, has been extraordinarily compact. Excepting two short periods of cooperation with the agrarians and the collective four-party cabinet during World War II, the social democrats have held office since 1932. The powerful Minister of Finance in 1974 had been a cabinet member since 1946. The government, nourished by Keynesian ideas since the 1930s and the heyday of the Stockholm School of Economics, together with the impetus from an enlightened trade union movement, has cooperated with business on the important matter of reaching consensus and increasing the prosperity of the people.

No social upheavals connected with World War II, as experienced in England, France, Japan, and the USSR, have disturbed the continuity of Swedish development. On the contrary, the Swedish pattern of science and technology during the war followed, albeit on an immensely smaller scale, the American experience. Mainly through conscious government funding and support of the aircraft industry, a small Swedish military-industrial complex was founded, based on SAAB and Swedish Flygmotor and supported by Bofors and the shipping industry. The aircraft industry, in particular, joined in the 1960s by the electronics firms have thus been able to support technologically advanced weapons systems which were funded via the defense budget. This lead to a uniformly high standard in technology and management. The Swedish military-industrial complex, like the state itself, has been a Weberian paradise: hard working, incorruptible, highly motivated Protestants cooperating with an efficient and dedicated bureaucracy.

171

The emergence of this complex during World War II has had several important implications for the industrial side of Swedish R&D. Development and research in Swedish industry, as in other states, is carried out by the big corporations—in 1972, 75 percent by the 50 largest firms.[5] The defense effort gave the government a natural sector in which to support R&D. Sweden avoided the French arsenal system for military procurement. Major defense corporations have been kept half in and half out of the defense business,[6] facilitating the spin off effect in both directions.

THE UNIVERSITY SYSTEM

Until the 1940s, the Swedish university system played little part in technological development. The traditional universities at Uppsala and Lund, supplemented by the academies at Stockholm and Gothenburg, supplied the cadres for a modernizing state--training its civil servants in law, theology, and medicine, and its gymnasium teachers in the arts and the basic sciences. Applied science and technology was delegated to the two Institutes of Technology business management to the Stockholm School of Economies. The university professors were civil servants, appointed by their peers and receiving their salary from the Ministry of the Church and Education. In 1914, the government allocated the equivalent of $5 million to R&D and in 1939 $1 million. In the interwar period, the governmental R&D effort was consistently 1 percent of the GNP. During World War II, the first timid efforts were undertaken to strengthen government support of science with the foundation of the Technical Research Council in 1942, as a result of an investigation by the Department of Commerce. Utilitarian ideas were also behind the Medical Research Council, the Atomic Research Council, and the Agricultural Research Council (established in 1945), the Natural Science Council (in 1946), and the Social Science and Humanities Councils (in 1947). Together they received in 1947 $1.4 million, very little indeed, compared to the funds given, say, the aircraft industry.

Throughout the 1950s, the council funds expanded from $1.4 to $5.4 million: Sweden entered the 1960s with only 3 percent of its R&D funds in this area. Prime Minister Erlander, Sweden's leading political figure from 1946 to 1969—who had begun his government career as a minister of education—maintained a benevolent interest in the field throughout the period. A committee on higher education was appointed in 1955, to overhaul the university system. Its results were published throughout the 1960s, foreshadowing the overwhelming and dramatic changes in the area of university training that took place in the 1970s. Still, the 1950s were the age of the high school in Sweden. The 1960s were the age of higher education and science policy.

If a date for the new age must be set, it is 1962. This year saw the establishment of the Science Advisory Council (SAC) and, through the council, the government's awakening to the impact of science and technology on the prosperity and welfare of the nation. The emergence in the 1960s of sectorial thinking in science and technology, and its impact on industrial R&D, can be traced in the activities of this council. Equally important is the parallel reorganization and transformation of higher education in the late 1960s and early 1970s, culminating in the present polarization of science policy against the background of latent antiscientism, if not antiintellectualism.

## THE ATTEMPT TO INSTITUTIONALIZE SCIENCE POLICY

A survey of the Swedish scene in 1962 gives the following result. In 1962, Sweden spent 1143 mkr on R&D (equivalent to $220 million) or 1.7 percent of the GNP. The funding of R&D was shared about equally by government and industry. Defense, including nuclear energy consumed about one-third of the funds—roughly $80 million a year. Industrial expenditure on R&D counted for 4 percent of the industrial output (1959) compared to 3.1 percent in Britain and 5.7 percent in the U.S. (1958).[7]

In the summer of 1962, a meeting of illustrious Swedes took place at Harpsund, the prime minister's summer residence, to plan the Science Advisory Council. Crucial in the preparation of this meeting of 30 prominent scientists, government representatives, and members of the business community had been two professors, Bror Rexed and Sven Brohult. Significantly, they represented—in their own way—the two poles of power in Sweden, social democracy and government on the one hand, and big business and technology on the other. Rexed, a professor of medicine from Uppsala was an old friend of the prime minister and an active social democrat. In the Uppsala student club Laboremus, he and Nils Elvander, a political scientist, had tried to advocate the ideas of Bernal on the social functions of science. Sven Brohult, on the other hand, was head of the Royal Swedish Academy of Engineering Science, which traditionally has excellent connections with the business community. That community too, symbolized by the Swedish Federation of Industry, had seen the need for a more systematic study and support of science policy options.

Several reasons existed why 1962 was the year of this step in Swedish science policy. The research councils had stagnated in their funding. Exactly as the OECD was to point out in their report on Sweden the following year, the councils allocated their funds in an incremental, bureaucratic manner. The main reason was, however, the importance of science and technology in international competition.

173

"We are leaving our idyllic world to face the harsh realities of the 1960s," said Rexed at the meeting. The 32-man Science Advisory Council, chaired by the prime minister, represented practically all branches of science and included 8 men from the technological and business community. Of its professed functions: observer of international developments, coordinator of science policy, and integrator of science with general policy—the observer function had, of course, always been filled by the invisible colleges of the scientific community of which Swedes were members not least in their selection of Nobel prize winners. The change was thus one of scale rather than substance, and the issue was the size of future science funds, which required a more formalized allocation procedure than before.

In the beginning, the SAC directed its activity towards the obvious. Inspired by the OECD visiting team, it turned its interest to R&D statistics and to mapping the domestic situation in various fields. [8] The stagnation of science council was overcome. In 1961, two special funds for technical R&D were created which added $10 million a year, and in 1965 the Bank of Sweden Tercentenary Fund more than trebled the money available to social science research, from $1 million to $4 million. The government research funds in fact expanded from $6.4 to $40 million in the 1960s, from 3 to 10 percent of the nation's total R&D resources. [9]

From the beginning, the policy of SAC was carried out by its executive committee, made up of key persons like Rexed and Brohult and attended by the key ministers and undersecretaries. While the formal meetings of the whole council were infrequent and served as the sounding board of the scientific community, it was intended that the working committee would become the policy instrument.

For various reasons this did not happen, mainly because of the different perspectives and goals of the members of the larger council. Whereas men like Rexed and Tiselius wanted to emphasize the life sciences and medicine as appropriate goals for Sweden, Hannes Alfven (later a Nobel laureate) was determined to push sciences that turned out to be too big for Sweden, such as astrophysics and astronomy. As a consequence of this endeavor and his opposition to the ill-fated Marviken nuclear reactor project, Alfven found himself commuting between California and Moscow, while the expansion in medicine continued. Those scientists who believed that a science policy directed by the council could be worked out soon became disillusioned.

In a sense, SAC quickly found its tasks, fulfilled them, and became—through the passage of time—obsolete. The main theme in 1965 through 1967 was the support of industrial R&D and the modernization of Swedish industry. Whereas business itself had already embarked upon this process, the debate in SAC made the choices explicit also to the government members and helped to familiarize the scientists with facts of commercial life. Out of the debate came the new "active industrial policy" which, as we shall see, failed.

But other problems existed. If the task of SAC was to centralize science policy, the logical action would be the appointment of a responsible minister, as in France and Britain. In fact, an effort was made in 1965 by Rexed to coordinate more power in the prime minister's office, but it was foiled by the resistance of other science bureaucrats. Despite the efforts of the executive committee, it quickly became obvious how hard it is to overcome the bureaucratic routine. The sponsoring of projects across traditional departmental lines became almost impossible. As a consequence, SAC became most effective in the department it controlled the most—the Department of Education in charge of the universities and the science council funds.

The most powerful reason behind the decline of SAC was inherent in politics generally. As the first enthusiasm for science policy as such evaporated, traditional politics reasserted itself. Gradually, Sweden set the international trend not to look upon science policy as something sui generis, but rather as a tool in the service of other policies.[10] As it became obvious that the nation's large development projects were funded through conventional funds, science as a means rather than as an end emerged. It became clear that the main Swedish effort had been within the realm of big science—defense and atomic energy.

## ADVANCED TECHNOLOGIES AND BIG SCIENCE

A comparison of government R&D expenditures in three European countries during the 1960s gives the result shown in Table 6.1.[11]

How do we explain these expenditures by a country traditionally believed to be a model welfare state with no aspirations beyond its borders?[12]

### Defense

The armed neutrality of Sweden in combination with the defense industry established during World War II explains the difference of magnitude between the Swedish and the Dutch efforts: two economies of equal size. The success of the investment was accentuated in the 1960s by the development of the largest project in the history of the nation—the multipurpose combat aircraft 37 Viggen by SAAB and the Swedish aircraft industry. For a period during the 1960s, Viggen absorbed about 50 percent of all defense R&D funds and thus more than 10 percent of all Swedish R&D funds—an Apollo project by Swedish standards.[13] Through the 1960s, Viggen and other military projects such as the electronic battle control system STRIL 60, the

175

TABLE 6.1

Percent of Government R&D Funds Allocated to Big Science

| | Defense, Atomic Energy, and Space | | | Defense Only | | |
|---|---|---|---|---|---|---|
| | France | Sweden | Germany | France | Sweden | Germany |
| 1961 | 70 | 70 | 38 | 40 | 47 | 22 |
| 1962 | 69 | 68 | 35 | 38 | 46 | 18 |
| 1963 | 66 | 70 | 38 | 36 | 46 | 21 |
| 1964 | 64 | 65 | 41 | 36 | 44 | 20 |
| 1965 | 65 | 62 | 39 | 40 | 44 | 20 |
| 1966 | 66 | 60 | 39 | 40 | 44 | 19 |
| 1967 | 61 | 58 | 45 | 35 | 44 | 20 |
| 1968 | 55 | 54 | 44 | 30 | 39 | 20 |
| 1969 | 56 | 41 | 42 | 31 | 31 | 19 |
| Average for 1961-68 | 64.5 | 63.5 | 41 | 37 | 44.5 | 20 |

Note: During most of the 1960s, Sweden devoted proportionally as much government funds to R&D supporting high politics as did the France which under de Gaulle aspired to great power status. The country devoted proportionally 50 percent more than Germany. Whereas about 50 percent of the French and German big science efforts went into defense, two-thirds of the Swedish funds did. The Swedish defense and atomic energy expenditures were substantial even in total.

Bofors battle tank S, the coastal defense missile robot 08, and the Navy submarine Sjoormen kept the expenditure up. [14] In the first half of the 1970s, the $200 million development of the engine of the Viggen interceptor version was the major expenditure.

Atomic Energy

Atomic energy provides a good example of how a small state (relying on Gilpin's second strategy)[15] can show considerable flexibility due to an alert business community. The Swedish atomic energy program, like that of the great powers, was from the beginning conceived in terms of military needs. In 1947, a joint government-business corporation, AB Atomenergi, was formed to direct the Swedish efforts. Stimulated by the U.N. conference on peaceful uses of atomic energy (Geneva, 1955), the Swedish plans were formulated. While the debate on Swedish nuclear weapons was under way (to be discontinued for a mixture of financial and moralistic reasons in 1959), the government played it safe and cast its 1956 plans in terms of energy

176

consumption and support of heavy industry in the face of future international competition. A Swedish line was chosen, relying on a natural uranium heavy water concept and based on Sweden's extensive resources of uranium—a dual-purpose reactor for both civilian and military uses. In 1956, an agreement was concluded on peaceful nuclear cooperation with the United States, including the import of enriched American uranium. A decision to develop a heavy water reactor at Marviken in 1959 led to a $100 million investment before its cancellation in 1970—the learning money paid by the Swedish government. [16] In 1963, business urged AB Atomenergi to move from the Swedish line to the enriched uranium, light-water reactors developed in the United States. By 1966, an agreement was concluded with America on the delivery of enriched uranium over the next thirty-year period, abandoning the heavy water strategy at a relatively early and inexpensive time in the game. [17] Two years later, government—realizing that it had little choice—nationalized AB Atomenergi and gave it a pure research function, while the commercial development was given to a new corporation, Aseaatom, jointly owned by the government and the traditional power corporation ASEA of the Wallenberg group. [18] By 1974, Aseaatom placed orders for seven Swedish reactors valued at several hundred million dollars. [19] With an R&D investment of 400 million, Sweden will emerge in the 1970s as the seventh or eighth energy power in the world with its first commercial reactor at Oskarishamn (constructed by ASEA) going into operation in 1971. Whether the reactors will be competitive on the international market is another question. So far only two have been sold, to Finland.

Defense and atomic energy, then, are outstanding examples of sectors never under the purview of the Science Advisory Council. In atomic energy, only the relatively small sums dedicated to university research ($4 million) and Sweden's participation in CERN

TABLE 6.2

Government R&D Expenditure, 1961-69
(Million 1960 U.S. dollars)

| | Defense | Times Sweden | | Atomic Energy | Times Sweden |
|---|---|---|---|---|---|
| U.K. | 5,500 | 9 | France | 2,100 | 8+ |
| France | 3,500 | 6 | U.K. | 1,350 | 5+ |
| Germany | 1,400 | 2+ | Germany | 1,150 | 5- |
| Sweden | 600 | | Canada | 460 | 2- |
| Canada | 480 | 4/5 | Sweden | 250 | |
| Netherlands | 50 | 1/12 | Japan | 180 | 2/3 |
| | | | Netherlands | 125 | 1/2 |

($ 8 million) are distributed via the Atomic Science Council; that is the Department of Education. What happened to the other sectors?

## A SECTORAL APPROACH TO SCIENCE AND TECHNOLOGY

A comparison between the government R& D expenditures of Sweden and the Netherlands at the beginning and the end of the 1960s reveals the Swedish trend. [20]

While Sweden still spends a much larger share on defense than the other country, Sweden's support of the technological basis of general industrial research and general services and education has moved towards the international norm during the 1960s. The most important factor in this development is the gradual acceptance of "sectoral thinking" in the support of science and technology.

Because R& D funds are allocated under departmental budgets, those sectors that have a natural base in a specific department have naturally been favored. Whereas defense technologies are well defined under the Defense Department, atomic energy has found an outlet in the energy sector. Simultaneously, the Department of Agriculture has found its Phoenix in the environmental issue, first raised by Rexed in SAC papers as early as 1964. The social sciences have a safe base in the welfare budget, as have medical science and housing research. In contrast, the Swedish space effort has never commanded more than 1 percent of the R& D budget. Simultaneously, Swedish industrial support for data systems has hovered at less than $ 1 million a year, which means that the main support of the Swedish computer industry has been channeled via the Defense Department funding the Viggen central digital computer.

The phenomenon of the sectoral thinking has made it more difficult to support technologies with many users or where the political power is split and fragmented. The most unlikely yet interesting field is the field of medical technology which, contrary to original expectations, has not become a success. The Swedish hospitals are controlled by the counties, or landsting, and each county anxiously guards its own budget, procuring the equipment that its own specialists (doctors) recommend. In addition, the invisible landsting party is one of the strongest pressure groups in Parliament, due to the fact that the leading bureaucrat in each of the 23 counties often is an M. P. In Parliament, the landsting politicians are thus able to fight any government reform of, say, centralization of medical equipment procurement.

The sectoral thinking has yet an additional drawback. Small nations like Sweden generally need one "R& D carrier" in each decade, that is, a big project that brings with it large R& D funds and thus is able to create spin off effects in the fields of technology and, above all, management. Throughout the 1960s, Viggen was such a

TABLE 6.3

Comparison Between Sweden and the Netherlands of
Government R&D Expenditures in percents

|  | 1961 | | 1969 | |
|---|---|---|---|---|
|  | Sweden | Netherlands | Sweden | Netherlands |
| Big Science | 74 | 16 | 41 | 19 |
| Economic | | | | |
| Development | 7 | 23 | 17 | 18 |
| General Welfare | 5 | 10 | 11 | 9 |
| Advancement of | | | | |
| R&D, Little | | | | |
| Science | 14 | 51 | 31 | 54 |

carrier. The problem now is that there is no project on the same
scale to take Viggen's place.

As a result, efforts are under way to create public markets for
technology and to coordinate the procurement of advanced technological
goods. So far, as the medical sector shows, the results are frustrating.

On the educational side, a slightly different sectoral approach
will meet greater success. The theme of the proposed future university
system, U 68, is division into five broad sectors: technical, administrative and economic, welfare, education, culture and information. [21]

Sectoral thinking is a major reason why SAC never achieved a
comprehensive science policy. If every sector takes care of its own
needs, what role is left for a general staff? Thus, the science council
was not the tool used for government intervention in the two structures
of technology and science. [22] Instead, the two chosen instruments
were the departments of industry and education. Let us investigate
why, from the government's point of view, the intervention in technology through the Department of Industry at first ended in failure
while the intervention in education was successful. Let us also
explore why the educational success of the government is deplored
by the technological structure of the nation.


INTERVENTION IN TECHNOLOGY: THE ACTIVE INDUSTRIAL POLICY


By 1967, when two-thirds of the nation's 25,000 R&D employees
were working in industry, it was becoming obvious that the big R&D
defense expenditure caused by Viggen would begin to taper off at the
end of the decade. This was, however, not the main reason behind
the government's new interest in an "active industrial policy." Rather,
the British Labour party experiments of 1965-66 seem to have been the

179

initiator. In 1967, a section of the Department of Commerce under the newly appointed cabinet minister Krister Wickman, took charge of the policy. A government investment bank was created, followed by a government R&D corporation SU modeled on the Wallenberg incentive corporation. In 1969, a Department of Industry was formed under Wickman, with a special undersecretary in charge of a conglomeration of government enterprises, AB Statsforetag. At the same time, the old Technical Research Council, together with a couple of other research funds were integrated into a Board for Technical Development and given greater resources than before. The industrial research associations receiving government money (9 out of 30) were also put under the leadership of the new board. Ambitious plans abounded. Unfortunately, the government support of technical R&D became thus entangled with government expansionism in the field of industrial enterprise.

Through a mixture of incompetence and politics, the activities of AB Statsforetag seemed (after three years) in shambles. [23] After a period of upheaval, a new management team stabilized the activities of the corporate group, now it is not much different from the corporations in the private sector; meanwhile, no one mentions "the new industrial policy." The outcome of the government technological drive is still uncertain. In a way, this was almost unavoidable from the beginning. The Technical Development Board has been forced to represent exactly the technologies and the general technical R&D that has no sector to catch on to. Of course, this could have been seen as a challenge, but bureaucratization and routine has so far taken its natural course. Every year, routine grants are doled out in small portions to a thousand small projects carried out by industry, the industrial branch research organizations, and the institutes of technology. Grantsmanship has turned into a lottery: the paperwork involved in applying for, evaluating, supporting, and studying research projects is becoming enormous. As usual, developing new fields through bureaucratic ukase has turned out to be impossible, especially if it takes at least $20 million a year to achieve significant results and the board only commands 10 percent of that amount for each field. In 1974, the head of the Technical Development Board, Professor Agdur, who had wished to reform it along the lines of the French ANVAR foundation, resigned due to his disagreement with the detailed supervision by the Department of Industry.


INTERVENTION IN EDUCATION: UNIVERSITY REFORM


In no area has the tension between utopia and reality emerged as strongly as in the area of higher Swedish education. One generation ago, Joseph Schumpeter shrewdly pointed out that one of the reasons why Swedish social democracy was so eminently sensible and prag-

180

matic was the fact that all university graduates were absorbed into the power apparatus and you thus got no unemployed discontented intellectuals as on the European continent. [24] Whatever the present Swedish planners of higher education have read, Schumpeter it is not.

Throughout the 1950s, the government paved the way for the war baby boom through high school, and in the 1960s the universities were bound to follow. In 1960, there was one university student for every 230 inhabitants in Sweden compared to one for every 505 in Britain. [25] In 1960, it was planned that the 30,000 students of 1960 would increase to 55,000 in 1970. [26] Three years later the estimate was up to 88,000. [27] In 1972, the figure was around 120,000: more than twice as many as envisaged a decade ago and 1.5 percent of the total population. [28]

The expansion of the system was prepared by royal commission studies beginning in 1955. By 1964, almost all power had been assembled at the Chancellor's Collegium (Universitets-konslersambetet—UKA), which, through its central bureaucracy and its faculty councils, makes all crucial decisions concerning higher education in Sweden. At the same time this development has effectively broken the power of the professors who relied on the original chair system, it has created exactly the tensions foreseen by Schumpeter. Let us first summarize the reforms and then trace the sources of discontent both on the part of the students, the faculty, and the consumers—that is, society at large.

In brief, Swedish reform is introducing an American-type university system without the latter's differentiation. The distinction is crucial. Through its size, resources, and flexibility, the American system is able to combine mass education and excellence, simply through the method of maintaining a wide variety of private and public institutions, from Harvard to South West Texas State Teachers College. Sweden, which has neither the size nor the flexibility, has introduced a system for mass education, rigorously ruled from the UKA, equally allocated funds from Stockholm, that achieves mass education but simultaneously loses quality. The result is essentially a welfare scheme, and as in all such schemes formality and bureaucracy have taken precedence over excellence. The combined result is an unfortunate misalliance of formal strictness and real sloppiness. Of course, some inertia of excellence has remained in traditional fields such as medicine, technology, and the natural sciences, not least because medicine and technology still have restricted intake and attract some of the best students. Even in these fields, however, complaints come from the older professionals. On the whole, everyone but the representatives of the UKA are at the present time unhappy. Some of the reasons are explored in the following pages.

The students' source of discontent is the most predictable one. Until recently, Sweden was a country of farmers, and the man of learning was symbolized by the clergy and, on a higher level, the doctor, the two traditional generational stepping stones in the Swedish circulation of classes. As late as a decade ago, to be an akademiker was a sign of respectability and social elevation. An akademiker was anyone with an academic degree from the high school teacher to the professor. When the government in the 1960s promised the children of blue- and white-collar workers and farmers that they too would study, the children drew the wrong conclusions. They believed that if you only passed your studentexamen (which has been abandoned) you could enter the university, get your degree, and settle into your new role as high school teacher or civil servant. What the government had given was, of course, a guarantee of the chance to enter the university, not to finish it and, still less, to obtain a respected and secure job afterwards. As a consequence, a student form of Luddism has emerged: protest actions against the weeding-out of poor students at the universities, actions against individual professors, and demands for participation in the decision-making process. As the number of students expanded, the undergraduate study reform PUKAS was introduced: similar to the American fixed, three-year period of study, with obligatory exams during and at the end of each term.

The Swedish student minirevolt in May 1968 thus followed the international pattern of international student unrest. In Sweden, the revolt was not caused by legitimate grievances over study conditions (as at the Sorbonne), foreign wars (as in the United States), or political oppression (as in Czechoslovakia and certain Latin American countries). It was largely a protest against the new demands of the government that the students from now on would be forced to study at a certain pace and with a specific goal in mind. It was the revolt of an essentially new petit bourgeois student body against an unfamiliar and, by Swedish standards, hostile environment.[29]

By now, the grievances have found a new and better rationale. The Swedish educational and social structure has simply not been able to accommodate all the new university graduates. According to some estimates, up to 4,000 students are out of work and continue their university studies beyond the B.A. level simply because they cannot get a satisfactory job. Because the expectations were still the old ones, the disillusion of many has been profound. At the same time, blue-collar jobs are being degraded as unworthy and debasing by the New Left. In fact, the reforms might have effects quite opposite to what the visionaries at the UKA had imagined. If a university degree becomes a necessary but not sufficient condition for a qualified job, where is a prospective employer to look for guidance? In a society only one generation removed from an essentially feudal career system shot through with a creed of "la carriere ouverte aux talents" a natural impulse might be to fall back on old boys networks—possibly with less upward mobility as a result. Who can spot a talent if everyone has the same grade?

The faculties are unhappy for other reasons. The centralization of power in the UKA has deprived the professors of their traditional dictatorial powers. Competition for research funds and increased bureaucratization has made life harder. Above all, the introduction of mass education, without the establishment of a hierarchy among the institutions of learning has led to lower standards imposed by a UKA for which "the flow of students" is the main criterion. Where three years of study were necessary, two are now sufficient—more efficient teaching is not the reason for the time reduction. Whereas formerly official accounting estimated that 50 percent of the universities' time was devoted to teaching and 50 percent to research, the new guide line is now 70-30 percent. At the same time, most of the teaching has been taken over by teaching assistants. As a consequence, several professors in fields where such steps can be taken have moved from the universities and institutes of technology to the private sector— to big business that offers freer working conditions, more travel, less bureaucracy, greater funds, and an absence of dull students.

Society, finally, has responded with mixed reactions. Several corporations have found it necessary to give new engineers on-the-job training for a period of time before they can handle the work that the older engineers took on immediately. In the graduate programs, the consequences cannot yet be evaluated. The recent switch from the old licentiat and doctorate system to an American type of Ph.D., four years after college, is attractive on paper. Again, the resources have, alas, not matched the intentions. The new program assumed that only the best students would go on, and that they would be given rigorous and personal training during the whole period. In fact, the practice has varied from one place and subject to another. In the American model the quality and significance of the Ph.D. varies, of course. In an extraordinary homogenous Sweden, the Ph.D. will resemble that from a good American state university, without that extra edge so necessary in international competition. [30]

## POLARIZATION?

The main problem with the present situation in Sweden is that the Palme government is interested in education rather than science. The vast expansion of the university system has taxed the teaching resources of the faculties. The new fiscal restraint has stopped the reform half way. As a consequence, research has suffered at the expense of teaching. The expansion is paralleled by a totally unprecedented drive in adult education at all levels—vocational, high school, and college. The insight that there is a lost generation of those between the ages of thirty and fifty who did not receive the benefit of higher education is obvious to the present government. In a blend of liberalism and social democracy, the new equality is to be achieved through the education of the workers—the Fabian impulse becomes policy when the Fabians have the government machinery at their instant command. [31]

These beliefs clash not only with the elitist notions of the few conservatives left in the country, of whom the professors have more than their share, but also with some of the liberal views of the business community. While the government Fabians build their beautiful domestic utopia, achieving mass education, equality, and justice within the country, industry feels the threat from international competition, an area where the only substitute for quality is politics. More dependent on the achievements of Swedish R&D capability than ever, the business community sees Sweden slipping and, in some areas, even falling behind. At the same time, the international trend against science as such has not left Sweden untouched. While most often the trend has taken the humane direction from the natural to the social sciences, from a blind enthusiasm over progress to a more fundamental questioning of what progress is all about, its less attractive consequences are painfully obvious in the meager literature on Swedish science policy. The only relatively comprehensive studies so far are three: two Marxist conspiracy-oriented studies depicting Sweden as a corporate state (and the U.S. as a country well in the hands of the fascist military-industrial complex), [32] and another published by a science policy panel appointed by TCO, the main federation of Swedish white-collar workers. [33] The latter publication gives us several clues to the present antiscience mood in the country, bordering on antiintellectualism.

Among the recommendations found in the TCO report are the separation of research and higher education, the creation of positions of exclusive teaching at the universities, the emphasis on "ability to cooperate" when appointing new professors, the belief that to stimulate crossfertilization all Ph.D. theses should be team efforts, and a full-scale attack on the successful part of the business community for their endeavors in R&D. [34] Especially harsh is the study on a report by the Engineering Academy, proposing a Swedish Institute for Futurology, funded jointly by government and business. The TCO study takes particular offense at the technology-oriented BNP maximizing approach of the report and its "Americanized" methods. "What is good for General Motors is not necessarily good for Sweden," lectures TCO. [35]

Even if the TCO study only caught a few straws in the wind, its temper seems to have been correct. On the educational side, the arguments of the UKA committees expanding the university reform (U 68) have a similar thrust. In U 68, an 828-page royal commission report drafted by three directors general and the undersecretary in the Ministry of Education, management terms abound. [36] The country is

184

to be divided into six hogskole (university) regions, and higher education fragmented to nineteen different places. Each region is to be endowned with a board made up of six representatives of society (politicians), two representatives of education and, "in forthcoming cases," research, one representative of the nonteaching staff, one student representative, and the managing director of the regional unit. In fact, a superficial examination of the report does not make it crystal clear whether one is dealing with students or, possibly, groceries. The violent reaction of all university staffs against the bureaucratic and parochial system the report envisages will most likely lead to substantial modifications in the final design of the future Swedish university system.[37]

Thus the Department of Education captured the university system whereas industry captured the Department of Industry. Why did the outcome of the battles differ? The answer lies in the terms countervailing power, sanctions, and personalities.

Obviously, the powerful industrial establishment had more resources and subtlety than the university system, the arguments of which always could be dismissed as "academic." The market mechanism provided the new industrial policy with more sanctions than U 68. If you fail in industry you have unemployment, and unemployment hurts politically. If your educational standards go down, it does not show for several years; the drawbacks are not tangible. Finally, and characteristically, the three cabinet members in charge of the new educational and industrial policy in the beginning were social democrats with little experience outside the government offices— Carlsson, Moberg, and Wickman. When the new industrial policy failed, the Department of Industry was taken over by Rune Johansson from the pragmatic, old-fashioned, nonacademic section of the party.

In early 1969, the Science Advisory Committee was reorganized. Twenty instead of thirty-two men were to become members, leaving Brohult and later the new president of the Engineering Academy, Professor Hambreaus, as the sole representatives of industry in the new council. More social scientists were included, marking the new emphasis on the consequences of science and technology. Almost all new members were social democrats. While Rexed remained as a member of SAC, he relinquished the post of secretary to another professor of medicine, Arne Engstrom.

Even so, SAC is bound to produce more heat than light, more discussion papers than results. The resources at its command are small compared to those available to big business and the treasury. By definition, SAC can do little about the problem that lies at the heart of the matter—the problem of Sweden's participation in Europe.

185

INTERNATIONAL INTEGRATION AND SWEDISH SCIENCE POLICY

While the new Science Advisory Council has been preoccupied with solving science priority problems, the international technological problems have made themselves felt. On March 18, 1971, the government announced that Sweden—for reasons of neutrality—could not and did not intend to become a full member of the European Common Market. The trade agreement given Sweden in the negotiations is described as insufficient by a unanimous industrial community. With Britain and Denmark as full members, 50 percent of Sweden's trade is with the enlarged European community. Even before the government announcement, the export industry was facing an uncertain future. There are more unsolved problems than ever in the period ahead. At the same time, the hard economic climate of the 1970s makes it imperative to rely on government R&D funds where earlier the banks or self-financing would do the job. These concerns have been amply mirrored by recent acts and statements.

Most important, business has declared that no matter what the policy of the government, it is going to concentrate its future expansion inside the Common Market, whether Sweden is a member, an associate, or neither. In 1972, SKF sold 93 percent of its production abroad; Atlas Copco, 88 percent; Sandvik, 88 percent; Alfa Laval, 84 percent; LME, 81 percent; Swedish Match, 69 percent; Electrolux, 69 percent; and Volvo, 70 percent.[38] Earlier, Sweden lost licensing agreements to American and Japanese firms covering all of Europe, because of the uncertainty over the market issue. In a spectacular but practical move, the Swedish-based multinational corporation SKF decided to relocate an R&D center to Holland.

Initially, the consequences of Sweden going it alone were felt rather lightly, mainly because Brussels failed in establishing a coordinated R&D policy. Over the long range, the Swedish prospects are dimmer. At the same time, a new imbalance is emerging in Swedish science policy. During the happy 1960s when everyone was on the Science Advisory Council, the council spoke for the nation. In the 1970s, it was mainly speaking for the government.

In 1972, a blue ribbon panel presented a report which led to the establishment of a four-man Secretariat for Futures Studies within the prime minister's office.[39] As expected, the report stressed the importance of a social perspective on the future, making the distinction between the clear-cut goals pursued by the large Swedish corporations and the more diffuse goals preferred by the government. Still, at that time, the public imbalance was really the other way around. The government has its secretariat, while the industry speaks with many tongues. No pole of counterpower has been established to the heavy influence of the Department of Education. A technology relying on a second-rate domestic base will end up living on borrowed time — and exhaust that too.

186

The politicization and integration of European technology will undoubtedly raise obstacles in Sweden's path. More and more states will be buying technology from themselves: huge projects will forever be lost for the corporation or country that is unable to participate in such planning at a very early stage. If Sweden is losing the battle of quality at a time when her traditional natural resources of iron ore, wood, and hydroelectric power are becoming irrelevant, then the traditional advantage of staying on the outskirts of European politics will indeed turn into a competitive disadvantage. If so, not even the most brilliant science policy can reestablish the balance.

## NOTES

1. Robert Gilpin, France in the Age of the Scientific State (Princeton: Princeton University Press, 1968), p. 21.

2. Sven Anders Soderpalm, Storforetagarna och det demokratiska genombrottet [Big Business and the Breakthrough of Democracy] (Lund: Gleerups, 1969).

3. Olle Gasslander, History of Stockholms Enskilda Bank to 1914 (Stockholm, 1962). The bank merged with Skandinaviska Banken in 1972.

4. Joseph Schumpeter, Theorie der Wirtschaftlichen Entwicklung (Vienna: Duncker An Humblot, 1912).

5. Svensk Industri, Industrins forsknings-och utvecklingsverksam-het. Delrapport fran industristrukturutredningen [Swedish Industry. R&D in Industry. Report from the Industrial Structure Committee] (Stockholm, 1974).

6. For a comparison with the United States, see Carl Kaysen, "Improving the Efficiency of Military Research and Development" in Public Policy, vol. XII, 1963.

7. OECD, Scientific Policy in Sweden (Paris, 1963), p. 18. In 1971, Sweden spent about $500 million, 1.5 percent of the GNP. About 50 percent was still paid by the government but two-thirds was performed by industry.

8. In 1963, the economist Ingvar Svennilson predicted that the Swedish R&D expenditure in 1973 would be $640 million, 2.9 percent of the GNP in 1973. In 1972, the figure in 1963 prices was about $400 million, 1.5 percent of the GNP. Ingvar Svennilson, Utveckling-sperspektiv for svensk forskning [Perspectives for Swedish Research], Science Advisory Council, June 15, 1963.

9. Forskning och utveckling. Rapport fran TCO's forskningsdele-gation [Research and Development. Report by the Research Study of the TCO. (TCO=Tjanstemannens Centralorganisation--Central Organi-zation of the Tjansteman white-collar workers.)] (Stockholm, 1970), p. 37.

10. The first ideas were formulated by a young political scientist; Sverker Gustavsson: "Forskning och politik" [Research and Politics], (Tiden, No. 3, 1966), followed by two articles by the President of the Federation of Swedish Industry, Axel Inveroth, "Malmedveted forskningspolitik" [Goal-oriented Research Policy] (Industriforbundets Tidskrift, March 1967), and "Staten industrin ochforskningen" [Government, Industry and Research] (Industriforbundets Tidskrift, April 1967). Gustavsson specifically criticizes "the science policy phraseology peddled by the OECD Science Policy Research Unit" (Tiden, No. 3, 1966): 152).

11. OECD Document SP(71) 10 (OECD: Paris, 1971) Annex, pp. 81, 106, 171.

12. Ibid., pp. 80, 170.

13. Ingemar Dorfer, System 37 Viggen: Arms, Technology and the Domestication of Glory (Oslo: Oslo University Press, 1973).

14. In FY 1961 through FY 1970, an average 9.4 percent of the Swedish military expenditure went to R&D. The corresponding figures in other countries were: USA 13.1 percent, Britain 12.7 percent, France 8.9 percent, and Germany 3.7 percent (Ibid., p. 44).

15. To select specific areas in science and technology which are important for the future development of national and industrial strength and concentrate R&D resources in these areas (Gilpin, op. cit., p. 147).

16. See Hannes Alfven, "Science, Technocracy and the Politico-Economic Power," Impact of Science on Society, no. 22 (January-June 1972): 85-93.

17. Svensk atomenergipolitik, Industridepartementet [Swedish Atomic Energy Policy, Department of Industry,] (Stockholm, 1970), p. 6.

18. In 1971, a Swedish electronics corporation was formed based on the same model—STANSAAB ELEKTRONIK AB, jointly owned by SAAB, the ITT group, and the Swedish Government Development Corporation, SU. In 1973, ITT left the partnership, which now is equally divided between SAAB and SU.

19. Westinghouse has been given the order for three reactors.

20. Based on figures in OECD Document SP(71) 10, op. cit.

21. SOU 1973: 2 Hogskolan SOU-Statens Offentliga Utredningar—Royal Commission Studies, published in consecutive order. SOU 1973: 2 is study number 2 for the year 1973. Higher Education] p. 45.

22. The important exception is military R&D. The conclusions of an investigation chaired by the new Science Advisory Council Secretary, Professor Engstrom, called for a coordination and centralization of the Swedish military R&D effort. (SOU 1970: 54, Forskning inom forsvars-sedtorn) [Research Within the Defense Sector]. Yet this is exactly the field where coordination has been rather good also in the past.

23. Items: Kalmar Verkstad developed a truck that they could not sell. The company was liquidated and its facilities taken over by

Volvo. SMT was to expand in the field of advanced machinery. When no market developed, 50 percent of the personnel were fired in 1972.

24. Joseph Schumpeter, Capitalism, Socialism and Democracy (New York: Harper Bros., 1950), p. 325. Note the British parallel in higher education and socialism.

25. Scientific Policy in Sweden, p. 14.

26. Ibid., p. 47.

27. Ibid., p. 14.

28. Eventually the market mechanism asserted itself. Between FY 1973 and FY 1974 the total number of students decreased by 8 percent, in the humanities by 20 percent.

29. In Stockholm, a few hundred students occupied their own student union. In most mass media this was considered bold. This is not surprising. Whereas Schumpeter's unemployed French intellectuals spent their time debating each other, some of Sweden's new surplus university graduates are addressing the public through the state monopoly radio and television. More specifically, they address and find a sounding board among the surplus students that came after them and did not find jobs, even in the mass media.

30. Under the old system, the doctoral thesis in the social sciences and humanities was all too often a proof of tenacity and effort rather than scientific brilliance. The new system will, it is hoped, weed out the less gifted scholar faster. A translation appeared in 1974, To Choose a Future (Royal Ministry of Foreign Affairs, Stockholm)

31. Who participates in adult education courses? Not the worker but the middle-class house-wife.

32. Ronny Ambjornsson, et. al., Forskning och politik i Sverige, Sovjet och USA [Research and Politics in Sweden, the Soviet Union and the United States] (Stockholm: Aldus Bonniers, 1969; Jan Annerstedt, Makten over forskningen [The Power Over Research] (Lund: Zenit, 1972).

33. Forskning och utveckling op. cit.

34. "It is untolerable", says the report "that SU has not been given the same opportunities as Incentive."

35. Ibid., p. 153. Try that statement again, substituting Volvo for GM.

36. SOU 1973: 2, Hogskolan, op. cit. The reaction is summarized in Hogskolan i framtiden. UKAs yttrande over U68s huvudbetankande "Hogskolan", Bilaga 2 [Higher Education in the Future. Comment by the Chancellor's Collegium on the Main Report of U68s, "Higher Education," appendix Z. ] (Stockholm: Universitetskanslersambetet, February 1974).

37. See, for instance, Torgny T. Segerstedt, Hotet mot den hogre utbildningen [The Threat to Higher Education] (Boras: Askild & Karnekull 1974), by the president of Uppsala University.

189

38. Veckans Affarer [Business Week] (August 2, 1973): 110.

39. SOU 1972: 59 Att valja framtid. A translation appeared in 1974, To Choose a Future (Royal Ministry of Foreigh Affairs, Stockholm). In fiscal 1975 almost a million dollars is allocated to pilot projects in "futures studies." A parliamentary contact group is to be formed deemphasizing the image of the secretariat as a government staff.

CHAPTER

# 7

## UNITED STATES
## SCIENCE POLICY
## IN TRANSITION
Jurgen Schmandt

The intent of this chapter is to put the major policy issues identified in the previous chapters into a comparative frame, and for comparative purposes to reconsider science policy in the light of U. S.
experience. While no full-fledged additional country study is intended,
the reader may compare some of the events and trends discussed in the
chapters on the USSR, the United Kingdom, France, Japan, and Sweden
with the situation in the United States, the one country that has
seemed to be ahead in formulating and coming to terms with new
policy issues raised by advances in science and technology.

Science policy during the 1960s found its identity as a new
responsibility of government, largely at the cost of its instrumental
nature. To be sure, science policy was always viewed as a tool
which could contribute to the solution of a variety of policy issues,
ranging from defense to foreign aid and urban development. In reality,
however, a single model of the impact of science on society was
assumed. It was one based on the particular experience in military
and, in the United States, space matters where science and technology
had become a dominant innovative force. As a result, science policy
began to be viewed by other agencies of government as an autonomous
policy area to be turned to when more traditional means of resolving
issues seemed ineffective.

Such high expectations allowed the new mechanisms for national
science policy temporarily to support basic research and science
education, but they failed to contribute significantly to the solution
of the major policy issues of the decade, domestic or international.
When it became obvious, at least in the United States, that science
policy could not be expected to provide "easy"—that is, technical—
solutions to complex and controversial political issues, the mood
changed to one that was more critical of science and technology.
There is now a real possibility in some countries that a coalition of
antiscientific attitudes on the part of the radical Left and disillusion-

191

ment with science on the part of pragmatic politicians will hamper efforts aimed at using science and technology as effective policy tools.

## SCIENCE POLICY RECONSIDERED

A less ambitious and less olympian view of the role of science and technology in policymaking is now called for. Instead of searching for a general strategy for turning knowledge into action—an endeavor with both utopian and promethian overtones—knowledge and knowhow need to be related to the specific institutional settings and value systems of particular policy areas. The instrumental character of science and technology as forms of knowledge and knowhow needs to be adapted to particular circumstances, so that science policy can become a serious policy tool.

The objective of this chapter is to spell out some implications of such an approach to science policy. To set the stage, some basic assumptions underlying the development of science policy during the last decade need to be reviewed first. Were they rooted in a particular view of the social role of science and technology, or has the special experience of the war and postwar periods led us to believe in a dependence on modern society on science and technology which may, in fact, be less than universal? This is not to deny that science and technology have shaped, and will continue to shape, the world in which we live. But the deliberate planning and building of society through massive use of science and technology is an art that man has not yet mastered. Unforeseen results of his action are sometimes so important as to jeopardize seriously the progress embodied in the original design. The art of building the new world cannot be developed in a mechanical, universal, and single-minded way. Distinctions and qualifications, values and wisdom need to be introduced into the process. Science and technology must be looked upon less as independent variables and more as one or two among a large number of dependent variables.

Once this is accepted and translated into organizations and programs, science policy can be restructured around a limited number of major policy functions. Even at the risk of losing some of its recently acquired identity, science policy must be integrated into the process of planning, implementing, and evaluating major areas of policy, broadly conceived so that issues can be seen in their interaction with other problems.

192

# SOME ASSUMPTIONS OF THE 1960s

Science policy, in the meaning with which we use the term today, came into its own during World War II. The experience gained in mobilizing science and technology for warfare constitutes the watershed separating the prehistory of science policy from its history, although science policy did not emerge in all of the warfaring nations. France left the war too early to be counted upon in this respect, and its deep-seated institutional divisions made it an unlikely candidate for developing the institutional alliances which are characteristic of modern science policy. Japan was fraught with competition between and among military and civilian participation on scientific research and policy matters. Germany, which is not the subject of a separate essay in this volume, was endowed with a rich tradition in the industrial utilization of science, but it failed to develop a science policy. Bureaucratic shortsightedness and Nazi arrogance contributed to viewing the task narrowly and urging scientists to develop miracle weapons. New weapons were indeed developed—the jet fighter and the guided missile. But such was the distrust between the leaders and the scientists that Germany's scientific potential was never successfully mobilized for the war effort.

Russia had geared its science and technology to the pursuit of national objectives from the time of the revolution onwards and as Loren Graham comments in his chapter on the Soviet Union, "consequently relatively few new principles needed to be established in order for political directives to flow throughout the scientific and technological establishment." In England and the United States, with traditional separations between action-oriented government agencies, centers devoted to learning and knowledge, and a private sector eager to translate new inventions into commercial growth and profits, the task of bringing such disparate institutions into the war effort seemed more difficult. But these countries managed to find new, flexible ways to mobilize science and technology for war. In the process they not only developed sophisticated new weapons in time to influence significantly the outcome of the war, but also invented administrative mechanisms which gradually established close working relations among government, industry, and the universities. These included such simple devices as the adjustment of the traditional government purchase contract to the purchase of university or industrial time and manpower—the R&D contract—permitting the scientist and engineer to work for the government while remaining in his normal institutional environment.

A new science advisory system introduced a small group of scientists—initially mostly physicists—into the government process of formulating and implementing decisions, and new management skills were developed for planning and executing large technological projects. Institutions such as national laboratories and "think tanks" were originated to concentrate research efforts in particular areas or to study issues of policy and strategy, thus providing government agencies with systematic and detached study capabilities. All this was energized by a new degree of mobility. Science advisors and administrators, though coming from different organizations, were concerned with the same issues and began to speak the same language.

These organizational, procedural, and behavioral innovations provided the foundations for modern science policy. They gave it institutional characteristics which, at least initially, were well suited to the special working needs of scientists and engineers and the knowledge requirements of government. While modified in many ways by national traditions and circumstances, the basic science policy mechanisms that were first created in England and the United States, were reproduced in many nations throughout the world during the 1950s and 1960s.

What was sought more or less successfully was the easy interchange of expertise, ideas, and people among government, industry, and universities in order to use the potential of science for policy objectives—an arrangement now widely criticized as the military-industrial-scientific complex. There is no question that the interpenetration of formerly separate institutions brought with it new issues of responsibility, accountability, and control. Critical observers— among them General Eisenhower in his well-known farewell address— pointed out dangers in the system long before the more broadly based attack on science and technology of the late 1960s forced the issue into the open.

Rather than emphasize the shortcomings of this system, it is necessary to understand it as highly imaginative and superbly successful response to a particular historical situation: science and technology had become so powerful that they could make a critical difference in responding to the challenges of national survival and world leadership. The union between government and independent institutions experienced in the production of knowledge and knowhow, organized in response to these challenges, represents the single most powerful and most visible effort of utilizing science and technology in the pursuit of major national goals. Despite talk about making use of science and technology for general welfare purposes, we still operate within the system of science and government relations created in response to the challenges of war and of international competition, accepting its basic philosophies and using its institutions and procedures.[1] The basic assumptions underlying science policy have been consistent during the last three decades in England and the United States, and since the late 1950s in other countries.

194

## Science Can and Does Determine Policy

The famous Einstein letter informing President Roosevelt of advances in nuclear physics and the possibility of developing an atomic bomb perfectly illustrates the new pattern of decisionmaking in national security matters which was to establish itself firmly in the years to come. The possibility of the new weapon was first conceived by a small group of scientists who themselves had been close to the theoretical work behind the new development. They were able to map out the path from scientific discovery to operational military hardware—the time and the resources needed.

The president's decision to go ahead was a policy determination responsive to the work and the vision of scientists—a group of people traditionally far removed from the shaping of public policy. The civilian bureaucracy and the military, unable to evaluate what was proposed, gambled on the advice of an apolitical group and entrusted members of this group with major responsibility for planning and implementing the project. The relationship that began to tie together government officials and scientists was one of trust and dependency. It worked well as long as the trust was not betrayed and the feeling of dependency did not become too great.

In the past, the options now provided by scientists had opened up gradually or as "miracles" that one could not plan for. Now, it appeared that radical changes in the power base of nations could be planned and brought about in the course of a few years through the combined powers of science and technology. This potential made of science and technology "master variables," relegating other variables, such as population, territory, quantity of natural resources, and training standards of the armed forces, into second rank. These others continued to be important, but only within a framework established by the "master variable."

The effects of this change for the policymaker were twofold. He found himself confronted with new policy issues which demanded his attention. Issues of military and domestic nuclear policy, space programs, communications satellites, weather modification, coal gasification—now figured on the decision agenda, where they had to be examined both for their intrinsic merit and their importance compared to other programs competing for limited public funds. Moreover, these additions to the policy agenda added an enormous degree of uncertainty and risk to the business of making decisions. While risk is inherent in all decisions, the situation is more difficult when the decisionmaker's crystal ball is less clear than that of his scientific advisor. Science and technology brought to professional administrators, diplomats, soldiers, and elected officials a new awareness of their own ignorance and uncertainty. These policymakers recovered their nerve only when they realized that the final decision remained theirs and had to be based on political considerations of which scientists knew as little as any other group. [2]

The experience has been likened to the realization of a baseball team that the boundaries of the playing field have been changed in the middle of the game. [3] To carry the analogy a step further, the boundaries were moved not by the players or the manager, but by the grounds keepers who suddenly became a major power factor. Based on this experience the first assumption of contemporary science policy is that science can—and to a considerable extent does—determine policy. In Robert C. Wood's words:

> It subtly shifts the emphasis of the persistent political question "Can we do this?" from the consideration of legal constraints to consideration of physical constraints. . . . The possession of technical know-how about physical matters gives the scientist direct initiative in proposing actions that are not available to other experts. [4]

### Scientists Make Policy

The prevailing assumption is that scientists increasingly find themselves in positions where more is asked from them than simply giving advice. They participate actively in the shaping of public decisions and, at times, even dominate this process. The experience in the war and the postwar periods of people like Vannevar Bush, James Conant, Karl Compton, or Robert Oppenheimer is the origin of this assumption. The benefits and risks of policy involvement on the part of presumably neutral and detached advisors were widely discussed during the 1960s, beginning with C.P. Snow's warnings against allowing a "scientific overlord" to usurp power at the apex of government. [5] Among those actively involved in shaping national science policies, the view prevailed that successful advice did indeed entail more than writing a report and returning to the laboratory.

In the U.K., Sir Henry Tizard's work contributed to a concept of science policy that emphasized the need for more than scientific discoveries and technical developments. Social innovations are also required to make use of technological advances: education, diffusion of information, logistics and maintenance, operational performance and changes in strategy, new administrative arrangements—all are part of the process of innovation. This broad view of scientific advice brought about a radical change in the way the British government conducted its business after the war. Prior to the war, a high government official pointedly expressed the traditional view that scientists had to be on tap, not on top: "It is against the rules of sound adminis-

196

trative practice to allow scientists to attend a meeting of higher officers. "[6] After the war, when Tizard was the principal science advisor to the government he "participated at the meetings of the Chiefs of Staff not only when he was specifically invited, but also when he himself thought that his presence might be useful. "[7]

A similar revolution in the ways in which advisors enter the policy process took place in the United States. But there as well very few advisors—I have called them "scientific statesmen"[8]—found themselves placed in positions where knowledge and action coalesced. Writing of the scientific advisory function, Harvey Brooks distinguishes five ways of providing scientific advice: (1) to analyze the technical aspects of major policy issues for policymakers, frequently with recommendations for decision or action, (2) to evaluate specific scientific or technological programs for the purpose of aiding budgetary decisions or providing advice on matters affecting public welfare or safety, (3) to study specific areas of science or technology for the purpose of identifying new opportunities for research or development in the public interest, or of developing coherent national scientific programs, (4) to advise on organizational matters affecting science, or a particular mission of an agency involving the use of science or scientific resources, (5) to advise on the selection of individual research proposals for support. [9] The borderline between advice and policymaking can become particularly blurred in the first category, where major decisions need to be made and where the vision, conviction, and perseverance of the scientific statesman can be instrumental in opening up a new policy alternative for his nonscientist colleagues in government. He may then indeed exercise more power than is ordinarily desirable for an advisor who is not accountable to the public. [10]

After a review of the British experience during World War II, C.P. Snow concluded in 1962: "If you are going to have a scientist in a position of isolated power, the only scientist among nonscientists, it is dangerous, whoever he is. . . . Whoever he is, whether he is the wisest scientist in the world, we must never tolerate a scientific overlord again. "[11] Until a new attitude of critical pessimism concerning science emerged, Snow's warning was ignored. The hope remained —though rarely openly expressed—that a top scientist could bring to the government a dimension of foresight and vision about policy that other mortals did not share.

Knowledge Institutions Will Become Dominant

The new preeminence of science and technology in public affairs is giving increased importance to those institutions which specialize in generating knowledge. The knowledge industry has become an important growth sector of the economy. Fritz Machlup, writing in 1962, found that the production of knowledge in the United States accounted for 29 percent of the national product, and was growing at about twice the rate of the rest of the economy. [12] By the late 1970s it is expected to represent over half of the total national product. [13]

The growth of universities has been a general trend in industrialized countries, partly due to the fact that a university education has become a prerequisite for attaining social status and qualifying for well-paying jobs. Universities have always had an important role as critical observer of political, social, and cultural developments. Now they are increasingly called upon to render direct services in defining and implementing national policy objectives. Clark Kerr put it this way: "The multiuniversity in America is perhaps best seen at work, adapting and growing, as it responded to the massive impact of federal programs beginning with World War II . . . . (The) university has become a prime instrument of national purpose."[14] Not-for-profit research organizations and think tanks of different kinds have mushroomed and play an important role as research, planning, and evaluative centers advisory to government.

During the 1960s it was widely assumed that knowledge institutions were developing into key instruments of social change and dynamic leadership in technologically advanced societies. They are viewed as agents of change and centers of power in the sense in which farms and industries played this role in the past. A society whose economy is based on advanced technology has an increasing demand for public rather than private decisionmaking. This leads to "the centrality of theoretical knowledge as the source of innovation and policy formulation in the society."[15]

The traditional classification of knowledge activities as part of the tertiary industries is outdated: ". . . knowledge has actually become the 'primary' industry, the industry that supplies to the economy the essential and central resource of production. . . . Knowledge is now the main cost, the main investment, the main product of the advanced economy and the livelihood of the largest group in the population."[16] It was an assumption of the 1960s that theoretical knowledge would become a dominant element in the process of policy formulation. Science policy mechanisms and approaches would advance this objective, permeating government with a new capability for change and innovation and ultimately rejuvenating the entire government apparatus.

Science Can Solve Social Problems

The success of science in revolutionizing national security policy and building, within a short time, a highly successful U. S. space program raised widespread expectations about using science and technology to alleviate a large number of economic and social ills. Over and over again, the "Apollo analogy" has been offered as a shortcut to social reform—to eradicate poverty and hunger, eliminate urban blight, reduce environmental damage, fight crime, and improve the international balance of payments. A combination of scientific and technical innovation and new management techniques would provide us with the weapons necessary to overcome whatever economic or social problem that we decided to attack—such was the optimistic assumption. A strategy of "technological fixes" or shortcuts" for the solution of social problems has been advanced on the grounds that technological solutions to social problems are often easier to effect than political or economic solutions. Such a strategy might not get to the roots of the problem, but it would alleviate pressures and allow us to "buy the time necessary to get at the cause of the social problem."[17]

This thinking was directly transposed into the political arena. President Johnson hoped that science and technology would play an important part in the war on poverty. When funds became scarce and the strategy of "maximum feasible participation" of the poor in program implementation resulted in conflicts with the mayors, the president maintained that new program solutions could be mapped out by relatively inexpensive investment in demonstration projects and related R&D activities.[18]

Soon after the SST project had been terminated by Congress, President Nixon entrused its former project director with a nationwide search for new national technological opportunities. In a message to Congress, Nixon expressed his hope that "the remarkable technology that took . . . Americans to the moon can also be applied to reaching our goals here on earth." The search was finally called off when Nixon and his advisers acknowledged

> that the context for stimulating technological innovation in the private sector is very different from that of the defense or space sectors, and that there were economic, political, legal, and institutional constraints—which pose significant obstacles to the President's often-repeated aim of "harnessing the wonders of science to the service of man."[19]

What was too easily forgotten was the emergency nature of the earlier projects, which not only allowed but demanded secrecy, custom-tailored institutional arrangements, hierarchically structured lines of authority, and nearly unlimited resources.

# THE ENVIRONMENT OF SCIENCE POLICY

As the four assumptions discussed above became the basis of science policy planning for the 1960s, it also became axiomatic that a modern government needed to have a central science policy office. An OECD report published in 1963 did its share to accelerate this thinking. It identified three tasks for such an office:

1. a national policy for science should be formulated;
2. the various scientific activities of the country should be coordinated;
3. there should be an integration of science with general policy. [20]

Since coordination is presumably more effective when exercised at a level of government higher than the agencies in need of coordination, it was only logical—and many countries followed this logic—to locate the science policy office at the level of the prime minister or the president. This, it was hoped, would carry with it the advantage of making available directly to the head of government advice concerning the contribution of science and technology to the solution of national problems.

This model of science policy planning and implementation, developed in the U.S. and U.K. during the 1960s, was conditioned by responses to the challenges of war and world leadership. It has tended to conceive of science as a relatively independent activity, capable of resolving major policy issues and functioning in the policy process at the very apex of government. The principal task at hand was seen as adjusting procedures, institutional arrangements, funding mechanisms, and action strategies which had first been improvised for large-scale programs concerned with radar, the atomic bomb, or the exploration of the moon to a much wider range of policy issues. It was rarely seen that new diversified mechanisms and strategies suited for linking knowledge to action in different policy areas might be required. The model succeeded in its original environment because technological innovations were accompanied by appropriate social innovations in the form of new institutions (like the wartime OSRD, or today's AEC and NASA), new management techniques, working patterns, and training programs. Tizard was successful because he had a broader view of innovation than the German leaders, who were only interested in new military hardware. What men like Tizard in England and Bush in the United States started, in time became a successful combination of scientific-technical innovation on the one hand and complementary social innovation on the other, capable of providing new solutions to urgent public needs.

But the success of yesterday can become a dangerously constraining factor tomorrow. This is what happened to science policy during the

200

1960s. At a time when it enjoyed considerable visibility as a new government responsibility, it operated with a serious built-in handicap. The unique situation of the war, when science had become a dominant variable in emergency conditions, was viewed as the general model for the science-society interaction. Insufficient attention was given to the social innovation which has to accompany technical innovation, and which is qualitatively different from one policy area to another. The wartime experience represents a particular strategy, not a universal one. It is not the only way to bring to bear on policy issues the problem-solving powers of science and technology. Better results can be expected from strategies for the utilization of science and technology which are developed in the context of specific policy issues, in which technical and social innovation are combined.

Science as an organized activity has existed for half a millennium, and technology became science-based more than a century ago. Although a comprehensive social history of science and technology, comparable in scope and detail to Arnold Hauser's Social History of Art, does not yet exist, [21] it is evident that social and technical change have always been intimately intertwined and that without understanding this process, science policy is in danger of operating from too narrow a base. Models for linking knowledge to social change and action can be found outside the primarily defense-oriented science policy effort of the 1950s and 1960s. They are needed to illustrate the process of change in its complexity, looking both at the scientific-technical components and at the economic, social, and political issues which may be at stake in any given policy area. Urban development identifies one problem horizon against which a problem-specific science policy effort needs to be defined.

Technology and Urban Form

Cities have always been highly versatile social organizations which, among other things, provide a favorable environment for technological advances. This is the case both with respect to the development of technology and its social utilization. Cities are built around a particular set of technological conditions. As technology changes, the functions, shape, and organization of cities change. This is a never-ending process, but there are times when the adjustment between technological and social conditions in the city is slow or delayed. Far-reaching changes in the technological conditions of urban life have not yet (or only insufficiently) led to a restructuring of the ways in which urban areas are developed, financed, and administered.

Conditions in the city core—traffic congestion, high residential density, soaring land cost, and pollution—have contributed to the mass

201

migration of manufacturers, retailers, and well-to-do residents to the suburbs. The central cities underwent little physical change to adapt to the new conditions, and little imagination or planning was addressed to the question of what should take the place of lost production and wealth. Meyer, Kain, and Wohl have concluded:

> The most serious problem of existing central business districts is that they were designed for an outdated set of technological conditions, the most serious single problem being an inadequate separation of truck, private vehicular, and pedestrian traffic. [22]

The modern large city was shaped by earlier advances in industrial and transportation technologies which put a premium on high density and central location. Today's city is no longer the beneficiary of technological change. It has been bypassed by the mainstream of technological innovation, both in its governance and in its physical dimension. The organization, management, and financial structure of central cities and their surrounding suburbs continues to be geared to an earlier set of technological and economic conditions. Technology has brought innumerable benefits to individual entrepreneurs and individual consumers. But citizens, politicians, and local governments have refused, by and large, to recognize or accept the implications of those structural changes for the governance of their cities. Social innovation has yet to catch up with technological innovation—a classic example of what William Ogburn called a "social lag."

We know well how to develop airports, highways, and telephone and electric power systems, but we do not really understand and are therefore unable to control the problems which arise when all these technologies operate simultaneously in a confined space. Technically and economically, city and suburb are one unit. But we do not have political mechanisms that are capable of developing urban areas as a unit. We are systematic about subsystems, but we do not have the political will, expertise, and institutions to be systematic about the system itself.

The shortcomings which cause these problems are not only gaps in knowledge. They go deeper and have to do with societal goals and values. But the knowledge component is important. Once it successfully combines hardware and systems-oriented knowledge, it can help in identifying action alternatives and their implications. To develop this knowledge component is the principal task for a science policy effort which is integrated into a national urban policy.

### The Agricultural Example

In introducing a broader view of innovation as the problem environment in which science policy has to operate, I have emphasized specifically the need for complementary attention to social as well as technical innovation. Science policy needs to consider both if it is to be successful. One condition for success which can be isolated fairly easily is the necessary institutional mechanism to translate knowledge into policy action. The centralized science policy effort of the 1960s gave little attention to this need.

Examples are found in a variety of domestic policy areas where institutional networks capable of combining knowledge-generating institutions with the tasks of instruction, diffusion of knowledge, technical assistance, and planning and implementation of action programs have been developed. Such examples include the improvement of public health standards, the development of municipal water and sewer systems or of the other public utilities, and—most recently—the construction of a nationwide, interstate highway system. In each case, a constellation of factors was needed to bring about movement from the old to a new state of affairs. The single most important factor, perhaps, is a goal and leadership in reaching it. A second factor is interest, which is closely related to people's values and goals. It can take many forms: fear of epidemics or of punishment, hope for personal profit, or commitment based on enthusiasm or idealism. Scientific and technical innovation plays a double role: it dramatizes the need for change by, for example, discovering the dangers of bacteria-infected water, and it can offer new solutions by inoculations against certain diseases. But there also needs to be a strong institutional actor prepared to identify with a cause, to lobby and fight for it.

The example of American science policy for agricultural improvement illustrates the institutional conditions for success. A century-long history of government promotion of research led to a diversified institutional system, linking federal, state, and county layers of government and creating a new type of research and educational institution, the land-grant colleges. While hardly comparable to the monolithic technological giants of NASA or the AEC, the Agricultural Research Service was instrumental in dramatically improving productivity and quality in American agriculture. It provides an early example of use of science and technology in a major domestic policy area, with particular benefits to an individual group and general benefits to the nation and the world.

Over the years, the work in the state experiment stations has led to results of outstanding scientific importance. The discovery of vitamins and of modern nutritional standards, as well as the development of streptomycin and dicoumarol represent well-known achievements. Assured financing—by means of a complicated allocation formula to each state and a superannuated institutional environment—have encouraged a good deal of marginal work. The fact remains, however, that for a period of several decades, a system of decentralized and diversified research institutions, supported and guided by the federal government, controlled locally, and integrated into teaching

203

institutions, proved highly successful in improving agricultural productivity by generating and applying scientific knowledge. Admittedly, the system served agriculture first and science second, exposing the land-grant institutions and their research activities to the acid criticism of academic scientists. Yet Eric A. Walker when president of the Pennsylvania State University remarked about relations between the federal government and American universities that:

> In casting around for models on which to base these arrangements we have almost completely overlooked the oldest active program of this sort in the country. Yet, ironically, it is probably the most successful of them all. I'm speaking here of the Federal support program for agricultural research. [23]

It is not intended to suggest the agricultural example as a general strategy for the integration of science in public policy. The fact that industrial cooperative research has not proved to be a vigorous factor of innovation was reaffirmed by a recent study of cooperative research associations in England. [24] Still, the experience of agricultural experiment stations in the United States seems to have been more productive and less marginal. To a certain extent, this was true with respect to the quality of scientific work, as measured by such criteria as number of publications and citation rates. Most important of all was the impact of agricultural research on farming in America. The research stations have been successful as agents of change, and as mediators between knowledge and action—whether the knowledge originated with them or not. As such, they played an important role in the nation's agricultural policy.

## THE CONCEPT OF SECTORAL SCIENCE POLICIES

For the future development of science policy, and in order to surmount the impasse of past assumptions, three criteria must be met: (1) Science policy will have to be related explicitly to major policy functions, such as economic development, defense, urban development, and health; (2) Science policy will have to be considered one intervention mechanism available to government among others, such as taxation, regulations of private activities, and subsidies; (3) Science policy will have to be designed with equal attention to scientific-technical innovation, per se, and to its social and institutional environment. While this development of sectoral science policy strategies should constitute the major thrust of the science policy effort—an effort aimed at decentralization, integration in a variety of policy functions, and building goal-related institutional mechanisms—

a need remains for a central science policy function devoted to an overview of science activities through research data analysis and promotion of fundamental and problem-oriented research.

The federal budget can provide an analytical framework for relating policy functions to R&D efforts. By analyzing the budget we can discover imbalances in present programs, over- or underallocation of R&D funds for particular policy functions, and the impact of new policy directives. In the long run, the functional analysis of R&D investments should help in developing methods for assessing payoffs from these investments. This in turn is a precondition for developing policies aimed at obtaining increased social dividends from R&D.

At the federal level in the United States, science and technology expenditures have remained around the $17 billion mark since 1967, a sizable part of federal spending. They equal, for example, the combined outlays for three important government tasks: the federal portion of spending for "Education and Manpower," "Natural Resources," and "Community Development and Housing."[25] To the extent that R&D investments lead to successful developments, they carry with them a long-term multiplier effect. This adds importance to the task of studying the ways in which generation of knowledge and achievement of political objectives can be coupled.

In examining the relation between policy and R&D functions, the U.S. federal budget document presents the analyst with special problems. And yet, publications analyzing the R&D budget are indispensable, even though they convey an impression of functional coherence not characteristic of the research and development items in the budget. During the budget planning and negotiation stages there is, in the U.S., no overall R&D budget. No part of government, no single committee of Congress is in charge of preparing or reviewing R&D expenditures as a separate budget item.[26]

To appreciate the dimensions of the task of analyzing the R&D budget in sectoral terms, we need a breakdown of governmental activities in a limited number of functions. The twenty-three categories used in the budget are too cumbersome to do justice to substantive connections. Some grouping into major policy functions seems desirable. Murray Weidenbaum, in a study of Congress and the federal budget, worked with only four functional groups: defense, public welfare, economic development, and general government.[27] Christopher Freeman uses four different functions: military and prestige, economic development, welfare, developing countries, and one special group, fundamental research.[28] A study by Leonard Lederman and Margaret Windus relates policy functions to R&D programs in twelve functional areas. They compute the amount of the federal budget allocated to each function and the amount of R&D expenditure within each function.[29] Their results, summarized in Table 7.1, indicate that no parallelism exists between program funding and R&D funding.

205

TABLE 7.1

Major Policy Functions: Their Percentage of the Federal Budget
and Their Part of Total R&D Funds
(Fiscal year 1971)

| Policy Functions | Percent of Federal Budget | Percent of R&D Funds |
|---|---|---|
| National Security | 39 | 54 |
| Income Security and Welfare | 30 | 0.3 |
| Health | 9 | 8 |
| Education, Knowledge, and Manpower | 5 | 8 |
| Commerce, Transportation, Communications | 5 | 3 |
| Agriculture and Rural Development | 3 | 2 |
| General Government | 2 | 0.1 |
| International Relations | 2 | 0.3 |
| Housing and Community Development | 2 | 0.5 |
| Natural Resources | 1.5 | 5 |
| Space | 1.5 | 18 |
| Environment | 0.5 | 1 |

Source: Lederman and Windus, op. cit., pp. 13, 17.

This is what one would have expected, given the wide variance in the reliance on technological advances in different policy areas.

For the sectoral analysis suggested here, twelve government functions is still too large a number. The Organization for Economic Cooperation and Development has classified government expenditures for R&D into six areas: national defense, space exploration, nuclear energy, economic development, community services, and advancement of science. The principal weakness of this breakdown is that it mixes policy functions (such as economic development) with the development of particular technologies (such as nuclear energy). To avoid this methodological flaw, I propose a division into six broad policy sectors, each grouping related government functions in terms of policy responsibilities rather than in terms of specific technologies, thus maintaining a view of R&D programs as instruments and not as ends in themselves. Strategies for R&D investments in each sector can thus be formulated in policy terms and not in terms of the needs and capabilities of specific technologies. The proposed sectors are:

1. National Security (including military assistance to other countries and arms control);

2. Economic Development (industry, commerce, and agriculture);

3. Infrastructure Development (energy, transportation, and communications);

4. Physical Environment (including space exploration, disaster prevention, meteorology, and maritime resources);

5. Human and Social Development (health, public welfare, education, and law and order);

6. Advancement of Science and Technology.

A breakdown of federal R&D funds according to these functions is given in Table 7.2. The first five functions view science and technology as means for achieving specific political ends. They provide the justifications and guidelines for the direction and size of scientific and technical investments. The sixth function is different from the other five because it views science as an end in itself, a national resource that receives public support to ensure the continued flow of knowledge. National efforts in research and development can be maintained only with continued support for basic research and advanced training of scientists and engineers.

Table 7.2 shows an interesting evolution of sectoral R&D investment in the decade 1963-73. The general shift from military to civilian R&D discerned by Freeman and his associates, working with OECD data, is confirmed here.[30] The very low level of support for the economic development sector is highlighted. Most of the R&D funding in this sector goes to the support of agricultural research, described in the earlier section on the historical role of agricultural research. Infrastructure R&D is experiencing modest growth, due largely to increases in transportation and energy R&D funding. These two sectors together, however, were only 8.4 percent of total federally-funded R&D in 1973, compared with 4.6 percent in 1963. Rapid increases for energy R&D are included in the 1974 and 1975 budgets, which reflects a shift from a one-sided nuclear energy emphasis to a diversified resource and development effort.

The physical environment sector, which was second to national security in 1963, due to the civilian space segment, remained the second largest in 1973. Space R&D alone increased to 28 percent of total federal expenditures in 1968; it declined to 15 percent by 1973. Increases in pollution control and resource development were of roughly the same order of magnitude as increases in transportation and energy R&D. The social programs sector increased from 5.5 percent of federally-funded R&D in 1963 to 12.1 percent in 1973. The dramatic change was in health-related research, which grew 188 percent to over 1.6 billion. Other areas of the social program sector also had important increases, suggesting the likelihood of significant long-term growth.

207

TABLE 7. 2

Federal R&D Expenditures by Function, 1963, 1968, and 1973
(millions of dollars)

| | 1963 (percent) | 1968 (percent) | 1973 (percent) |
|---|---|---|---|
| National Security | | | |
| DOD-military[a] | 6, 791 | 7, 964 | 8, 252 |
| AEC-military | 482 | 609 | 609 |
| International Relations | 10 | 20 | 27 |
| Total | 7, 283 | 8, 613 | 8, 888 |
| Percent of annual total | 64. 2 | 52. 7 | 53. 5 |
| Economic Development | | | |
| Commerce and Industry | 1. 5 | 14. 4 | 9. 6 |
| Agriculture | 139 | 226 | 301 |
| Total | 141 | 240 | 311 |
| Percent of annual total | 1. 2 | 1. 4 | 1. 8 |
| Infrastructure | | | |
| Energy | 265 | 345 | 452 |
| Communications[b] | 14 | 26 | 81 |
| Transportation | 112 | 366 | 563 |
| Total | 391 | 741 | 1, 096 |
| Percent of annual total | 3. 4 | 4. 5 | 6. 6 |
| Physical Environment | | | |
| Pollution Control | 66 | 109 | 249 |
| Resource Development | 106 | 196 | 323 |
| Space-civilian | 2, 430 | 4, 577 | 2, 930 |
| Total | 2, 602 | 4, 882 | 3, 502 |
| Percent of annual total | 22. 9 | 29. 8 | 21. 1 |
| Social Programs | | | |
| Health | 594 | 1, 125 | 1, 607 |
| Education | 10 | 87 | 156 |
| Economic Security | 22 | 98 | 171 |
| Community Development | . 2 | 6 | 53 |
| Crime Control | - | . 6 | 23 |
| Total | 626 | 1, 317 | 2, 010 |
| Percent of annual total | 5. 5 | 8. 0 | 12. 1 |
| Advancement of Science and Technology | | | |
| General Science | 273 | 520 | 726 |
| Technology Improvement | 23 | 24 | 50 |
| Office of Science and Technology | - | 1. 2 | 2. 2 |
| Total | 296 | 545 | 778 |
| Percent of annual total | 2. 6 | 3. 3 | 4. 6 |
| Total | 11, 339 | 16, 332 | 16, 585 |
| | 100. 0 | 100. 0 | 100. 0 |

a  Includes Office of Emergency Preparedness.
b  Includes Postal Service.
Source: Based on NSF, Funding by Function, Table C 1 (NSF 72-313).

208

Advancement of science and technology, which involves principally the budget of the National Science Foundation, remained small — exceeding only the economic development sector both in 1963 and 1973. Yet despite the relatively modest funding allocated in this sector of the R&D budget, the growth from 1963 (2.6 percent) to 1973 (4.6 percent) was better than 160 percent in absolute terms. The "balance-wheel" function of federal support for basic research appears to have been operating with some success. In addition, significant new funds for problem-oriented R&D were flowing through the program of Research Applied to National Needs (RANN) and through the new energy-related R&D initiatives.

Each of these six sectors requires a separate rationale for the investment of public funds in R&D. Moreover, considerable variation in program justification, financing procedure, and institutional mechanisms is evident in each. The total picture suggests a broad effort toward achieving major national goals through the application of science and technology, but the sectoral approach also reveals major imbalances of effort within sectors. These can often be traced to particular historical circumstances —the space program is an obvious and recent example. While these imbalances are specific to the U.S. R&D budget, the illustration of a sectoral analysis independent of operational and organizational categories may be applied to the science policy of any industrial nation.

The preceding remarks indicate the scope and direction of a sectoral analysis of R&D spending and its part in policy development. The analysis itself remains to be undertaken.


## CONCLUSIONS


The relations between knowledge and action are controlled by institutional structures and patterns of behavior. To a degree, these are specific to national societies. The structures and patterns examined here are principally those of the United States, though in the early postwar years they were to a significant extent shared among nations that had been wartime allies, especially the United Kingdom. The underlying assumptions that strongly affected the character of these years, continuing into the late 1960s, were based on success in organizing and directing science first for war and then for an armed, nuclear peace. Assumptions about the utility of science, the role of scientists, the function of knowledge institutions, and the impact of science on social problems which had been generated in the war and early postwar years remained dominant for nearly a quarter of a century.

The history of complex social problems in which science has played an important part, for example, the evolution of urban form and the application of research to agriculture, shows the importance of social invention interacting with scientific discovery. One of the neglected lessons of British success in World War II was the combination of operations research with weapons research. Large-scale, defense-related technological undertakings in the United States, specifically the Manhattan and Apollo projects, teach the same lesson.

New assumptions are required if science is to begin to fulfill its promise—largely rhetorical in recent years—in the formulation and execution of public policy. These assumptions must begin with the description of broad national goals, independent of the operational and organizational arrangements in being. By grouping programmatically R&D activities of the government in major, goal-oriented sectors, it will be possible to begin assessing the balance of expenditure among competing goals, and within sectors among related but competing claimants for R&D resources. Science cannot solve all social and human problems; but each social and human problem can, in some degree, be shaped by the tools of science.

## NOTES

1. For an analysis of new organizational arrangements (developed during and after World War II) which provided the foundations of modern science policy, see Don K. Price, Government and Science (New York: Oxford University Press, 1954), esp. chapts. 3 and 5. A useful reader, drawing on a variety of sources—Congressional hearings, White House press releases, annual reports of the Carnegie Institution, documents of the National Academy of Science, etc. —is James L. Penick et al. , The Politics of American Science: 1939 to the Present, revised edition (Cambridge: MIT Press, 1972).

2. See Albert Wohlstetter, "Strategy and the Natural Scientists, " in Robert Gilpin and Christopher Wright, eds. , Scientists and National Policy-Making (New York: Columbia University Press, 1964), pp. 217 ff.

3. Emmanuel G. Mesthene, "The Impacts of Science on Public Policy, " Public Administration Review 27 (1967): 98.

4. Robert C. Wood, "The Rise of an Apolitical Elite, " in Gilpin and Wright, eds. , op. cit. , p. 54.

5. C. P. Snow, Science and Government (New York: Mentor Books, 1962).

6. Quoted in Earl of Birkenhead, The Professor and the Prime Minister: The Official Life of Professor F. A. Lindemann (Boston: Houghton Mifflin, 1962), p. 198.

7. Sir Henry Tizard, A Scientist In and Out of the Civil Service, Twenty-second Haldane Memorial Lecture, Birkbeck College, London, March 9, 1955, p. 15.

8. Jurgen Schmandt, "Le 'Scientific Statesman'," Les Etudes Philosophiques, no. 21 (April-June 1966): 165-86.

9. Harvey Brooks, "The Scientific Adviser," in Gilpin and Wright, eds., op. cit., p. 75 f.

10. Jurgen Schmandt, op. cit. I have traced here the origins and defined the "job characteristics" of the scientific statesman.

11. C.P. Snow, op. cit., appendix, p. 118.

12. Fritz Machlup, The Production and Distribution of Knowledge in the United States (Princeton: Princeton University Press, 1962), p. 374.

13. Peter F. Drucker, The Age of Discontinuity (New York: Harper & Row, 1968), p. 263.

14. Clark Kerr, The Uses of the University (Cambridge: Harvard University Press, 1964), pp. 45, 87.

15. Daniel Bell, "The Measurement of Knowledge and Technology," in Eleanor Sheldon and Wilbert E. Moore, eds., Indicators of Social Change (Russel Sage Foundation, 1968), p. 157. See also Daniel Bell, The Coming of Post-Industrial Society (New York: Basic Books, 1973), p. 20.

16. Peter F. Drucker, op. cit., p. 264.

17. Alvin M. Weinberg, "Social Problems and National Scio-Technical Institutes," in Applied Science and Technological Progress, A Report by the Committee on Science and Public Policy, National Academy of Sciences for the committee on Science and Astronautics, U.S. House of Representatives (Washington, D.C.: U.S. Government Printing Office, 1967), p. 416. See also Amitai Etzioni, "'Shortcuts' to Social Change?" The Public Interest 12 (Summer, 1968): 40-50.

18. OECD, "Science and the Great Society," Reviews of National Science Policy: United States (Paris, 1969): 289-303.

19. John M. Logsdon, "Towards a New Policy for Technology: The Outlines Emerge," Technology Review 75 (1972): 37.

20. OECD, Science and the Policies of Governments (Paris, 1963), p. 34. The writer bears some responsibility for, as a recent convert to the cause of science policy, he helped to prepare the report.

21. A useful overview of the field is given in Technology and Social History, Harvard University Program on Technology and Society, Research Review No. 8, 1971.

22. J. Meyer, J. Kain, M. Wohl, The Urban Transportation Problem (Cambridge: Harvard University Press, 1965), p. 13.

23. E.A. Walker, "Reorganization for Progress," 74th Annual Meeting, American Association of Land-Grant Colleges and State Universities (processed) (Washington, D.C.: November 1960). Quoted in H.C. Knoblauch et al., State Agricultural Experiment Stations: A History of Research Policy and Procedure, U.S. Department of Agriculture Miscellaneous Publications 904 (Washington, D.C.: Government Printing Office, 1962).

24. P. S. Johnson, "The Role of Co-operative Research in British Industry, " Research Policy, 1 (1971-72): 349 f.

25. Their respective portions of the federal budget for 1972 amounted to 3. 8 percent for education and manpower, 1. 9 percent for natural resources, and 2. 0 percent for community development and housing. R&D outlays accounted for 7. 3 percent. See American Enterprises Institute for Public Policy Research, Overview of the Federal Budget, Fiscal 1972, Legislative Analysis No. 2, 92nd Congress, February 1971, table 5.

26. Personal communication from William D. Carey, formerly with the Office of Management and Budget (now with Arthur D. Little).

27. Murray L. Weidenbaum and John Saloma, III, Congress and the Federal Budget (Washington, D. C.: American Enterprise Institute for Public Policy Research, 1965), p. 6.

28. C. Freeman et al. , "The Goals of R&D in the 1970's, " Science Studies, 1 (1971): 357-406.

29. Leonard Lederman and Margaret Windus, Federal Funding and National Priorities: An Analysis of Programs, Expenditures and Research and Development (New York: Praeger, 1971).

30. C. Freeman et al. , op. cit.

SOVIET UNION

Deutscher, Isaac. Soviet Trade Unions: Their Place in Soviet Labor Policy (New York, Royal Institute of International Affairs, 1950).

DeWitt, Nicholas. Education and Professional Employment in the USSR (Washington: National Science Foundation, 1961).

Field, Mark. Soviet Socialized Medicine (New York: Free Press, 1967).

Gill, Richard R. "Problems of Decisionmaking in Soviet Science Policy," Minerva, vol. v (Winter, 1967): 198-208.

Graham, Loren R. "Science Policy and Planning in the USSR," Survey (July 1967): 61-79.

_____ "Reorganization of the Academy of Sciences," in Peter Juviler and Henry Morton, eds., Soviet Policy-Making (New York, 1967), 133-61.

_____ The Soviet Academy of Sciences and the Communist Party, 1927-1932 (Princeton, 1967).

_____ Science and Philosophy in the Soviet Union (New York, 1972).

Greenberg, Linda Lubrano. "Soviet Science Policy and the Scientific Establishment," Survey, vol. 81 (Autumn 1971): no. 4, 51-63.

_____ "Policy-making in the USSR Academy of Sciences," Journal of Contemporary History, vol. 8 (1973): no. 4, 67-80.

Joravsky, David. The Lysenko Affair (Cambridge: Harvard University Press, 1970.

Korol, Alexander G. Soviet Education for Science and Technology (Cambridge: MIT Press, 1957).

_____ Soviet Research and Development: Its Organization, Personnel and Funds (Cambridge: MIT Press, 1965).

Kramish, Arnold. Atomic Energy in the Soviet Union (Stanford: Stanford University Press, 1959).

Medvedev, Zhores A. The Rise and Fall of T. D. Lysenko (New York: Columbia University Press, 1969).

_____ The Medvedev Papers: The Plight of Soviet Science (New York: Columbia University Press, 1971).

Organization for Economic Cooperation and Development, Science Policy in the USSR (Paris, 1969).

Sakharov, Andrei D. Progress, Coexistence and Intellectual Freedom (New York: Norton, 1970).

Schwartz, Solomon M. Labor in the Soviet Union (New York: Praeger 1952).

Survey, "Report on Soviet Science," No. 52, July 1964, special issue.

Turkevich, John. "Soviet Science in the Post-Stalin Era," Annals of the American Academy of Political and Social Science, vol. CCCIII (January 1956): 139-51.

Vucinich, Alexander. Science in Russian Culture, 1861-1917 (Stanford: Stanford University Press, 1970).

_____ The Soviet Academy of Sciences (Stanford, Hoover Institute Studies, 1956).

GREAT BRITAIN

A Framework for Government Research and Development. Cmd. 4814 (London: HMSO), 1971.

Advisory Council on Scientific Policy. Annual Reports, 1947-1948 to 1963-1964 (London: HMSO).

Ashby, Sir Eric. Technology and the Academics (London: Macmillan, 1958).

Bernal, John Desmond. The Social Function of Science (London: George Routledge & Sons, 1939).

Calder, Nigel. Technopolis: Social Control of the Uses of Science (London: MacGibbon & Kee, 1969).

Cardwell, D. S. L. The Organisation of Science in England: A Retrospect (London: William Heinemann, 1957).

Central Advisory Council for Science and Technology. Technological Innovation in Britain (London: HMSO, 1968).

Ciba Foundation. Symposium on Decision-Making in National Science Policy (Boston: Little, Brown, 1968).

Clark, Ronald W. Tizard (Boston: MIT Press, 1965).

Committee of Enquiry into the Organisation of Civil Science (Trend Report), Cmd. 2171 (London: HMSO, 1963).

Committee on Higher Education. Higher Education (Robbins Report), Cmd. 2154 (London: HMSO, 1963, 6 vols.).

Committee on Manpower Resources for Science and Technology. The Brain Drain (Jones Report), Cmd. 3417 (London: HMSO, 1967).

_____ The Flow into Employment of Scientists, Engineers and Technologists. (Swann Report), Cmd. 3760 (London: HMSO, 1968).

Council for Scientific Policy. Enquiry into the Flow of Candidates in Science and Technology into Higher Education (Dainton Report), Cmd. 3541 (London: HMSO, 1968).

_____ Report of a Study on the Support of Scientific Research in the Universities (Massey Report), Cmd. 4798 (London: HMSO, 1971).

_____ Report on Science Policy. Cmd. 3007 (London: HMSO, 1966).

_____ Second Report on Science Policy. Cmd. 3420 (London: HMSO, 1967).

_____ Third Report of the Council for Scientific Policy. Cmd. 5117 (London: HMSO, 1972).

Framework for Government Research and Development. Cmd. 5046 (London: HMSO, 1972).

Gowing, Margaret. Britain and Atomic Energy, 1939-1945 (London: Macmillan, 1964).

Habakkuk, H. J. American and British Technology in the Nineteenth Century (Cambridge: The University Press, 1967).

Hailsham, Lord (Quintin Hogg). Science and Politics (London: Faber, 1963).

Hobsbawm, E. J. Industry and Empire: The Making of Modern English Society. vol. II, 1750 to the Present Day (New York: Pantheon, 1968).

Industrial Research and Development in Government Laboratories: A New Organisation for the Seventies (Green Paper) (London: HMSO, 1970).

Landes, David S. The Unbound Prometheus: Technological Change and Industrial Development in Western Europe from 1750 to the Present (Cambridge: The University Press, 1969).

Layton, Christopher. European Advanced Technology: A Programme for Integration. P. E. P. (London: Allen & Unwin, 1969).

MacLeod, Roy M. "The Support of Victorian Science: the Endowment of Research Movement in Great Britain, 1868-1900." Minerva, IX (April 1971): 197-230.

_____ and Andrews, E. Kay. "The Committee of Civil Research: Scientific Advice for Economic Development 1925-1930." Minerva, VII (Summer 1969): 680-705.

_____ "The Origins of the D. S. I. R.: Reflections on Ideas and Men, 1915-1916." Public Administration (London). 48 (Spring 1970): 23-48.

Melville, Sir Harry. The Department of Scientific and Industrial Research. New Whitehall Series No. 9 (London: Allen & Unwin, 1962).

Nicholson, Max. The System: The Mismanagement of Modern Britain (New York: McGraw-Hill, 1969).

Office of the Minister for Science. Report of the Committee on the Management and Control of Research and Development (Zuckerman Report) (London: HMSO, 1961).

O. E. C. D. Reviews of National Science Policy: United Kingdom/Germany (Paris: OECD, 1967).

Palmer, Arthur. "The Select Committee on Science and Technology." In Alfred Morris, ed., The Growth of Parliamentary Scrutiny by Committee: A Symposium (London: Pergamon Press, 1970).

Peck, Merton J. "Science and Technology." In Richard E. Caves, et al., Britain's Economic Prospects (Washington: Brookings Institution, 1968): 448-484.

Rose, Hilary, and Rose, Stefan. Science and Society (Harmondsworth: Penguin Books, 1969).

Select Committee on Science and Technology, House of Commons Report, Session 1966-67, United Kingdom Nuclear Reactor Programme. H.C. 381 (London: HMSO, 1967).

_____ Second Report, Session 1968-69. Defence Research. H.C. 213 (London: HMSO, 1969).

_____ Third Report, Session 1968-69. The Natural Environment Research Council. H.C. 400 (London: HMSO, 1969).

Smith, Bruce L. R., and Hague, D.C., eds., The Dilemma of Accountability in Modern Government: Independence Versus Control (London: Macmillan, 1971).

Snow, C.P. (Lord Snow). Science and Government (New York: Mentor Books ed., 1962).

_____ The Two Cultures: and a Second Look (New York: Mentor Books, 1964).

The Reorganisation of Central Government. Cmd. 4506 (London: HMSO, 1970).

Vig, Norman J. Science and Technology in British Politics. (London: Pergamon Press, 1968).

_____ and Walkland, S. A. "Science Policy, Science Administration and Parliamentary Reform," Parliamentary Affairs, 19 (Summer 1966): 281-294.

Walkland, S.A. "Parliament and Science Since 1945." In A. H. Hanson and Bernard Crick, eds., The Commons in Transition (London: Fontana/Collins, 1970), pp. 152-66.

_____ "Science and Parliament: the Origins and Influence of the Parliamentary and Scientific Committee." Parliamentary Affairs, 17 (Summer and Autumn 1964): 308-320, 389-402.

_____ "Science and Parliament: the Role of the Select Committees of the House of Commons." Parliamentary Affairs, 18 (Summer 1965): 266-278.

Williams, Roger. Politics and Technology (London: Macmillan, 1971).

Zuckerman, Sir Solly. Beyond the Ivory Tower: The Frontiers of Public and Private Science (London: Weidenfeld and Nicolson, 1970).


FRANCE


Aron, Raymond. The Great Debate. Translated by Ernest Powel, (New York: Doubleday, 1965).

Caute, David. Communism and the French Intellectuals, 1914-1960 (New York: Macmillan, 1964).

Dubois, Rene. Pasteur and Modern Science (New York: Doubleday, 1960).

Furniss, Edgar. De Gaulle and the French Army (New York: The Twentieth Century Fund, 1964).

Gilpin, Robert. France in the Age of the Scientific State (Princeton: Princeton University Press, 1968).

_____ "Technological Strategies and National Purpose," Science, vol. 169 (July 31, 1970): 441-448.

Goldschmidt, Bertrand. The Atomic Adventure. translated by Peter Beer (New York: Pergamon Press, 1964).

Guerlac, Henry. "Science and French National Strength," in Edward M. Earle, ed., Modern France (Princeton: Princeton University Press, 1951).

Hoffmann, Stanley. In Search of France (Cambridge: Harvard University Press, 1963).

Kowarski, Lew. "Psychology and the Structure of Large-Scale Physical Research," Bulletin of the Atomic Scientists, vol. V (June-July 1949): nos. 6-7.

Layton, Christopher. European Advanced Technology (London: Allen and Unwin, 1969).

Quinn, James B. "National Planning of Science and Technology In France," Science, vol. 150 (November 19, 1965): 993-1903.

Scheinman, Lawrence. Atomic Energy Policy in France under the Fourth Republic (Princeton: Princeton University Press, 1965).

JAPAN

Bellah, Robert N. Tokugawa Religion (New York: Free Press, 1957.

Boffey, Philip. "Japan (I): On the Threshold of an Age of Big Science?" Science, vol. 167 (January 2, 1970): 31-35.

_____ "Japan (II): University Turmoil Is Reflected in Research," Science, vol. 167 (January 9, 1970): 147-152.

_____ "Japan (III): Industrial Research Struggles to Close the Gap," Science, vol. 167 (January 16, 1970): 264-267.

Blewett, John E., S.J., ed. and trans. Higher Education in Postwar Japan (Tokyo: Sophia University Press, 1965).

Dore, Ronald. Education in Tokugawa Japan (Berkeley: University of California Press, 1965).

Ellingworth, Richard. "Japanese Economic Policies and Security," Adelphi Papers. No. 90 (London: International Institute for Strategic Studies, October 1972).

Guillain, Robert. The Japanese Challenge (New York: Lippincott, 1970).

Halloran, Richard. Japan, Images and Realities (New York: Knopf, 1969).

Hashimoto, U. "An Historical Synopsis of Education and Science in Japan from the Meiji Restoration to the Present Day," Impact of Science on Society, vol. XII (1963): no. 1, 3-24.

Hirschmeier, Johannes, S.J., The Origins of Entrepreneurship in Mieji Japan (New York: Cambridge University Press, 1964).

Imai, Ryukichi, "The Non-Proliferation Treaty and Japan," Bulletin of the Atomic Scientists, vol. XXV (May 1969: no. 5, 2-7; and "Japan and the World of SALT," Bulletin of the Atomic Scientists, vol. XXVII (December 1971): no. 12, 13-16.

219

Japan, Ministry of Education, Japan's Growth and Education (Tokyo, 1963).

Jequier, Nicolas. Le Defi Industriel Japonais (Lausanne: Centre de Recherches Europeennes, 1970).

Journal of World History, "Society, Science and Technology in Japan," vol. IX, no. 2, 1965.

Kobayashi, Tetsuya. General Education for Scientists and Engineers in the United States of America and Japan. Comparative Education Dissertation Series, no. 6 (Ann Arbor: University of Michigan, 1965).

Langdon, Frank C., Japan's Foreign Policy. (Vancouver: University of Vancouver Press, 1973).

Lockwood, William W. The Economic Development of Japan, 1868-1938 (Princeton: Princeton University Press, 1964).

_____ "Japan's New Capitalism," in William W. Lockwood, ed., The State and Economic Enterprise in Japan (Princeton: Princeton University Press, 1965).

Long, T. Dixon. "Science and Government in Japan," in Svensk Naturvetenskap 1967 (Stockholm, 1967): 296-315.

_____ "Policy and Politics in Japanese Science: The Persistence of a Tradition," Minerva, vol. III, no. 3 (Spring 1969): 426-453.

MacKay, Alan. "An Outsider's View of Science in Japan," Impact of Science on Society, vol. XII (1962): no. 3, 177-202.

Maddison, Angus. Economic Growth in Japan and the U.S.S.R. (London: George Allen and Unwin, 1969).

Morley, James W. "Growth for What? The Issues of the 70's" in Gerald L. Curtis, ed., Japanese-American Relations in the 1970s (Washington, D.C.: Columbia Books, 1970).

New Scientist, "The Rise of Japanese Technology," vol. XXXVI (November 16, 1971): supplement, 1-32.

Olson, Lawrence. "The Elite, Industrialism, and Nationalism in Japan," in Kalman Silvert, ed., Expectant Peoples (New York: American Universities Field Staff, 1963): 398-426.

_____ Japan in Postwar Asia (New York: Praeger, 1970).

Organization for Economic Cooperation and Development, Reviews of National Science Policy—Japan (Paris, 1967).

Passin, Herbert. Society and Education in Japan. (New York: Columbia University Teacher's College Press, 1965, 1965).

Stone, P.B. Japan Surges Ahead. (New York: Praeger, 1969).

Tsuji, Koyoaki. "Decisionmaking in the Japanese Government," in Robert Ward, ed., Political Development in Modern Japan. (Princeton: Princeton University Press, 1968).

Tuge, Hideomi. Historical Development of Science and Technology in Japan. Series on Japanese Life and Culture, vol. 5, (Tokyo: Kokusai Bunka Shinkokai, 1961).

UNESCO, Science Policy and the Organization of Research in Japan. (Paris: Science Policy Studies and Documents, 1968).

Wakaisumi, Kei, "The Problem for Japan," in Alistair Buchan, ed., A World of Nuclear Powers? (Englewood Cliffs, New Jersey: Prentice-Hall, 1966); 76-87.

Ward, Robert E. "Reflections on the Allied Occupation and Planned Political Change in Japan," in Robert Ward, ed., Political Development in Modern Japan (Princeton: Princeton University Press, 1968): 477-535.

Yanaga, Chitoshi. Big Business and Politics in Japan (New Haven: Yale University Press, 1968).

SWEDEN

Alfven, Hannes. "Science, Technocracy and the Politico-Economic Order." Impact of Science on Society, no. 22 (January-June 1972): 85-93.

Brohult, Sven. "Problems Associated with Swedish Research Policy." Svenska Handelsbanken Quarterly, No. 2, 1965.

Dorfer, Ingemar. "System 37 Viggen: Science, Technology and the Domestication of Glory." Public Policy, vol. 17 (1968): 201-229.

_____ System 37 Viggen: Arms Technology and the Domestication of Glory (Oslo: Oslo University Press, 1972).

Gasslancder, Olle. History of Stockholms Enskilda Bank, Stockholm, 1962.

Kaysen, Carl. "Improving the Efficiency of Military Research and Development." Public Policy, no. 12 (1963): 219-273.

Kramish, Arnold. Atlantic Technological Imbalance: An American Perspective (London: Institute for Strategic Studies, 1967).

Organization for Economic Cooperation and Development. Scientific Policy in Sweden (Paris, 1964).

Palme, Olof. "Science, Technology and Swedish Society." Impact of Science on Society, no. 22 (January-June 1972): 73-84.

Science and Technology in Sweden, Science Advisory Council (Stockholm, 1970).


UNITED STATES


Baxter, James Phinney. Scientists Against Time (Boston: Little, Brown, 1946).

Brooks, Harvey. The Government of Science (Cambridge: MIT Press, 1968).

Bush, Vannevar. Modern Arms and Free Men (New York: Simon and Shuster, 1949).

_____ Pieces of the Action (San Diego: Morrow, 1970).

Dupre, Stefan, and Sanford Lakoff. Science and the Nation: Policy and Politics (Englewood Cliffs: Prentice-Hall, 1962).

Dupree, A. Hunter. Science in the Federal Government. (Cambridge: Harvard University Press, 1957).

_____ "Central Scientific Organization in the United States," Minerva, vol. 1 (Summer 1963): no. 4, 453-469.

Gilpin, Robert. American Scientists and Nuclear Weapons Policy (Princeton: Princeton University Press, 1962).

_____ and Christopher Wright, eds., Scientists and National Policy-making (New York: Columbia University Press, 1964).

Green, Harold P., and Alan Rosenthal. Government of the Atom: The Integration of Powers. (New York: Atherton, 1963).

Greenberg, Daniel S. The Politics of Pure Science (Baltimore: Johns Hopkins University Press, 1967).

Jacobson, Harold K., and Eric Stein. Diplomats, Scientists and Politicians: The United States and the Nuclear Test Ban Negotiations (Ann Arbor: University of Michigan University Press, 1966).

Lakoff, Sanford A., ed. Knowledge and Power (New York: Free Press, 1966).

Leiserson, Avery. "Scientists and the Policy Process," American Political Science Review, vol. LIX (June 1965): 408-416.

Lederman, Leonard, and Margaret Windus. Federal Funding and National Priorities (New York: Praeger, 1971).

Logsdon, John. The Decision to Go to the Moon (Cambridge: MIT Press, 1970).

Maddox, John. "American Science: Endless Search for Objectives," Daedalus, vol. 101 (Fall 1972): 129-40.

Mesthene, Emmanual G. "The Impacts of Science on Public Policy," Public Administration Review, vol. XXVII (June 1967): 97-104.

_____ "How Technology Will Shape the Future," Science, vol. 161 (July 12, 1968): 135-44.

National Academy of Sciences—National Research Council. Basic Research and National Goals (Washington: U.S. Government Printing Office, 1965).

Organization for Economic Cooperation and Develokment. Reviews of National Science Policy: United States (Paris, 1968).

_____ Science and the Policies of Governments (Paris, 1963).

Orlans, Harold, ed. Science Policy and the University (Washington, D.C.: Brookings, 1968).

Penick, James L., Jr., et. al. The Politics of American Science: 1939 to the Present (Cambridge: MIT Press, 1972).

Perl, Martin. "The Scientific Advisory System: Some Observations," Science, vol. 173 (September 24, 1971): 1211-1215.

Price, Don K. Government and Science. (New York: Oxford University Press, 1954).

_____ The Scientific Estate. (Cambridge: Harvard University Press, 1965).

Reagan, Michael D. Science and the Federal Patron. (New York: Oxford University Press, 1969).

Skolnikoff, Eugene B. Science, Technology, and American Foreign Policy. (Cambridge: MIT University Press, 1967).

Smith, Alice Kimball. A Peril and a Hope: The Scientists' Movement in America, 1945-1947 (Chicago: University of Chicago Press, 1965).

Strickland, Donald A. The Atomic Scientists' Movement, 1945-46, (Lafayette: Purdue University Press, 1968).

United States, House of Representatives. Federal Policy, Plans and Organization for Science and Technology. Committee on Science and Astronautics, Ninety-Third Congress, Second Session (June 1974).

_____ National Science Foundation. Science Indicators, 1972 (Washington, 1973).

Van Dyke, Vernon. Pride and Power: The Rationale of the Space Program (Urbana: University of Illinois Press, 1964).

von Hippel, Frank, and Joel Primack, "Public Interest Science," Science, vol. 178 (October 6, 1972): 39-43.

Weinberg, Alvin. Reflections on Big Science (Cambridge: MIT Press, 1968).

Wiesner, Jerome B. Where Science and Politics Meet (New York: McGraw-Hill, 1965).

231

# ABOUT THE EDITORS AND CONTRIBUTORS

T. DIXON LONG is Associate Professor of Political Science at Case Western Reserve University in Cleveland. He has been a staff member of the Directorate for Scientific Affairs of the Organization for Economic Cooperation and Development (OECD) in Paris, and in 1973-74 he was a resident Fellow in the Office of the Foreign Secretary, National Academy of Sciences, Washington, D. C.

Dr. Long was the rapporteur for the OECD's Review of National Science Policy—Japan; he has published articles in Minerva and Science Studies and has prepared reviews for Technology and Culture and American Political Science Review.

Dr. Long holds a B.A. from Amherst College, an M.A. from the Fletcher School of Law and Diplomacy, a Certificate from the East Asian Institute, and a Ph. D. from Columbia University.

CHRISTOPHER WRIGHT is consultant for natural and environmental sciences to the Rockefeller Foundation in New York. He was Director of the Institute for the Study of Science in Human Affairs at Columbia University from its inception in 1966 to 1972. Before that, he was Executive Director of the Council for Atomic Age Studies at Columbia and a lecturer in the Department of Political Science and the School of International Affairs.

Mr. Wright is coeditor, with Robert Gilpin, of Scientists and National Policy Making; he has contributed chapters to a number of books including the Britannica Yearbook of Science and the Future and Uniting Europe in the 1970s. He has published articles in the Bulletin of the Atomic Scientists, UNESCO Journal of World History, Daedalus, and Vista and has prepared reviews for the Political Science Quarterly and Science.

Mr. Wright holds an A.B. and an A.M. degree in philosophy from Harvard University, and he was a Fulbright Scholar at Oxford University.

LOREN R. GRAHAM is Professor of History at Columbia University and a member of the staff of the Russian Institute. He teaches both general history of science and Soviet intellectual history at Columbia.

Dr. Graham has published many articles and books in his areas of interest, including The Soviet Academy of Sciences and the Communist Party (1967) and Science and Philosophy in the Soviet Union (1972). The latter book was nominated for the 1973 National Book Award in history. Professor Graham has been a Guggenheim Fellow and a Member of the Institute for Advanced Study (1969-70). He holds a B. S. from Purdue University and an M.A. and Ph. D. from Columbia University.

NORMAN J. VIG is Associate Professor of Government and International Relations at Carleton College. He is the author of Science and Technology in British Politics and coauthor of Politics in Advanced Nations: Modernization, Development and Contemporary Change.

Dr. Vig was a Fulbright Scholar at the University of Manchester in 1961-62 and received his Ph.D. from Columbia University in 1966. He conducted research on British science policy in London in 1965, 1966, and 1970.

ROBERT G. GILPIN, JR. is Professor of Politics and International Affairs at Princeton University. He has been a Congressional Fellow of the American Political Science Association, a Fellow in the Science and Public Policy Program at Harvard University, and a Guggenheim Fellow. Professor Gilpin is the author of American Scientists and Nuclear Weapons Policy, France in the Age of the Scientific State, and coeditor of and contributor to Scientists and National Policy Making. He has contributed articles to Science, Foreign Policy, Public Policy, and a number of other periodicals. Dr. Gilpin holds a B.A. from the University of Vermont, an M.S. from Cornell University, and Ph.D. from the University of California, Berkeley.

INGEMAR N.H. DORFER is Assistant Professor of Political Science at Uppsala University, Sweden. He is currently serving as a Special Assistant in the Swedish Ministry of Defense. Dr. Dorfer's publications include Communications Satellites (Stockholm: Swedish International Peace Research Institute, 1969), System 37 Viggen: Arms, Technology and the Domestication of Glory (Oslo: Oslo University Press, 1973), and a chapter in Frank B. Horton III, Anthony C. Rogerson, and Edward L. Warner III, eds., Comparative Defense Policy (Baltimore: Johns Hopkins University Press, 1974). He has published articles and reviews in Public Policy, Research Policy, and Cooperation and Conflict, as well as numerous Swedish newspapers and periodicals. Ingemar Dorfer holds a fil kand and a politices magister from the University of Lund, Sweden, and a Ph.D. in Government from Harvard.

JURGEN SCHMANDT is Professor at the LBJ School of Public Affairs, The University of Texas, Austin. He has been Associate Director of the Program on Technology and Society at Harvard University, and director of the program on national science policies in the Directorate for Scientific Affairs, Organization for Economic Cooperation and Development in Paris, France. Professor Schmandt is coauthor of a number of federal policy assessments published by the LBJ School of Public Affairs, principal author of the report to the House Committee on Science and Astronautics titled Science Policy in the Nineteen Seventies, and he was rapporteur for OECD's Reviews of National Science Policy: France. His articles and reviews have appeared in American, French, and German periodicals. Dr. Schmandt holds the Ph.D. in Political Philosophy from the University of Bonn.